Vocational Development and Guidance

Papers by
W. Wesley Tennyson, C. Todd Strohmenger,
Edwin L. Herr et al.

MSS Information Corporation
655 Madison Avenue, New York, N.Y. 10021

Library of Congress Cataloging in Publication Data

Main entry under title:

Vocational development and guidance.

    1. Vocational guidance--Addresses, essays, lectures.
2. Occupations--Addresses, essays, lectures.
I. Tennyson, Willard Wesley, 1924-
HF5381.V54   ·371.4'25   73-12105
ISBN 0-8422-7160-0

TABLE OF CONTENTS

CREDITS AND ACKNOWLEDGEMENTS

Baal, Ione T., "Careers Unlimited," *American Vocational Journal*, 1969, 44:30-32.

Bailey, Larry J., "Theories of Vocational Behavior," *Journal of Industrial Teacher Education*, 1968, 5:4-19.

Bailey, Larry J.; and Dennis C. Nystrom, "A Rationale for Career Development at the Elementary School Level," *Journal of Industrial Teacher Education*, 1972, 9:5-10.

Bjorquist, David C.; and H.C. Kazanas, "Should We Teach Career Information?" *Man/Society/Technology*, 1970, 30:92-95.

Carey, E. Niel, "Vocational Guidance for All: Is Differentiated Staffing the Answer?" *American Vocational Journal*, 1970, 45:68-69.

Cote, Theodore J., "The Counselor's Most Logical Helper," *American Vocational Journal*, 1968, 43:11-12, 55.

Cote, Theodore J., "Vocational Guidance European Style," *American Vocational Journal*, 1970, 45:24-26.

Crites, John O., "Appraising the Appraisal Instruments," *American Vocational Journal*, 1968, 43:22-24, 53.

Fisher, Eleanore; and James B. Van Hoven, "The Guidance-Administration Team," *Educational Leadership*, 1972, 29:695-698.

Gribbons, Warren D.; and Paul R. Lohnes, "A Five-Year Study of Students' Educational Aspirations," *Vocational Guidance Quarterly*, 1966, 14:66-69.

Gysbers, Norman C.; and Earl J. Moore, "Career Guidance: Program Content and Staff Responsibilities," *American Vocational Journal*, 1972, 47:60-62.

Herr, Edwin L., "Contributions of Career Development to Career Education," *Journal of Industrial Teacher Education*, 1972, 9:5-14.

Lavender, John, "Occupational Versatility: Key to Careers," *Educational Leadership*, 1972, 30:215-217.

Law, Gordon F., "A Regular Place for Guidance," *American Vocational Journal*, 1969, 44:27-28, 60.

Law, Gordon F., "Vocational Education Is Service," *American Vocational Journal*, 1968, 43:41-56.

Pautler, Albert J., "Occupational Education in Career Development," *Educational Leadership*, 1972, 30:237-240.

Pratzner, Frank C., "Development of the Self-Concept: A Theoretical Framework and Suggestions for Classroom Action Research," *Journal of Industrial Teacher Education*, 1969, 7:31-37.

Prediger, Dale J., "Obtaining Test Information Relevant to Vocational Program Choice," *Journal of Industrial Teacher Education*, 1972, 9: 15-20.

Pucel, David J., "The Centour Methodology Applied to Vocational Student Counseling and Admission," *Journal of Industrial Teacher Education*, 1969, 7:5-12.

Pucel, David J.; Howard F. Nelson; Darrell Heitzman; and David N. Wheeler, "Vocational Maturity and Vocational Training," *Journal of Industrial Teacher Education*, 1972, 9:30-38.

Sievert, Norman W., "The Role of the Self-Concept in Determining an Adolescent's Occupational Choice," *Journal of Industrial Teacher Education*, 1972, 3:47-54.

Slakter, Malcolm J.; and Stanley H. Cramer, "Risk Taking and Vocational or Curriculum Choice," *Journal of Counseling Psychiatry*, 1969, 18: 127-132.

Strohmenger, C. Todd; and Harold L. Henderson, "Career Development: Pandora's Box or Cornucopia?" *Educational Leadership*, 1972, 30: 261-263.

Tennyson, W. Wesley, "Career Development," *Review of Educational Research*, 1968, 38:346-366.

Tesh, Betty, "What Can a Counselor Do?" *Today's Education*, 1973, 62:28-29.

Wellman, Frank E.; and Norman C. Gysbers, "Main Question Is: Did the Program Make a Difference?" *American Vocational Journal*, 1971, 46:47-50.

PREFACE

This volume, the second in MSS' Series on Vocational Education, considers questions of career development, the role of guidance in the school, vocational training, the relation of self-concept to vocational choice, and occupational information. Papers deal with theories of vocational behavior, the success of vocational education programs, and testing information.

Career Development

Career Development

Work as a prominent feature of the lives of adults has long attracted the
interest of social and behavioral scientists. A perusal of contemporary
literature bears witness to the growing awareness that occupational motives
and behaviors are the result of a complex process of development and experience. Vocational or career development as an area of investigation has
been concerned with trying to understand the elaborate socialization process
required to transform the child into the working adult, as well as to
discover the manner in which work is related to the life styles of adults in
the labor force.

Distinguishable characteristics of vocational development, including research reportedly under way which marks this field as a viable one for
study, were to be found in Borow's volume entitled *Man in a World at
Work* (1964), a compilation sponsored by the National Vocational Guidance Association. Holland (1964) provided a carefully documented review
of systematic programs of research which approach career development
from a psychological orientation. The newer trends in theory and research
may be viewed in perspective by consulting Williamson's historical treatise
(1965). Walz (1963) and Perrone (1966) have reported in the *Review
of Educational Research* the status of research activity in this field of inquiry since 1962. Borow (1966) summarized research directly concerned
with vocationally relevant phenomena in children and youth. The significance of research in career development and vocational guidance was
recognized through financial support given by the U.S. Office of Education
during the past three years (Scates and Brittain, 1967).

Theory Construction and Testing

Vocational psychology during the decade of the 1950's, partly in reaction to criticisms of classical trait-measurement approaches to occupational behavior and partly because of greater sophistication with respect
to human development, gave explicit attention to theory building. Concerted efforts were made to construct heuristic concepts and propositions
of a dynamic nature which would serve to explain the process by which
vocationally relevant behavior is developed and expressed. More recently,
the literature has revealed an increasing interest in empirical research
designed to test the earlier speculations and assumptions and to refine and

10

give systematic structure to theory. Although these newer approaches to the study of career behavior promise to bring vocational development into the mainstream of behavioral science, it cannot be assumed that in the immediate future there will be any diminution in number of studies which investigate differential choice behavior by utilizing classical trait theory of personality. Cooley (1964) made the point that the trait-and-factor problem today is not simply the task of relating a test score to some final occupation, but rather a consideration of the pattern of attributes that are related to the sequence of decisions a young person makes in establishing himself in the work world. The use of computers and multivariate methods of prediction should encourage those researchers who desire to probe the limits and capabilities of classical trait theory.

Theoretical Formulations

Important precursors and continuing stimulants to the developmental emphasis in research on vocational behavior have been the 20-year longitudinal Career Pattern Study under the direction of Super, and the Harvard Studies in Career Development directed by Tiedeman. Super and his colleagues have drawn upon self-concept theory to provide testable hypotheses regarding the exploratory and decision-making process. Many of their earlier formulations integrating aspects of theory with elements of vocational behavior were summarized in one work (Super and others, 1963). The fourth in a series of monographs (Super and others, 1967) treated the years of transition from school to college and to work. Approximately 200 men in their mid-twenties who had first been studied 10 years earlier were followed up with interviews. An objective was to determine the extent to which floundering and trial precede establishment in an occupation, and the relationship between such career behavior and antecedent measures designed to assess vocational maturity and traditional personality and achievement variables.

The process of fashioning a vocational identity was seen by Tiedeman and O'Hara (1963) to involve cognitive mechanisms of differentiation and integration which are set into motion through recognition of a problem or present unsatisfactory situation. Their conceptualization of an anticipatory stage of vocational development with substages of exploration, crystallization, choice, and clarification was verified by Harren (1966) with male college students.

Theory underlying current programmatic and longitudinal research assumes that long-term vocational behaviors occur within an ordered sequence of life stages in which there is a progression of necessary learning experiences and a mastery of coping techniques. The notion of invoking the concept of developmental tasks and relating such tasks to vocational life stages holds promise of increasing our understanding of the motives and behavior which have relevance for career. Havighurst (1964), adding

11

to the work of others, proposed a six-stage schema of vocational development, specifying ages and principal tasks or behaviors corresponding to
each stage. Havighurst's conceptualization, while helpful, lacks the specificity needed in identifying representative vocational developmental tasks.

Gribbons and Lohnes (1966a) launched a longitudinal study in 1958
designed to investigate the vocational behavior of 111 adolescent subjects
as they progressed through a sequence of developmental stages. Projecting
follow-ups to the age of 30 years, the investigators adopted the strategy
of intensive interviewing every two years. A multidimensional scaling of
early vocational maturity resulted in an instrument named Readiness for
Vocational Planning.

Programmatic research on career-oriented behavior now under way at
the University of Iowa was described by Crites (1965b). The Vocational
Development Project has utilized an empirical-analytical approach in
theorizing about vocational maturity and the interrelationships among
various components of this construct. Through extensive cross-sectional
sampling, Crites (1965a) managed to develop and standardize readily
employable instruments for measuring aspects of vocational behavior.

Although differences in orientation among theorists may be more apparent than real, certain occupational psychologists have been less concerned with portraying the experiences that shape vocational patterns at
various developmental stages than with studying the specific act of occupational selection as an expression of personality. Bordin, Nachmann, and
Segal (1963), for example, articulated a framework based upon analytic
theory which attempts to identify the gratifications different kinds of work
can offer. They traced these gratifications to physiological functions pre-
sumed necessary to their achievement, with emphasis upon early experiences leading to particular modes of obtaining gratification.

Roe's formulation, suggesting that basic parental attitudes of acceptance,
concentration, and avoidance influence the child's later vocational choice,
has stimulated lively research interest. Utton (1962) and Switzer and
others (1962) found no clear confirming evidence that early parental
management of the child is related to vocational behavior; however, the
adequacy of the test in both studies may be questioned because of
methodological problems centering around the means used to have college
students recall their backgrounds. In contrast, closely related propositions
about field of choice deduced from psychoanalytic theory were supported
in one study using retrospective interview data (Galinsky, 1962). Efforts
to construct more sensitive measures for obtaining data on family-child
relations were reported by Roe and Siegelman (1963) and by Brunkan
and Crites (1964). Green and Parker (1965) used the Roe and Siegelman
instrument to obtain data on parent-child relations from 355 seventh
graders. When these data were related to occupational choices, classified
according to a person or nonperson orientation, equivocal results were
found. There was some evidence that parent attitudes may affect boys and

girls differently. Brunkan (1965) reaffirmed the findings of others who have put Roe's hypotheses to test, but his study holds implications for future research. By manipulating the choice variable, Brunkan sought to control conscious or reality factors which may mask the influence of parental attitudes in occupational selection. Future researchers should recognize that the relationship between early childhood experience and vocational choice may have been overly simplified by Roe, and that her theory does not give sufficient attention to the many possible factors which interact and affect career decisions.

A stream of research has been generated by Holland's model of vocational choice behavior, a model which he regards also as a theory of personality. The model includes a six-category typology of psychosocial environments. Predictions can be made that individuals will choose occupations that are in categories consistent with their personality types. The theory, and most of the empirical studies exploring it, were reported in a book by Holland (1966). A major limitation of the research, acknowledged by Holland, is that it was conducted with atypical samples consisting of National Merit Scholars. A study by Osipow, Ashby, and Wall (1966) used a normal sample of college students, and the data revealed that although large proportions of the subjects chose occupations consistent with the theory, many did not. Methodological limitations in assigning students to personality type groups may have led to an underestimation of the predictive value of the theory. Holland's contention that modal orientations may be inferred from typical vocational interest inventories was confirmed in one study which compared *Strong Vocational Interest Blank* scores with vocational choices classified according to one of the six major personality categories (Wall, Osipow, and Ashby, 1967).

Phrased in the tradition of trait-and-factor theory, Project Talent was designed to delineate a system of personality measures from follow-ups with a large, representative sample of high school students, with predictive validity for career and life adjustment criteria (Flanagan and others, 1962). Findings from the first follow-up studies undertaken when each grade was one year out of high school were reported recently by Flanagan and Cooley (1966). In addition to providing normative data with respect to post-high school experiences, the investigators reported information establishing the predictive usefulness of the "Talent" battery with ninth graders. Five-year, 10-year, and 20-year studies are planned.

Critique of Theories

Tempered criticisms of vocational development formulations were found in the literature, pointing to the incompleteness of current theory. Tyler (1967) stated that much of what is being discovered about the stages through which an individual passes in preparing to find his place in the work world cannot be generalized beyond middle-class males. LoCascio

(1967) showed how theories of vocational development tend to emphasize the continuous, uninterrupted, and progressive aspects of behavior, and thus appear to have limited significance for the disadvantaged, whose development probably is characterized best as discontinuous. Noting the strict adherence of the theorists to taxonomies based on positive attitudes toward work, Zytowski (1965) proposed that avoidance behavior be studied. Lyon (1965) underscored the need for occupational researchers to relate theory to cultural determinants rather than to conceptualize exclusively in terms of a universally applicable developmental psychology. Accepting the developmental approach, Beilin (1963), however, cautioned that there is danger in focusing on normative data and conceptions to the neglect of studying cognitive learning. An overall analysis was made by Carkhuff, Alexik, and Anderson (1967), who applied an inductive-deductive schema of theory building to contemporary vocational development formulations. These analysts concluded that none of the present theories satisfies the criteria of a comprehensive model, and they offered the opinion that theoretical breakthroughs may be held back by the need of researchers to continually relate their data to preconceived constructs which do not change with the acquisition of data.

It is encouraging to note from this review that psychologists are beginning to champion sound conceptual models of vocational behavior and are evidencing a lively interest and involvement in putting theoretical propositions to test. That much of the present knowledge provided by research may not permit generalization to large segments of the population, particularly to women and to those who live in marginal socioeconomic circumstances, constitutes a theoretical and practical problem of considerable importance.

Additional References: LoCascio (1964); Super (1964).

Correlates of Vocational Development

Many studies have been directed toward examining the processes by which concepts of work are acquired and vocational motives expressed.

Occupational Stereotypes

Research has consistently shown that there is high agreement in perceptions of occupations when a prestige dimension is imposed by the investigator. Hodge, Siegal, and Rossi (1964) compared prestige rankings of occupations with similar rankings obtained in 1947 in a widely cited study by North and Hatt of the National Opinion Research Center. A coefficient of correlation of 0.99 resulted. Gunn (1964) interviewed elementary children to determine when and in what manner the prestige motive is manifested. She found that children as early as the third grade were beginning to confer status to jobs based upon service criteria, while at the seventh-grade level a social class hierarchy had emerged in their perceptions. Socioeconomic differences in values were associated with disparities in ranks assigned by senior high school subjects.

Where psychological dimensions of vocational stereotypes have been studied, results are conflicting. Bohn (1966) investigated the relationship between psychological needs and measured vocational interests, interpreting the findings as supporting current vocational stereotypes. Gonyea (1963), on the other hand, permitted subjects greater freedom in choosing relevant dimensions and found a heterogeneity of vocational perceptions not indicated by previous research. That a person's image of his chosen occupational role may change was shown by James (1965), who found that discrepancies between perceived self-expectations and concepts of persons in the chosen occupation motivate attitude change leading toward congruity.

Educational and Occupational Aspirations

A review by Haller and Miller (1963) showed level of occupational aspiration to be an important variable in the study of social mobility behavior of youth. In a seven-year follow-up of high school junior and senior boys, Miller and Haller (1964) found a crude measure of level of aspiration to be the best predictor among 50-odd variables of the prestige accorded to the occupation in which the individual was eventually employed. To meet the need for an adequate research instrument to measure the variable, Haller and Miller (1963) constructed the Occupational Aspiration Scale. The instrument appears to offer a practical and reliable measure for determining differential levels of occupational aspiration; however, predictive validity of the instrument, its fakeability, and its appropriateness for girls remain open questions.

The variety of social stimulus variables found to be associated with level of aspiration and the lack of attention, in some instances, to proper control, make it difficult for those who wish to draw dependable inferences. Krauss (1964) discovered that educational aspirations of lower-class youth were related to the educational experiences of family members and peers. The effect of perceived economic opportunity on aspirations was apparent in a study by Henderson (1966). He found that poverty-stricken youth, when compared with middle-class Negroes, projected a significantly greater difference in ideal and real aspirations. Appalachian youth who stay in that geographical area were studied by Stevic and Uhlig (1967) and were found to have significantly lower occupational aspirations than those who migrate to a residential area near an urban center. Sewell and Orenstein (1965) tested the relationship between size of community residence and occupational choice of youth. Controlled factors of intelligence and socioeconomic status failed to account for the lower aspirations of male youth from rural and smaller communities. Career patterns reflecting aspiration

15

levels of rural youth were studied by Nelson and McFarland (1962). Among rural male graduates of 70 high schools in Minnesota who were followed up six years later, less than one-third sought formal post-high school training and less than 50 percent of those in the upper half of their graduating classes continued in school. Few of those who did go on chose to enter trade or technical schools. These studies seem to suggest that the level of one's aspirations is contingent to a degree upon opportunities and experiences available within one's frame of social reference.

Psychological characteristics and personal orientations tending to produce the experience of success in occupationally related areas of behavior were found to be associated with levels of aspiration. Gribbons and Lohnes (1966b), reporting findings of longitudinal research over a five-year period, disclosed that adolescents with intelligence slightly above average tended to lower the level of their aspirations, whereas over half the youngsters classified as having IQs below 105 persisted in their preferences for the professions. Perrone (1964-65) found that students whose aspirations led them to enroll in two-year post-high school programs were intellectually, socioeconomically, and educationally between those who terminated their education at high school or before and those who attended four-year colleges or universities. Motivational elements common to academic achievement were found by Farquhar and Payne (1963) to function similarly in occupational aspirations. The effects of fear of failure in organization of occupational aspirations were studied by Burnstein (1963). As fear of failure increased, prestige of occupations aspired to decreased.

Career Decision-Making Behavior

The literature was replete with investigations of the career process from initial attraction to a field of work through subsequent modifications of vocational choice to job entry. Parker (1962) sampled 29,000 seventh graders in Oklahoma and found the majority, 67 percent of the boys and 66 percent of the girls, expressing a certain definiteness about their future. In a 12-year longitudinal study of the vocational choices of children, Tyler (1964) concluded that boys who prefer a career in science crystallize their interests between the ages of 10 and 14. The interests of career-oriented girls begin to take shape at or before the age of 14.

As suggested by the theory of career patterning, a discernible change in factors associated with decision making at different ages was noted. O'Hara (1962), in a study of fourth-, fifth-, and sixth-grade pupils, confirmed the hypothesis that choices made at this stage of development are more closely related to interests than capacities. Following eighth graders over a two-year period, Gribbons (1964) found increasing awareness of interests and values and their relation to occupational decisions, along with greater awareness and accuracy of appraisal of abilities. He noted, however, that many youngsters at the tenth-grade level were not yet ready to make educational and prevocational decisions. Contrary to theoretical suppositions that values do not assume an important role in the vocational development of early adolescence, Gribbons and Lohnes (1965) concluded that value statements even among eighth graders are relatively free of fantasy elements, and remain constant throughout high school.

Evidence of a continued preeminence of the interest factor in vocational decision making of adolescents was found in several studies. Mierzwa (1963) selected science and nonscience criterion groups of eleventh-grade students and related multisystems of data to persistence of career choice. The effectiveness of the interest system to discriminate science and nonscience groups remained constant over a two-year period, although ability and environmental systems were shown to increase in effectiveness. Madaus and O'Hara (1967) found differences in the multivariate vocational interest patterns of high school boys classified according to nine broad categories based upon stated occupational choice. The study showed that these differences were more specific than science-nonscience differences found in previous research. Career choices of 650 male high school seniors were assessed by Astin (1967a) on the basis of their personal characteristics when they were in ninth grade. Among the 26 antecedent variables studied, measured interests and expressed career choice at the ninth-grade level were the best predictors of career outcomes at the twelfth grade.

Although criteria for evaluating realism of vocational choice have been found wanting (Hewer, 1966), it seems logical that decisions based on reality factors should lead to greater realism with advancing age. Defining realism in terms of level of vocational choice, Hollender (1967) showed that the concept was related to both age and grade. The shift with age from a reliance primarily upon interests in vocational decision making was noted by Montesano and Geist (1964), who, in contrasting ninth- and twelfth-grade boys, found the older students taking into account more factors related to their abilities and to occupational requirements and conditions of work. Hall (1963) observed that high school seniors compared with sophomores and juniors more frequently described themselves as being able to make a choice and to base their choices upon realistic factors in work. Decision making was viewed by Dilley (1965) as a function of vocational maturity, and he found the ability in twelfth-grade students to be associated with intelligence, achievement, and participation in extracurricular activities.

Vocational decision making was conceptualized by Hershenson and Roth (1966) as a process in which (a) the range of possibilities is narrowed and (b) those remaining are strengthened. According to Gross (1967), the direction of choice is less a matter of moving *toward* a solution of a problem than it is a moving *away* from a situation that is undesirable. Borow (1966) accented this line of thinking by stating that vocational decision making appears to be marked by a kind of occupational foreclosure in which many fields of work may be eliminated prematurely. Empirical support for the view was provided in Nelson's (1963) study of the knowledge and interest of elementary and secondary school students toward 16 selected occupations. Whereas the younger children, and those of lower IQ and socioeconomic status, tended to respond positively to all occupations, the responses of older and brighter youngsters were more pointedly negative. Nelson concluded that the occupational elimination process starts early in the elementary grades.

Implicit in a number of theories is the assumption that personality characteristics differentiate individuals preferring various fields of work. Crites (1963) found type of motivation to be a factor of importance in interest development. The primary motivational characteristic differentiating interests was a bipolar one of social service versus outdoor, science, and technology (working with people rather than things). In research on origins of interests in children, Roe and Siegelman (1964) obtained statistically significant correlations, though generally of a low order, between measures of early experience and adult preference for social activities. Oppenheimer (1966) confirmed the findings of a number of studies which have shown that people prefer occupations perceived as congruent with their self-concepts. A mediating variable, labeled self-esteem, was found to be related to eventual occupational choice in two studies (Korman, 1966, 1967). Kinnane and Gaubinger (1963) sought to determine with college freshmen the relation of general life values to values held important in work. The resulting correlations were significant, but low. One may conclude that descriptive and response correlated studies attempting to shed light on the interactions of personal traits and pre-employment occupational behavior have not, to the present time, provided convincing evidence in support of the predicted relationships.

Patterns of vocational change over time are of particular interest to those concerned with vocational education and manpower training. Super (1967) employed a variety of scales and judgment-making procedures to assess the vocational progress of young men from ages 18 to 25. Throughout these post-high school years, approximately one-third of the subjects engaged in behavior adjudged to be floundering. At age 25, one-fifth of the men still had not developed stabilizing vocational coping behavior. Of secondary interest, less than two-fifths of the subjects actually entered one of the occupations specified while in high school, a finding in line with the results of other research. Studies of career change among students in vocational-technical schools were not found, but Nichols (1964) investigated shifts in vocational choice of more than 6,000 highly able men and women during four years of college. Significant net changes occurred in all major fields except biology and speech. Astin (1967b) analyzed career change in samples of subjects of varying levels of educational attainment and found a consistent shift away from science and engineering fields and toward careers in business and education.

Interpretation of the data from research on career decision-making behavior raises serious questions about the wisdom of imposing vocational directions or curriculum choices on adolescents while in high school. Although the data testify to a healthy maturation of vocational motives and behavior during the adolescent years, including an increasing awareness of reality factors affecting vocational choice, the number of students making decisions based upon irrelevant and inaccurate information and the pattern of choice change during the early adult years argue for flexibility in educational programing. What effect specialized vocational training has in stabilizing career aspirations remains a question for investigation.

Sources of Influence

Multiple factors have a bearing on the development of work-relevant behavior. Unfortunately, the attention given to studying personal variables involved in vocational decision making has not been matched by an equal concern for understanding the influence of significant reference groups or the effect of providing information about job requirements and employment opportunities.

From the inception of the vocational development process, the family constitutes a highly significant reference group. Elder (1963) showed how family childrearing practices foster the development of achievement potential. Kinnane and Pable (1962) verified a number of hypotheses regarding the relationship between work values and family background dimensions, including cultural stimulation, family cohesiveness, social mobility, and adolescent independence. Evidence of the importance of the father's influence on vocational development was provided in a study by Marr (1965). Subjects who, at the age of 25, indicated a commitment to a field were contrasted with those who did not. A higher proportion of those having made a choice were found to have a father or father substitute whom they accepted. Steimel and Suziedelis (1963) found that predominance of perceived influence by one parent over that of the other had a demonstrable effect on the direction of interest development. Subjects reporting father influence measured more typically masculine interests. The investigators suggested that parental occupational and educational level may account for the perceived predominance of influence. Parental influence on work values of women was studied by Kinnane and Bannon (1964). The predominance of perceived influence by a father whose level of education and training was superior to that of the mother appeared to result in a lower work-value orientation on the part of the daughter.

Stump, Jordan, and Friesen (1967) cited a need for research to explicate the effect of cultural contexts on vocational development. Smelser (1963) analyzed socioeconomic histories of 93 families over an extended period of time and concluded that sons from the upward mobile families were the most aspiring as adolescents and the most dominant in their adult self-appraisals. In a study of sixth-grade boys in the Boston area, Maccoby (1962) found modest support for the hypothesis that middle-class children, in contrast to those from lower working classes, prefer occupations which offer authority and responsibility roles.

The impact of social and cultural restrictions on the occupational socialization process was the focus of several studies. Chansky (1965), matching 100 Negro and 100 Caucasian ninth-grade students on aptitude, found significant differences in the vocational interests of the two races. Negro youth were more interested in occupations calling for social interaction, money exchanges, verbal fluency, and computational manipulations. Caucasians were inclined to occupations involving a concern with nature and machines. Comparing children in grades three through six from the inner city with a representative group from suburbia, Clark (1967) reported that middle-class boys and lower-class girls express a significantly greater preference for white collar and professional occupations. In their perceptions of occupations, both lower-class boys and girls were significantly less able to supply appropriate job titles to stimulus figures, suggesting that some job models lack relevance for young people who are economically deprived. Himes (1964) drew the conclusion that race and class establish institutionalized conditions under which lower class Negro youth are socialized to certain work-related cultural deprivations which influence both their acceptance and performance as workers.

Other influences were singled out as being instrumental in the formation of work-related attitudes and values. From their study of 1,105 working males aged 25 to 64, Duncan and Hodge (1963) concluded that formal education is becoming a more potent factor than father's occupation in the son's level of occupational achievement. The potential influence of the counselor as a molder of attitudes was shown in a study by Krumboltz and Varenhorst (1965). Ninth-grade pupils were asked to indicate the extent of their agreement with three statements, each of which was attributed to a different one of three communicator groups: parents, peers, and counselors. Although the study was not designed to test influences specific to vocational behavior, the results clearly indicated the power of the counselor to shape attitudes.

De Fleur (1963) found that children between ages 6 and 13 increase their knowledge of occupational roles and status and that personal contact is a more effective educational influence than either television programs or general culture. Tennyson and Monnens (1963-64), on the assumption that elementary reading texts may influence vocational aspirations, analyzed the reading series of six publishing companies. They found a disproportionate emphasis given to professional, service, and outdoor occupations and an equivalent lack of attention given to clerical, skilled, semiskilled, and unskilled occupations. The influence of occupational information on vocational attitudes was demonstrated in a study by Osipow (1962), in which descriptive information eliminated differences in perception that apparently existed as a result of presentation of job titles alone. Few studies were found which dealt with the influence of school subjects, work experience, or peer pressure upon the development and expression of vocational motives.

Occupational Status and Performance

Prediction of Vocational Success

The efficacy of psychological measures to predict career performance continued as a pragmatic question of interest to researchers. An extensive survey of the literature by Super and Crites (1962) provided data on the usefulness of tests in predicting training and job success. The findings, which were generally consistent with earlier summaries, indicated a gap between training and job performance. Thorndike (1963) suggested that prediction of performance in school and work training programs may be the most one can expect from our present test batteries. When the task is viewed as that of providing individual guidance, the researcher may find logic in the approach of Cooley (1964), who made short-term predictions of educational and career decisions at successive stages of development.

Crawford (1964) reported the use of a variety of aptitude test batteries designed to predict successful performance in some 55 different curriculums at Los Angeles Trade-Technical College. Counselors in Georgia were provided data by Bottoms (1965) which enabled them to use the *Dailey Vocational Test* in relating student abilities to performance in area vocational-technical school programs. Banas and Nash (1966) correlated scores on selected scales of the *General Aptitude Test Battery* with a composite criterion to test the hypothesis that work performance of nonhandicapped subgroups of skilled, clerical, and nonskilled was more predictable than that of handicapped subgroups. Results showed a pattern of consistently lower validities for the handicapped, suggesting that aptitude measures typically used in selection may not be appropriate for persons with physical disabilities.

Although no studies were found which predicted success within an occupation from a measure of interest, evidence of the value of such inventories for predicting occupational choice or differentiating occupational groups continued to mount. D. P. Campbell (1966a,b) marshalled substantial data to show that scales of the *Strong Vocational Interest Blank*, developed in the 1930's, hold up in current cross-validations. Clark (1961), employing the *Minnesota Vocational Interest Inventory*, demonstrated that differentiated interest patterns exist among men who work at skilled and semiskilled occupations.

The prediction task in vocational education may be confounded by a philosophical disagreement over whether tests are to be used to predict individual career behavior or to make decisions regarding large numbers of candidates for various programs. Borow (1966) has shown that the conditions which apply in predicting normative behavior for personnel selection do not ordinarily obtain in vocational counseling, where one person's characteristics must be statistically related to a large number of occupational performance sets.

Personality Differences Among Occupational Groups

Only a few studies were reported in which the principal focus was on occupational group differences. The problem of relating personality attributes and roles of workers in various occupations is a formidable one, not only because of the tolerance within any given occupation for satisfying widely varying needs, but also because variables of age, education, and socioeconomic background interact to affect either personality or occupational role.

Segal and Szabo (1964), deriving hypotheses from psychoanalytic theory, found that accounting students contrasted with creative writing students exhibited closer positive identification with their parents and expressed more accepting attitudes toward authority and people in general. Personality characteristics of male and female junior college students enrolled in trade and vocational courses were analyzed by Stewart (1966). Noncognitive variables explored included sources of life satisfaction, risk-taking attitudes, impulse expression, estheticism, and abstraction. The population was found to be psychologically different from junior college students who are in nonvocational programs and from student populations in four-year colleges and universities. Gray (1963) was able to draw personality descriptions for secondary teachers, accountants, and mechanical engineers based upon differences found with the *Edwards Personal Preference Schedule* and a values inventory. Controlling age and experience factors, Gunderson and Nelson (1966) assessed differences among several Navy occupational groups on 31 personality and value scales. Most of the variance in test scores was accounted for by dichotomizing the six occupational specialties into the two broad categories of "white collar" (administrative and technical) and "blue collar" (mechanical, electrical, construction, and cooks). The latter group indicated greater needs for support, conformity, and rigidity in social relationships. Three occupational groups, classified on a person-thing—directed continuum, were studied by Miller (1962) and found to differ when personality dimensions were analyzed. The findings suggested that personality variables in relation to work may in some instances be value-oriented and in others function-oriented.

Worker Adjustment

Worker satisfaction, motivation, and productivity are often discussed as factors in vocational adjustment. Robinson, Conners, and Whitacre (1966) reviewed studies of job satisfaction completed in 1964-65, supplementing earlier reviews. Dawis, England, and Lofquist (1964) published a theory of work adjustment in which the interaction between the individual and his work environment is defined in terms of two concepts— "satisfactoriness" and "satisfaction." Weiss and others (1964a,b) reported on the development and construct validity of the Minnesota Importance Questionnaire, a measure of an individual's vocational needs. Five components of satisfaction were analyzed in a study by Carlson and others (1962) with handicapped and nonhandicapped workers possessing varying levels of skill. Among the nonhandicapped blue-collar workers, the "human relations" factor tended to have a larger significance in the satisfactions of the nonskilled than of the skilled. For the white-collar workers, a dominant factor was "satisfaction with the conditions of work," including satisfaction with supervision and compensation. A later publication by Carlson and others (1963) reported criterion measures of the worker's satisfactoriness to his employer.

Kornhauser (1962) found that factory workers performing in occupations in which well developed skills are applied show greater mental health than those limited to repetitive machine-paced operations. Mulvey (1963) was able to relate degree of adjustment to career pattern in a study of women between the ages of 37 and 47. She reported that most well adjusted women had a career pattern midway between housewife and full-time career. Lodahl and Kejner (1965) defined job involvement as a multidimensional attitude that can be scaled with adequate, but not high, reliability. The construct was found to be most affected by organization conditions and learned value orientations. Work role relationships within organizations were analyzed in a national survey by Kahn and others (1964), who found role conflict to have been experienced by about one-half of the workers in their sample. Paloli (1967) investigated the relationship between contrasting organizational types created in the laboratory setting and the distribution of three types of role strains—role uncertainty, role disparity, and role incompatibility. Modest support was found for the hypothesis that role uncertainty and role disparity would be more frequent in a relatively unstructured organization. It was further observed that emphasis on work rules was more directly associated with the frequency of role incompatibility than any other organizational feature.

Fundamental questions about what makes for a satisfied and productive worker remain to be answered. Since most of what is known about attitudes toward work has been learned through study of individuals for whom the ability to work is not a social problem, the current interest in the handicapped worker is a development of practical significance. The influence associates have on worker productivity has been studied extensively, but little is known about how differences in satisfaction with various aspects of one's vocation may result from different reference group pressures. Most importantly, there is need to research the elaborate socialization process required to transform the playing child into the working adult.

Facilitation of Career Development

Difficulties encountered by young people today in comprehending the intricate relationships of occupational life have prompted a growing interest in experimentation with procedures and media by which adequate information may be communicated. Katz (1963) explicated a schema for considering the use of curriculum choices and in-school decisions as part of a systematic program of career guidance. A conceptual model developed by Martin (1967) has provided a base for the design of new types of guidance materials and instructional approaches centering upon career planning for noncollege-bound and culturally disadvantaged youth. Her research has identified several important behavior elements related to vocational development. Drews (1965) demonstrated that a program which offers encouragement, models, and guidelines produces changes in attitude towards learning and towards career among gifted girls. Her materials formed the basis for a new career social studies program which is a radical departure from the usual vocational guidance course. Boocock (1967) reported the results of field tests with the Life Career Game, a simulated environmental tool for teaching decision making. The game was found to be useful in arousing student interest, communicating factual information about career decisions, and providing young people a realistic, if vicarious, experience with certain aspects of adult life. Shirts (1966) adapted the Life Career Game for use with sixth graders. Although the game evoked a high degree of pupil interest, an experimental group which played the game did not make a significant gain in vocational maturity over a control group.

Krumboltz and Thoresen (1964) reported the first in a series of carefully controlled experiments designed to evaluate the success of reinforcement counseling procedures in effecting changes in vocational behavior. Verbal reinforcement of information-seeking responses during the interview resulted in greater exploration of relevant occupational and educational information outside of the counseling situation. Model reinforcement presented through an audio-taped counseling interview proved more effective than verbal reinforcement alone in the case of males. The findings of this study were substantiated in later research by Krumboltz and Schroeder (1965) and by Thoresen and Krumboltz (1967).

Research and operational use of new technologies for processing information comprised the subject matter of a conference summarized by

Campbell and others (1966). A model system providing for microfilm storage, retrieval, and dissemination of occupational information was reported in use in San Diego County (Pierson, Hoover, and Whitfield, 1967). Ellis and Wetherell (1966) described the need for equipment required in a computerized system for presenting career-information. A prototype computer-based occupational information system was developed and described by Impellitteri (1967). One unique feature of the system is that information can be selectively presented in accordance with the individual's abilities as measured by the *General Aptitude Test Battery*. Hoyt and Cochran (1965) described a research program designed to collect, analyze, and disseminate data useful in the guidance of persons contemplating attendance at trade, technical, or business schools after leaving the secondary school.

Several national conferences have sought to find ways of stimulating research in career development and improving vocational guidance practice. Suggested guidelines for research and practice relative to guidance in vocational education were presented by R. E. Campbell (1966). Ashcraft and others (1966) identified concepts of occupational behavior and work in a changing society which have relevance for school curriculum planning. McDaniels (1966) compiled background papers and task-oriented group reports presented at a conference on the vocational aspects of counselor education. Many of the suggestions forthcoming from this conference are ready for prompt field tryout.

Summary

A strong beginning has been made to establish firmly or to contradict by empirical means the fundamental assumptions on which theory of vocational development rests. While contemporary formulations and research were found to fall short in important respects, an impressive body of knowledge about vocational development and behavior has accumulated. Concerted efforts are needed to start translating existing theory into practice. The potential of vocational education for providing exploratory experiences that develop broad occupational awareness remains an important topic for which there is need of research.

Bibliography

ASHCRAFT, KENNETH B., and OTHERS. *A Report of the Invitational Conference on Implementing Career Development Theory and Research Through the Curriculum.* Washington, D.C.: National Vocational Guidance Association, 1966. 205 pp.
ASTIN, HELEN S. "Career Development During the High School Years." *Journal of Counseling Psychology* 14: 94-98; March 1967. (a)

ASTIN, HELEN S. "Patterns of Career Choices over Time." *Personnel and Guidance Journal* 45: 541-46; February 1967. (b)

BANAS, PAUL A., and NASH, ALLAN N. "Differential Predictability: Selection of Handicapped and Non-Handicapped." *Personnel and Guidance Journal* 45: 227-30; November 1966.

BEILIN, HARRY. "Discussion." *Personnel and Guidance Journal* 41: 780-82; May 1963.

BOHN, MARTIN J., JR. "Psychological Needs Related to Vocational Personality Types." *Journal of Counseling Psychology* 13: 306-309; Fall 1966.

BOOCOCK, SARANE S. "The Life Career Game." *Personnel and Guidance Journal* 46: 328-34; December 1967.

BORDIN, EDWARD S.; NACHMANN, BARBARA; and SEGAL, STANLEY L. "An Articulated Framework for Vocational Development." *Journal of Counseling Psychology* 10: 107-16; Summer 1963.

BOROW, HENRY, editor. *Man in a World at Work*. Boston: Houghton Mifflin Co., 1964. 606 pp.

BOROW, HENRY. "Development of Occupational Motives and Roles." *Review of Child Development Research: Volume 2*. (Edited by Lois Wladis Hoffman and Martin L. Hoffman.) New York: Russell Sage Foundation, 1966. pp. 373-422.

BOTTOMS, GENE. *Counselor's Guide to Georgia Area Vocational-Technical Schools*. Atlanta, Ga.: State Department of Education, 1965. 39 pp.

BRUNKAN, RICHARD J. "Perceived Parental Attitudes and Parental Identification in Relation to Field of Vocational Choice." *Journal of Counseling Psychology* 12: 39-47; Spring 1965.

BRUNKEN, RICHARD J., and CRITES, JOHN O. "An Inventory To Measure the Parental Attitudes Variables in Roe's Theory of Vocational Choice." *Journal of Counseling Psychology* 11: 3-11; Spring 1964.

BURNSTEIN, EUGENE. "Fear of Failure, Achievement Motivation, and Aspiring to Prestigeful Occupations." *Journal of Abnormal and Social Psychology* 67: 189-93; August 1963.

CAMPBELL, DAVID P. "Stability of Interests Within an Occupation over Thirty Years." *Journal of Applied Psychology* 50: 51-56; February 1966. (a)

CAMPBELL, DAVID P. "The Stability of Vocational Interests Within Occupations over Long Time Spans." *Personnel and Guidance Journal* 44: 1012-19; June 1966. (b)

CAMPBELL, ROBERT E., editor. *Guidance in Vocational Education: Guidelines for Research and Practice*. Leadership 2, A National Interdisciplinary Seminar Sponsored by the Center for Vocational and Technical Education. Columbus: Ohio State University, January 12-14, 1966. 181 pp.

CAMPBELL, ROBERT E., and OTHERS. *Systems Under Development for Vocational Guidance: A Report of a Research Exchange Conference*. Columbus: Ohio State University, 1966. 70 pp.

CARKHUFF, ROBERT R.; ALEXIK, MAE; and ANDERSON, SUSAN. "Do We Have a Theory of Vocational Choice?" *Personnel and Guidance Journal* 46: 335-45; December 1967.

CARLSON, ROBERT E., and OTHERS. *The Measurement of Employment Satisfaction*. Minnesota Studies in Vocational Rehabilitation: XIII, Industrial Relations Center, Bulletin No. 35. Minneapolis: University of Minnesota, 1962. 189 pp.

CARLSON, ROBERT E., and OTHERS. *The Measurement of Employment Satisfactoriness*. Minnesota Studies in Vocational Rehabilitation: XIV, Industrial Relations Center, Bulletin No. 37. Minneapolis: University of Minnesota, December 1963. 74 pp.

CHANSKY, NORMAN M. "Race, Aptitude, and Vocational Interests." *Personnel and Guidance Journal* 43: 780-84; April 1965.

CLARK, EDWARD T. "Influence of Sex and Social Class on Occupational Preference and Perception." *Personnel and Guidance Journal* 45: 440-44; January 1967.

CLARK, KENNETH E. *Vocational Interests of Nonprofessional Men*. Minneapolis: University of Minnesota Press, 1961. 129 pp.

COOLEY, WILLIAM W. "Research Frontier: Current Research on the Career Development of Scientists." *Journal of Counseling Psychology* 11: 88-93; Spring 1964.

CRAWFORD, MARGARET L. "Selection and Guidance of Students for Technical and Vocational Education." *American Vocational Journal* 39: 14-15, 32; April 1964.

CRITES, JOHN O. "Vocational Interest in Relation to Vocational Motivation." *Journal of Educational Psychology* 54: 277-85; October 1963.

CRITES, JOHN O. *Measurement of Vocational Maturity in Adolescence: I. Attitude Test of the Vocational Development Inventory.* Psychological Monographs: General and Applied, Vol. 79, No. 2 (Whole No. 595). Washington, D.C.: American Psychological Association, 1965. 36 pp. (a)

CRITES, JOHN O. "Research Frontier: The Vocational Development Project at the University of Iowa." *Journal of Counseling Psychology* 12: 81-86; Spring 1965. (b)

DAWIS, RENÉ V.; ENGLAND, GEORGE W.; and LOFQUIST, LLOYD H. *A Theory of Work Adjustment.* Minnesota Studies in Vocational Rehabilitation: XV, Industrial Relations Center, Bulletin No. 38. Minneapolis: University of Minnesota, January 1964. 27 pp.

DE FLEUR, MELVIN L. "Children's Knowledge of Occupational Roles and Prestige: Preliminary Report." *Psychological Reports* 13: 760; December 1963.

DILLEY, JOSIAH S. "Decision-Making Ability and Vocational Maturity." *Personnel and Guidance Journal* 44: 423-27; December 1965.

DREWS, ELIZABETH MONROE. "Counseling for Self-Actualization in Gifted Girls and Young Women." *Journal of Counseling Psychology* 12: 167-75; Summer 1965.

DUNCAN, OTIS DUDLEY, and HODGE, ROBERT W. "Education and Occupational Mobility: A Regression Analysis." *American Journal of Sociology* 68: 629-44; May 1963.

ELDER, GLEN H., JR. "Achievement Orientations and Career Patterns of Rural Youth." *Sociology of Education* 37: 30-58; Fall 1963.

ELLIS, ALLAN B., and WETHERELL, CHARLES B. *The Computer and Career Decisions.* Cambridge, Mass.: Harvard University, 1966. 20 pp.

FARQUHAR, WILLIAM W., and PAYNE, DAVID A. "Factors in the Academic-Occupational Motivations of Eleventh Grade Under- and Over-Achievers." *Personnel and Guidance Journal* 42: 245-51; November 1963.

FLANAGAN, JOHN C., and COOLEY, WILLIAM W. *Project Talent, 1-Year Follow-Up Studies.* Pittsburgh, Pa.: University of Pittsburgh, 1966. 387 pp.

FLANAGAN, JOHN C., and OTHERS. *The Talents of American Youth 1: Design for a Study of American Youth.* Boston: Houghton Mifflin Co., 1962. 240 pp.

GALINSKY, M. DAVID. "Personality Development and Vocational Choice of Clinical Psychologists and Physicists." *Journal of Counseling Psychology* 9: 299-305; Winter 1962.

GONYEA, GEORGE G. "Job Perceptions in Relation to Vocational Preference." *Journal of Counseling Psychology* 10: 20-26; Spring 1963.

GRAY, JAMES T. "Needs and Values in Three Occupations." *Personnel and Guidance Journal* 42: 238-44; November 1963.

GREEN, LAURENCE B., and PARKER, HARRY J. "Parental Influence Upon Adolescents' Occupational Choice: A Test of an Aspect of Roe's Theory." *Journal of Counseling Psychology* 12: 379-83; Winter 1965.

GRIBBONS, WARREN D. "Changes in Readiness for Vocational Planning from the Eighth Grade to the Tenth Grade." *Personnel and Guidance Journal* 42: 908-13; May 1964.

GRIBBONS, WARREN D., and LOHNES, PAUL R. "Shifts in Adolescents' Vocational Values." *Personnel and Guidance Journal* 44: 248-52; November 1965.

GRIBBONS, WARREN D., and LOHNES, PAUL R. *Career Development.* Weston, Mass.: Regis College, 1966. 302 pp. (a)

GRIBBONS, WARREN D., and LOHNES, PAUL R. "Occupational Preferences and Measured Intelligence." *Vocational Guidance Quarterly* 14: 211-14; Spring 1966. (b)

GROSS, EDWARD. "A Sociological Approach to the Analysis of Preparation for Work Life." *Personnel and Guidance Journal* 45: 416-23; January 1967.

GUNDERSON, E. K. ERIC, and NELSON, PAUL D. "Personality Differences Among Navy Occupational Groups." *Personnel and Guidance Journal* 44: 956-61; May 1966.

GUNN, BARBARA. "Children's Conceptions of Occupational Prestige." *Personnel and Guidance Journal* 42: 558-63; February 1964.

HALL, DONALD W. "The Vocational Development Inventory: A Measure of Vocational Maturity in Adolescence." *Personnel and Guidance Journal* 41: 771-75; May 1963.

HALLER, ARCHIBALD O., and MILLER, IRWIN W. *The Occupational Aspiration Scale: Theory, Structure and Correlates.* Technical Bulletin 288, Agricultural Experimental Station. East Lansing: Michigan State University, 1963. 132 pp.

HARREN, VINCENT A. "The Vocational Decision-Making Process Among College Males." *Journal of Counseling Psychology* 13: 271-77; Fall 1966.

HAVIGHURST, ROBERT J. "Youth in Exploration and Man Emergent." *Man in a World at Work.* (Edited by Henry Borow.) Boston: Houghton Mifflin Co., 1964. pp. 215-36.

HENDERSON, GEORGE. "Occupational Aspirations of Poverty-Stricken Negro Students." *Vocational Guidance Quarterly* 15: 41-45; September 1966.

HERSHENSON, DAVID B., and ROTH, ROBERT M. "A Decisional Process Model of Vocational Development." *Journal of Counseling Psychology* 13: 368-70; Fall 1966.

HEWER, VIVIAN H. "Evaluation of a Criterion: Realism of Vocational Choice." *Journal of Counseling Psychology* 13: 289-94; Fall 1966.

HIMES, JOSEPH S. "Some Work-Related Cultural Deprivations of Lower-Class Negro Youths." *Journal of Marriage and the Family* 26: 447-49; November 1964.

HODGE, ROBERT W.; SIEGEL, PAUL M.; and ROSSI, PETER H. "Occupational Prestige in the United States, 1925-63." *American Journal of Sociology* 70: 286-302; November 1964.

HOLLAND, JOHN L. "Major Programs of Research on Vocational Behavior." *Man in a World at Work.* (Edited by Henry Borow.) Boston: Houghton Mifflin Co., 1964. pp. 259-84.

HOLLAND, JOHN L. *The Psychology of Vocational Choice.* Waltham, Mass.: Blaisdell Publishing Co., 1966. 132 pp.

HOLLENDER, JOHN W. "Development of a Realistic Vocational Choice." *Journal of Counseling Psychology* 14: 314-18; July 1967.

HOYT, KENNETH B., and COCHRAN, LEE W. "Communicating Guidance Information to Specialty Oriented Students." *Audiovisual Instruction* 10: 49-53; January 1965.

IMPELLITTERI, JOSEPH T. "A Computerized Occupational Information System." *Vocational Guidance Quarterly* 15: 262-64; June 1967.

JAMES, FLEMING, III. "Occupational Choice and Attitude Change." *Journal of Counseling Psychology* 12: 311-15; Fall 1965.

KAHN, ROBERT L., and OTHERS. *Organizational Stress: Studies in Role Conflict and Ambiguity.* New York: John Wiley and Sons, 1964. 470 pp.

KATZ, MARTIN. *Decisions and Values: A Rationale for Secondary School Guidance.* New York: College Entrance Examination Board, 1963. 67 pp.

KINNANE, JOHN F., and BANNON, SR. M. MARGARET. "Perceived Parental Influence and Work-Value Orientation." *Personnel and Guidance Journal* 43: 273-79; November 1964.

KINNANE, JOHN F., and GAUBINGER, JOSEPH R. "Life Values and Work Values." *Journal of Counseling Psychology* 10: 362-66; Winter 1963.

KINNANE, JOHN F., and PABLE, MARTIN W. "Family Background and Work Value Orientation." *Journal of Counseling Psychology* 9: 320-25; Winter 1962.

KORMAN, ABRAHAM K. "Self-Esteem Variable in Vocational Choice." *Journal of Applied Psychology* 50: 479-86; December 1966.

KORMAN, ABRAHAM K. "Self-Esteem as a Moderator of the Relationship Between Self-Perceived Abilities and Vocational Choice." *Journal of Applied Psychology* 51: 65-67; February 1967.

KORNHAUSER, ARTHUR. "Toward an Assessment of the Mental Health of Factory Workers: A Detroit Study." *Human Organization* 21: 43-46; Spring 1962.

KRAUSS, IRVING. "Sources of Educational Aspirations Among Working-Class Youth." *American Sociological Review* 29: 867-79; December 1964.

KRUMBOLTZ, JOHN D., and SCHROEDER, WADE W. "Promoting Career Planning Through Reinforcement." *Personnel and Guidance Journal* 44: 19-26; September 1965.

KRUMBOLTZ, JOHN D., and THORESEN, CARL E. "The Effect of Behavioral Counseling in Group and Individual Settings on Information-Seeking Behavior." *Journal of Counseling Psychology* 11: 324-33; Winter 1964.

KRUMBOLTZ, JOHN D., and VARENHORST, BARBARA. "Molders of Pupil Attitudes." *Personnel and Guidance Journal* 43: 443-46; January 1965.

LoCASCIO, RALPH. "Continuity and Discontinuity in Vocational Development Theory." *Personnel and Guidance Journal* 46: 32-36; September 1967.

LODAHL, THOMAS M., and KEJNER, MATHILDE. "The Definition and Measurement of Job Involvement." *Journal of Applied Psychology* 49: 24-33; February 1965.

LYON, RHEE. "Beyond the Conventional Career: Some Speculations." *Journal of Counseling Psychology* 12: 153-58; Summer 1965.

MACCOBY, ELEANOR E. "Class Differences in Boys' Choices of Authority Roles." *Sociometry* 25: 117-19; March 1962.

28

McDaniels, Carl, editor. *Conference on Vocational Aspects of Counselor Education Held at Airlie House, Warrenton, Virginia, December 12-15, 1965.* Washington, D.C.: George Washington University, 1966. 101 pp.

Madaus, George F., and O'Hara, Robert P. "Vocational Interest Patterns of High Schools Boys: A Multivariate Approach." *Journal of Counseling Psychology* 14: 106-12; March 1967.

Marr, Evelyn. "Some Behaviors and Attitudes Relating to Vocational Choice." *Journal of Counseling Psychology* 12: 404-408; Winter 1965.

Martin, Ann M. *A Multimedia Approach to Communicating Occupational Information to Noncollege Youth.* Pittsburgh, Pa.: University of Pittsburgh, December 1967. 265 pp.

Mierzwa, John A. "Comparison of Systems of Data for Predicting Career Choice." *Personnel and Guidance Journal* 42: 29-34; September 1963.

Miller, I. W., and Haller, A. O. "A Measure of Level of Occupational Aspiration." *Personnel and Guidance Journal* 42: 448-55; January 1964.

Miller, Sutherland, Jr. "Relationship of Personality to Occupation, Setting, and Function." *Journal of Counseling Psychology* 9: 115-21; Summer 1962.

Montesano, Nicholas, and Geist, Harold. "Differences in Occupational Choice Between Ninth and Twelfth Grade Boys." *Personnel and Guidance Journal* 43: 150-54; October 1964.

Mulvey, Mary Crowley. "Psychological and Sociological Factors in Prediction of Career Patterns of Women." *Genetic Psychology Monographs* 68: 309-86; November 1963.

Nelson, Richard C. "Knowledge and Interests Concerning Sixteen Occupations Among Elementary and Secondary School Students." *Educational and Psychological Measurement* 23: 741-54; Winter 1963.

Nelson, Theodore M., and McFarland, Keith N. "Occupational Patterns of Rural Youth." *Vocational Guidance Quarterly* 10: 164-66; Spring 1962.

Nichols, Robert C. "Career Decisions of Very Able Students." *Science* 144: 1315-19; June 12, 1964.

O'Hara, Robert P. "The Roots of Careers." *Elementary School Journal* 62: 277-80; February 1962.

Oppenheimer, Ernest A. "The Relationship Between Certain Self Constructs and Occupational Preferences." *Journal of Counseling Psychology* 13: 191-97; Summer 1966.

Osipow, Samuel H. "Perceptions of Occupations as a Function of Titles and Descriptions." *Journal of Counseling Psychology* 9: 106-109; Summer 1962.

Osipow, Samuel H.; Ashby, Jefferson D.; and Wall, Harvey W. "Personality Types and Vocational Choice: A Test of Holland's Theory." *Personnel and Guidance Journal* 45: 37-42; September 1966.

Paloli, Ernest G. "Organization Types and Role Strains: An Experimental Study of Complex Organizations." *Sociology and Social Research* 51: 171-84; January 1967.

Parker, Harry J. "29,000 Seventh Graders Have Made Occupational Choices." *Vocational Guidance Quarterly* 11: 54-55; Autumn 1962.

Perrone, Philip A. "Technicians: Somewhere In-Between." *Vocational Guidance Quarterly* 13: 137-41; Winter 1964-65.

Perrone, Philip A. "Vocational Development." *Review of Educational Research* 36: 298-307; April 1966.

Pierson, Glen N.; Hoover, Richard; and Whitfield, Edwin A. "A Regional Career Information Center: Development and Process." *Vocational Guidance Quarterly* 15: 162-69; March 1967.

Robinson, H. Alan; Connors, Ralph P.; and Whitacre, G. Holly. "Job Satisfaction Researches of 1964-65." *Personnel and Guidance Journal* 45: 371-79; December 1966.

Roe, Anne, and Siegelman, Marvin. "A Parent-Child Relations Questionnaire." *Child Development* 34: 355-69; June 1963.

Roe, Anne, and Siegelman, Marvin. *The Origin of Interests.* Washington, D.C.: American Personnel and Guidance Association, 1964. 98 pp.

29

SCATES, ALICE Y., and BRITTAIN, CLAY V. "Description of the Office of Education Research and Development Program on Career Development and Vocational Guidance: Part II." *Journal of Counseling Psychology* 14: 572-82; November 1967.

SEGAL, STANLEY J., and SZABO, RUTH. "Identification in Two Vocations: Accountants and Creative Writers." *Personnel and Guidance Journal* 43: 252-55; November 1964.

SEWELL, WILLIAM H., and ORENSTEIN, ALAN M. "Community of Residence and Occupational Choice." *American Journal of Sociology* 70: 551-63; March 1965.

SHIRTS, R. GARRY. *Career Simulation for Sixth Grade Pupils.* San Diego, Calif.: San Diego County Department of Education, 1966. 41 pp.

SMELSER, WILLIAM T. "Adolescent and Adult Occupational Choice as a Function of Family Socioeconomic History." *Sociometry* 26: 393-409; December 1963.

STEIMEL, RAYMOND J., and SUZIEDELIS, ANTANAS. "Perceived Parental Influence and Inventoried Interests." *Journal of Counseling Psychology* 10: 289-95; Fall 1963.

STEVIC, RICHARD, and UHLIG, GEORGE. "Occupational Aspirations of Selected Appalachian Youth." *Personnel and Guidance Journal* 45: 435-39; January 1967.

STEWART, LAWRENCE H. *Characteristics of Junior College Students in Occupationally Oriented Curricula.* Berkeley: University of California, 1966. 49 pp.

STUMP, WALTER L.; JORDAN, JOHN E.; and FRIESEN, EUGENE W. "Cross-Cultural Considerations in Understanding Vocational Development." *Journal of Counseling Psychology* 14: 325-31; July 1967.

SUPER, DONALD E., and CRITES, JOHN O. *Appraising Vocational Fitness.* New York: Harper and Row, 1962. 688 pp.

SUPER, DONALD E., and OTHERS. *Career Development: Self-Concept Theory.* New York: College Entrance Examination Board, 1963. 95 pp.

SUPER, DONALD E., and OTHERS. *Floundering and Trial After High School.* Career Pattern Study: Monograph IV. Cooperative Research Project No. 1393. New York: Teachers College, Columbia University, 1967. 334 pp.

SWITZER, DAVID K., and OTHERS. "Early Experiences and Occupational Choice: A Test of Roe's Hypothesis." *Journal of Counseling Psychology* 9: 45-48; Spring 1962.

TENNYSON, W. WESLEY, and MONNENS, LAWRENCE P. "The World of Work Through Elementary Readers." *Vocational Guidance Quarterly* 12: 85-88; Winter 1963-64.

THORESEN, CARL E., and KRUMBOLTZ, JOHN D. "Relationship of Counselor Reinforcement of Selected Responses to External Behavior." *Journal of Counseling Psychology* 14: 140-44; March 1967.

THORNDIKE, ROBERT L. "The Prediction of Vocational Success." *Vocational Guidance Quarterly* 11: 179-87; Spring 1963.

TIEDEMAN, DAVID V., and O'HARA, ROBERT P. *Career Development: Choice and Adjustment.* New York: College Entrance Examination Board, 1963. 108 pp.

TYLER, LEONA E. "The Antecedents of Two Varieties of Vocational Interests." *Genetic Psychology Monographs* 70: 177-227; November 1964.

TYLER, LEONA E. "The Encounter with Poverty—Its Effect on Vocational Psychology." *Rehabilitation Counseling Bulletin* 11: 61-70; Fall 1967.

UTTON, ALDEN C. "Recalled Parent-Child Relations as Determinants of Vocational Choice." *Journal of Counseling Psychology* 9: 49-53; Spring 1962.

WALL, HARVEY W.; OSIPOW, SAMUEL H.; and ASHBY, JEFFERSON D. "SVIB Scores, Occupational Choices, and Holland's Personality Types." *Vocational Guidance Quarterly* 15: 201-205; March 1967.

WALZ, GARRY R. "Vocational Development Process." *Review of Educational Research* 33: 197-204; April 1963.

WEISS, DAVID J., and OTHERS. *Construct Validation Studies of the Minnesota Importance Questionnaire.* Minnesota Studies in Vocational Rehabilitation: XVIII, Industrial Relations Center, Bulletin No. 41. Minneapolis: University of Minnesota, December 1964. 76 pp. (a)

WEISS, DAVID J., and OTHERS. *The Measurement of Vocational Needs.* Minnesota Studies in Vocational Rehabilitation: XVI, Industrial Relations Center, Bulletin No. 39. Minneapolis: University of Minnesota, April 1964. 101 pp. (b)

WILLIAMSON, E. G. *Vocational Counseling: Some Historical, Philosophical, and Theoretical Perspectives.* New York: McGraw-Hill Book Co., 1965. 229 pp.

ZYTOWSKI, DONALD G. "Avoidance Behavior in Vocational Motivation." *Personnel and Guidance Journal* 43: 746-50; April 1965.

30

CAREER DEVELOPMENT:
PANDORA'S BOX OR CORNUCOPIA

C. Todd Strohmenger
Harold L. Henderson

EDUCATION for Career Development could be considered to be in the stage of "becoming." The manner in which individual programs are conceived and managed will determine whether the movement will "become" just a semantic fad or the major trend in education that it deserves to become.

It would be presumptuous of the present writers to attempt to state the ultimate definition of career development education. However, some dimensions of the term and issues to be resolved may be illustrated by citing statements from a 1972 publication of the National Center for Occupation Education at North Carolina State University at Raleigh (Morgan *et al.*, 1972). The 39 projects described in the synopsis are diverse, both geographically and in the nature of programs offered, thus providing the contrasts necessary to clarify some major issues.

The Matter of Scope

One important consideration is the "for whom" issue. Opening statements of nearly all project summaries show that most programs include all grade levels. There is apparent agreement that children must be reached early if any program is to be effective. The question of which youngsters to reach finds different answers, however. Even though some projects are being implemented in phases, the fact that percentages of students participating at the various levels range from one percent to 100 percent suggests that this deserves considerable thought.

The stated goals and objectives reveal that some projects are limiting the target population of their programs for career development. Typical statements are: "train and place youth, particularly the actual and potential dropout"; "provide training in job entry skills to students previously not enrolled in vocational programs"; and "improve the status, scope, and image of vocational-technical education and promote expansion."

At the opposite end of the continuum are such global goals as: "develop the vocational maturity of all students"; "these goals are being reached by applying the career education concept to all courses in all grade segments"; and "the career education program spans grades 1-12 with 100 percent participation of the students."

Although each of the limited goals is commendable, one wonders if they are considered a portion of a total effort to provide education for career development for all children, as suggested in the broad goal statements. If some program developers reach a limited target population in the belief that they have "taken care of" career development education, then a real issue of scope does exist. A narrow coverage does not seem to harmonize with the sight of unemployed college graduates or the phenomenon of degree-holding adults entering technical schools in order to qualify for jobs.

The Change Agents

By whom should the program be generated, offered, and monitored? The telltale marks of two segments of the education community are visible in the objectives of the projects cited in the Raleigh publication. The guidance influence is evident in such terminology as: "clarify capabilities and potential," "develop a positive self-image," and "provide guidance and educational opportunities." Vocational educators have probably contributed such phrases as: "development of job entry skills," "develop a positive attitude toward vocational education," and "assistance in initial placement."

Both the counselor and the vocational educator have much to contribute to the career development movement and should rejoice in its popularity. Perhaps we are seeing a true milestone of education taking shape as it shakes the millstone of hoary academia from its shoulders. However, a jockeying for position, control, or credit by the guidance, vocational, or other segment of the educational scene is not a conflict that is needed in this "becoming" stage of career development education.

There is need for the curriculum director and administrator to assume their proper leadership roles and draw upon the best minds from all facets of community and school, utilizing guidance and vocational personnel as prime resource persons. It is evident that many of the programs reported

33

in the Raleigh study have taken this route.

There are some very obvious characteristics of good curriculum that should need no elaboration here. However, during this period of "becoming," with its diverse activities and term definitions, some of the basic principles of curriculum and learning may be slighted **as educators struggle to meet project deadlines and other pressures.**

Considering the tenuous nature of the terminology and the directions of the movement, care should be taken to define terms and state specific goals and terminal behavioral objectives within the limits of those defined terms (Mager and Beach, 1967).

The requirement that career development education begin early in the student's experience creates the problem of vertical curriculum design. It may be too tempting to divide the program into elementary, junior high, and high school segments and assign to each of them "developmental" tasks or objectives toward which to work. Education for career development should not have to make the historical mistake made by other curriculum areas by developing the three levels in isolation. Cannot these new programs be "born" as total programs, K through 12, with recurring themes, reinforced learning, common information systems, and truly developmental approaches?

It is obvious, as one reads career development literature, that there is as yet no general agreement concerning the nature of this human developmental process. Therefore, the subject matter content that would best contribute to this process cannot be identified with certainty. The variety of theories and notions upon which programs are being built, however, can be an asset. The wealth of practical information that is accumulated should bring about a refinement of our understanding of the process and identification of relevant curriculum content.

The effectiveness of various activities should also receive critical attention. "Hands-on" experiences, field trips to industry, and exposure to information about jobs will not guarantee that the desired learning will take place. Widely published evaluations of these various techniques are needed if the movement is to mature.

A Unique Role for Evaluation?

The most difficult yet the most critical aspect of any program is the matter of evaluation (Suchman, 1967). Evaluation can play a unique role during this stage of "becoming" that is characterized by diverse meanings and activities.

Provided each program defines its use of terms and uses them in articulating specific program objectives, the mass of evaluation material generated regarding concepts, process, techniques, and materials could bring order out of chaos. Too often, low profile programs are retained because no one is threatened by their existence. Specific career education programs must be retained only if they are viable, and should be changed as required; and both decisions must be reached on the basis of sound research. Furthermore, programs need to be compared by creative research designs that are constructed during program development, not after implementation.

Dropping the Other Shoe

We have been looking at some of the issues that must be faced by the local educators who must conceive and manage the programs. The flurry of activity directed toward education for career development is all related to a larger issue in education. This issue is discussed in detail in a U.S. Department of Health, Education, and Welfare publication that should be required reading for all educators (*Career Education*, 1971). President Nixon's 1970 call for massive reform in education is being answered in part by Sidney P. Marland, Jr., U.S. Assistant Secretary for Education, who has designated career education as a national priority.

Features of career education as outlined at the national level include: the restructuring of basic subjects around the theme of career development; extensive guidance and counseling for decision making; and studying careers in relation to major fields of occupations so that students leaving high school will be prepared for either employment in a job of their choosing or additional education in institutions of advanced standing.

In addition to this "in-house" approach to education for career development, a new direction is taking shape that is based upon writers such as Coleman. In view of ". . . the drying up of family functions and the specialization of economic activities . . ." where do the young people belong? Coleman's answer is that " . . . if they are to have the opportunity for moving to adulthood . . . they . . . belong where everyone else is, and where the action is: inside the economic institutions where the productive activities of society take place" (Coleman, 1972, p. 17).

The "employer based" programs represent another facet of the movement to provide education for career development. During the stage of "becoming," this facet can be a nourishing activity for the total movement. The "either-or" question is irrelevant at this time. As we learn from both "in-house" and "off-campus" programs, a rational foundation may be developed for a new order of education.

In the meantime, curriculum directors and administrators will have their hands full in facing the issues that accompany any effort to provide education for career development. The manner in which these issues are met will become evident as the "in-house" facet of the movement flourishes or as it deteriorates and becomes another semantic fad. Let us make certain it succeeds.

References

Career Education. DHEW Publication No. (OE) 72-39. Washington, D.C.: Superintendent of Documents, U.S. Government Printing Office, 1971.

J. S. Coleman. *How Do the Young Become Adults?* Grant No. OEG-2-7-061610-0207, Project No. R16J2C, Report No. 130. Presented at the American Educational Research Association, Chicago, Illinois, April 4, 1972. Baltimore, Maryland: The Johns Hopkins University, May 1972.

R. F. Mager and K. M. Beach, Jr. *Developing Vocational Instruction.* Palo Alto, California: Fearon Publishers, 1967.

R. L. Morgan, A. B. Moore, M. W. Shook, and B. Sargent, editors. *Synopses of Selected Career Education Programs: A National Overview of Career Education.* Career Education, Volume 1. Raleigh: North Carolina State University, National Center for Occupational Education, April 1972.

E. A. Suchman. *Evaluative Research: Principles and Practice in Public Service and Social Action Programs.* New York: Russell Sage Foundation, 1967.

CONTRIBUTIONS OF CAREER DEVELOPMENT TO CAREER EDUCATION

by
Edwin L. Herr

The term "Career Education" has come into American educational parlance both suddenly and surely. The U.S.O.E. has identified it as a national priority. Commissioner Marland (1971) has suggested that the implementation of Career Education "may set aside forever the whole question of the dropout." In addition, he has described it as "a new order of education concerned with the usefulness and self-realization of every individual" (U.S. Department of Health, Education and Welfare, 1971, p. iii). Associate Commissioner Worthington has described Career Education as "a bold new design for education that will effect a blend of academic, general and work skills learning so that individuals passing through the system will be ready for economic self-sufficiency, for a personally satisfying life, for new learning experiences appropriate to career development and avocational interests" (Worthington, 1971).

The concepts being used to describe Career Education indicate that the term includes a complex set of expectations and goals. However, it is apparent that the shifting emphases attached to vocational education legislation during the 1960's stimulated the momentum presently culminating in Career Education. Indeed, the Exemplary Programs and Services Branch, Division of Vocational and Technical Education, U.S.O.E. (1971) has indicated that Part D, Section 142(c) of the Vocational Education Amendments of 1968 actually represent "early attempts to structure operating models of what is now coming to be referred to as a K through 12 'career education system.' The roots for such a system go back into many years of basic research on career development theory" (Exemplary Programs and Services Branch, Division of Vocational and Technical Education, U.S.O.E., 1971).

At a gross level, Career Education represents a composite of what might be described as education for productivity (employability skills) and education for choosing (career development). This combination of emphases seems to be reflected in the recent position paper on Career Education adopted by the National Association of State Directors of Vocational Education. Among the essential characteristics of Career Education to which they gave their support were the following selected examples:

1. Career Education is not synonymous with Vocational Education but Vocational Education is a major part of Career Education.

5. Career Education involves extensive orientation and exploration of occupational opportunities.

7. Career Education is a continuum that begins at kindergarten and extends throughout education.

9. Career Education includes specific preparation for occupations.

10. Career Education assures realistic occupational choices.

12. Career Education permits each student to realistically assess personal attributes as a part of setting life goals (National Association of State Directors of Vocational Education, 1971).

These excerpts reflect continued assurance that the historical contribution of vocational education, preparing man for his work, is not only a useful but vital component of Career Education. Indeed, with the pervasive acceptance of the cluster concept, the occupational model for preparation has been enlarged in scope and in its relevance to the current realities of the occupational structure. But the implications of these excerpts do not stop with reasserting the validity of preparing people to work. They also support the importance of another emphasis, that of the career model.

The career model is broader than the occupational model because it includes attention not only to the acquisition of skills important to employability in particular occupations but also to the factors—attitudes, knowledge, self-concepts—which motivate or impede career literacy, identity and choosing. In the career model, the individual is conceived as moving along one of a number of possible pathways through the educational system and on into and through the work system (Super, 1969). This model emphasizes the importance to the individual of having the skills which will permit him to make informed choices as freely as possible among the multiple opportunities available to him. Of central concern here is helping the individual to see himself as having choices and as having personal characteristics which can be used to evaluate and order the choices available. The career model places its emphasis on helping persons develop preferences and facilitating the execution of plans by which their preferences can be implemented.

In order to choose as freely as possible, one needs knowledge not only about what is available to choose but also about the characteristics of oneself which might be emphasized in thinking about one's choices. The latter requires in addition to knowledge, emphases upon values, interests, and attitudes as these regard:

1. Self-characteristics

2. Environmental alternatives (occupational, educational, personal, social options)

3. The decision-making process itself

39

Career development is essentially the body of speculation and research which is focused upon understanding and describing the above factors and others important to education for choosing. Borow has suggested that theories and research conceived to examine vocational or career development are in reality, "a search for the psychological meaning of vocationally relevant acts (including the exploratory vocational behavior of youth) and of work itself in the human experience" (Borow, 1961). Within this context, recent perspectives on career development view vocational behavior as a continuing and fluid process of growth and learning. Thus, they attach considerable importance to the individual's self-concept(s), his developmental experiences, and his interaction with the situational circumstances in which he finds himself—e.g., family, values, school climate, community reward systems.

A major point of emphasis in career development theory is that education for choosing is a long-term process which has its beginnings early in the life of the child. Put more directly, how children are taught to think about themselves and about work in pre-school and elementary school is considered by many theorists to have important pre-vocational implications for later adult orientations or commitments to or away from work and one's place in it. This means that the foundations for work attitudes are laid not when a student first encounters machine shop or auto mechanics in the tenth grade, or direct work experience whenever that occurs, but many years earlier.

Since personality development and career development seem to be intimately tied together, some theorists also view career development as a continuing attempt to implement one's self-concept or to express one's personality. In one sense, the way one approaches decision-making or career choices is indicative of how one is handling his identity search. Speaking to this matter, Galinsky and Fast (1966) have asserted that, "In our society one of the most clear-cut avenues through which identity concerns are expressed is the process of making a vocational choice . . . . choosing a vocation involves a kind of public self-definition that forces one to say to the world, 'This is what I am.' "

Such an emphasis on education for choosing or on the importance of facilitating career development may be perceived by some as an unnecessary luxury irrelevant to the demands of the real world. While such a conclusion might have had validity several decades ago, it is not descriptive of the present nor of the future as the outlines of the latter are becoming visible. For example, Drucker maintains that the current attacks by youth upon depersonalization, manipulation, corporate society and the "Establishment" actually obscure their real concerns with what he contends is the "burden of decision" confronting them in the current plenitude of opportunity which characterizes this nation. He contends specifically that, "The society of organizations (modern-America's corporate nature) forces the individual to ask of himself: 'Who am I? What do I want to be? What do I want to put into life and what do I want to get out of it?' " (Drucker, 1969, p. 248). Thus, the level of opportunity available in this society also creates a level of personal responsibility for what one is and what he becomes unprecedented in human society. At another level Toffler speculates that the future may bring with it the heightened possibility of "decision stress" as a ramification of "overchoice." He describes the latter as follows:

> Ironically, the people of the future may suffer not from an absence of choice, but from a paralyzing surfeit of it. They may turn out to be victims of that peculiarly super-industrial dilemma: overchoice (Toffler, 1970, p. 26).

The observations of Drucker and of Toffler are either frightening or exciting depending upon how they are viewed. Regardless of such an orientation, however, they certify that education must acknowledge directly, through programmatic efforts, ways of helping persons acquire the information processing and choice behaviors which reinforce the reality of personal power to affect one's life. Such an intent seems to weave throughout descriptions of Career Education.

Career education and career development speak not to certain segments of the population exclusively, but rather to the importance of education for choosing among all students. Operationally, this requires that Career Education do more than simply reinforce or applaud those persons who already possess the characteristics about which it is concerned while simultaneously labeling those who do not already have such skills as losers or unteachable. Instead, Career Education must focus on developing the characteristics important to choosing, planning and employability in as many students as possible. Relevant here is Gysbers' observation that "Career exploration programs should not be seen as strickly a mining operation in which only those with certain talents are chosen, but as more of a farming approach in which all individuals are provided with opportunities to grow and to develop" (Gysbers, 1969). The distinction between mining and farming in this quotation goes beyond the literal interpretation made. It also suggests the differences between allowing career development to occur by chance and happenstance or to be facilitated purposefully and sequentially.

CAREER DEVELOPMENT: CONTENT CONSIDERATIONS

Currently, research and theory about career development are principally descriptive of what happens if there is no planned intervention in the process. However, because they indicate that career development differs among persons and groups, it is evident that career development is modifiable. In other words, career development does not unfold unerringly from some chromosomal or genetic mechanism but is primarily a function of learned responses, whether negative or positive in their characteristics or in their results. Given such a reality, the educator is faced with such questions as, "How does one match intervention in career development to the capacities and the characteristics of

41

students at different educational levels?'' Or, ''If programs to facilitate career development are to be implemented, what major themes ought they promote?'' There are many possible answers to these questions. Table 1 inventories some of them (Herr, 1971).

TABLE 1

EXAMPLES OF THEMES FOR CAREER DEVELOPMENT AT DIFFERENT EDUCATIONAL LEVELS

Elementary School

>*Prime considerations*: Formation of self-concept, developing a vocabulary of self and environmental alternatives.

Factors

>Formulating interests
>Developing a vocabulary of self
>Developing a vocabulary of work
>Developing rudiments of basic trust in self and others
>Developing rudiments of initiative
>Developing rudiments of industry
>Developing rudimentary knowledge of fundamentals of technology
>Differentiating self from environment
>Formulating sex social role
>Learning rudiments of social rules
>Learning fundamental intellectual, physical and motor skills

Junior High School

>*Prime considerations*: Translation of self-concept into vocational terms; dealing with exploratory needs with purpose and with intent.

Factors

>Using exploratory resources
>Relating interests and capacities
>Identifying personal strengths which one wants to exploit in formulating a vocational preference
>Understanding the interdependence of the educational and occupational structures
>Differentiation of interests and values
>Developing implications of present-future relationships
>Accepting one's self as in process
>Relating changes in the self to changes in the world
>Learning to organize one's time and energy to get work done
>Learning to defer gratification, to set priorities
>Acquiring knowledge of life in organizations
>Preparation for role relationships
>Preparation for level and kind of consumption

Prime considerations: Formulating plans to execute implementation of self-concept and generalized preference.

Factors

Refine and particularize as necessary junior high school factors
Relating interests and capacities to values
Planning for specific occupation or intermediate educational alternative
Acquiring information necessary to execute specific plans
Achieving mature relationship with peers of both sexes
Achieving emotional independence of parents and other adults

The factors identified in Table 1 have been drawn from the perspective of several theorists and researchers who have identified the characteristics of career development phenomena at different life periods essentially equivalent to the elementary, junior high and senior high school levels (Havighurst 1964; Gesell, Ilg and Ames, 1956; Erikson, 1950; Super, Starishevsky, Matlin and Jordaan 1963). These factors, while gross, provide the outlines for a structure by which the educational process can be harmonized with the child's natural development. These career development emphases once identified can be refined so that the specific knowledge, relationships, and attitudes associated with them can be described. In keeping with current concerns about the need for accountability, these career development emphases and their elements can be translated into behavioral objectives to which different educational experiences can be related (Herr and Cramer, 1972).

CAREER DEVELOPMENT: PROCESS CONSIDERATIONS

While the career development literature represents a repository from which can be gained insights into much of the substance of Career Education, this literature also speaks to the matter of process. For example, Roeber (1965-66) suggested that all contacts with people, things, and ideas have potential for influencing career development. Such an assertion is particularly valid if these contacts are purposefully and systematically addressed to such an expectation (Herr, 1970; Herr and Cramer, 1972). Thus, in addition to possibilities of facilitating career development through courses designed expressly for such purposes, computer-mediated activities, simulations, gaming, and other relatively new processes, there are and will remain specific instructional courses which offer the promise of influencing career development regardless of what else exists to serve such a need. Teachers of English, mathematics, sciences, social studies as well as vocational educators of whatever focus need to be helped to include in their instructional goals attention to both the educational and vocational implications of the course they teach. Questions which individual teachers need to address are: In what ways are the attitudes, skills, and approaches to problem-solving inherent in this subject manifested in life beyond the school? What workers or what further educational opportunities require or elaborate the content being pursued in this course? How can student learning about the content of this course be used also to stimulate their consideration of personal preference and competency? How can students be helped to constantly project their own answers to questions such as knowing what I know myself, how would I likely perform in a particular future academic or vocational role related to the content of this course?

Career development insights, then, accent the need to tailor educational responses to the characteristics of the student populations with whom we are dealing. They reinforce the equally important point that many techniques presently exist to facilitate career development but are not yielding maximum effect because they are not conceived as ways of providing inexperienced young people opportunities to bring reality to personal planning about vocational or educational goals, of projecting their own characteristics into the future implications of current educational content, or of reality-testing current personal behavior within a protective climate.

CAREER DEVELOPMENT: CLIMATE CONSIDERATIONS

Career development theory and research speak not only to content and process dimensions of Career Education but also to the climate in which it must be nurtured. If Career Education is to work, a climate supporting career development must occur in the school. It is clear that people develop their self-concepts, their perceptions of personal worth or lack thereof, from other people. They also incorporate belief systems about alternatives, the worth of personal planning, and the other notions implicit in career development to the degree that these concepts are valued and their importance reinforced by people from whom they seek feedback: teachers, counselors and administrators.

Students can hear from adults that one should consider a spectrum of occupational alternatives, those requiring post-secondary education as well as those which do not, but if, in fact, they are made to feel put-down everytime they consider an alternative other than one which is technical or semi-professional, the message gets distorted. If adults talk about the importance of vocational education and are permitted to snub vocational education students, the latter's confusion is extended. If students hear about the dignity of all work but are provided information about only a few ways of working, decision-making freedom is reduced and being informed is an impossibility. These are matters of climate as well as matters of process or content.

SUMMARY

In summary, while still incomplete and in a continuing state of need for

44

better answers and more comprehensive theory, contributions of career development to career education include:

1. Awareness that students need a comprehensive body of information which links what they are doing educationally to future options which will be available to them in education and in work.

2. Awareness that students need to be able to assess elements of the self, incorporate their meaning, and relate the relevance of self information to the choices with which they will be confronted. Without such linkages, feelings of powerlessness, of being unable to affect one's future, have a tendency to result.

3. Awareness that implicit in Career Education programs is the need to help students first see themselves as *some one* before they can see themselves effectively as *some thing* (Tennyson, 1967). Unless a student knows what personal resources he has to commit or wants to commit to planning and choosing or the outcomes he seeks from life, he has no particular guidelines by which he can decide whether any possible option is of value to him.

4. Awareness that to be effective, career development is not simply another add-on to current curricula. Rather, the development of constructive vocational identity and behavior—career development—is a process which begins in childhood and continues throughout school life. Consequently, educational objectives must be developed which encompass knowledge, attitudes, and skills fundamental to career development. These objectives must be tied to activities or experiences likely to facilitate the accomplishment of these objectives. Finally, the resulting objectives and experiences must be placed along a developmental time line integral to the educational process and responsive to the developing characteristics of students. Facilitation of career development can not be isolated only in units or in career days but must be reinforced by and woven through curricular emphases and the attitudes of those who monitor this process.

5. Awareness that as in any developmental emphasis, individuals will differ in their readiness for career development or the ways by which to approach the tasks subsumed by it. Career development is not necessarily linear or continuous. Thus, monitoring prescribing, and modeling among a range of educational experiences will be required to serve the needs of students at different developmental levels.

6. Awareness that in facilitating the process of formulating preferences and decision-making ability, contexts must be provided by which students can figuratively or literally project themselves into career roles and in a simulated or actual way be able to act out and test them for themselves. This will require more effective and more extensive use within curricula of group processes, gaming techniques, role playing, case studies, simulation, work-study, and work itself as a means for behavior modification. To implement the latter in a comprehensive way means that the community must be a participant in Career Education. Beyond paying the tab, it must comprehensively serve as an exploratory and employability laboratory in its role as the school extended.

These six implications from career development are important anchor points for the shaping of Career Education. Collectively, they add promise to the heritage of this society that not only does each man have as a basic right the choice of an occupation, but that also he is entitled to the assistance and the preparation to choose well and to experience the dignity and the fulfillment that such a condition permits.

REFERENCES

Borow, H. Vocational development research: Some problems of logical and experimental form. *Personnel and Guidance Journal,* 1961, 40, 21-25.

Drucker, P. *The age of discontinuity.* New York: Harper and Row, 1969.

Erikson, E.H. *Childhood and society.* New York: W. W. Norton, 1950.

Exemplary Programs and Services Branch, Division of Vocational and Technical Education, U.S. Office of Education. Background on the design, development, and implementation of vocational exemplary projects funded under Part D, Section 142(c) of the Vocational Education Amendments of 1968. Washington, D.C.: The Branch, U.S. Office of Education, 1971.

Galinsky, M.D. and Fast, I. Vocational choice as a focus of the identity search. *Journal of Counseling Psychology,* 1966, 13, 89-92.

Gesell, A., Ilg, Frances L., and Ames, L. *Youth: The years from ten to sixteen.* New York: Harper and Row, 1956.

Gysbers, N. Elements of a model for promoting career development in elementary and junior high schoool. Paper presented at the National Conference on Exemplary Programs and Projects Section of the Vocational Education Act Amendments of 1968, Atlanta, Georgia, March, 1969.

Havighurst, R.J. Youth in exploration and man emergent. In H. Borow (Ed.) *Man in a World at Work.* Boston: Houghton Mifflin, 1964.

Herr, E.L. *Decision-making and vocational development.* Guidance Monograph Series IV. Boston: Houghton Mifflin, 1970.

Herr, E.L. Curriculum considerations in career development programs K-12. Paper presented to the Ohio State Department of Education Project on Guidelines for Career Development Programs K-12. Columbus, Ohio, June 7, 1971.

Herr, E.L. and Cramer, S.H. *Vocational guidance and career development in the schools: Toward a systems approach.* Boston: Houghton Mifflin, 1972.

Marland, S.P., Jr. Career education—a new frontier. Paper presented at the Third Annual Conference of the Pennsylvania Personnel and Guidance Association, Pittsburgh, Pennsylvania, November 15, 1971.

National Association of State Directors of Vocational Education. *Position paper on career education.* Adopted at Las Vegas, Nevada, September 17, 1971.

Roeber, E.C. The school curriculum and vocational development. *The Vocational Guidance Quarterly,* 1965-66, 14, 87-91.

Super, D.E. Vocational development theory: Persons, positions, and processes. *The Counseling psychologist,* 1969, 1, 2-9.

Super, D.E., Starishevsky, R., Matlin, N. and Jordaan, J.P. *Career development: Self concept theory.* New York: College Entrance Examination Board, 1963.

Tennyson, W.W. The psychology of developing competent personnel. *American Vocational Journal,* 1967, 42, 27-29.

Toffler, A.A. *Future shock.* New York: Bantam Books, 1970.

United States Department of Health, Education, and Welfare. *Career education.* Washington, D.C.: U.S. Government Printing Office, 1971.

Worthington, R.M. Comprehensive personnel development for career education. Paper presented at the Fourth Annual Leadership Development Seminar for State Directors of Vocational Education, September 1971, Las Vegas, Nevada.

The teaching of separate, distinct vocational skills can be irrelevant and isolated as the classical curriculum. Accordingly, vocational teacher educators should lead the way in preparing vocational teachers whose primary concern is not in reproducing themselves by instructing in this or that skilled craft alone, but rather in facilitating self-learning for career development.

The men and women who have been taught to think of themselves as machinists or nurses, or even instructors, will be especially subject to the shocks of future change. Those who best survive the future will consider themselves (as do those today who are achieving the greatest success) not so much as persons who have a certain role or do a particular job, but as persons involved in the experiences and the processes that result in an extension of themselves along a time-space continuum of interrelationships, renewal, and reconstruction. It is no longer sufficient to be somebody who can do something worthwhile. Human development is essentially the development of functions which can be used in many ways to achieve changing goals. Thus, man is a multiplicity of media! And the finest development of humanity is in terms of career in the sense that one is becoming an ongoing process, using oneself— using one's own uses—voluntarily, deliberately, and intellectually.

Willers, J.C. The quality of life in the seventies and implications for vocational teacher education. In R.N. Evans and D.R. Terry (Eds.), *Changing the role of vocational teacher education.* Bloomington, Ill.: McKnight and McKnight, 1971, p. 10.

A RATIONALE FOR CAREER DEVELOPMENT AT THE ELEMENTARY SCHOOL LEVEL

by

Larry J. Bailey and Dennis C. Nystrom

Recent years have witnessed an increased interest in implementing programs variously described as "vocational guidance," "occupational information," and "careers." A comprehensive survey of such programs has been completed by Bailey (1970). With few exceptions, however, these programs fall far short of facilitating the type of behavior they seek to promote. A universal weakness of the programs is that they emphasize vicarious experiences rather than direct; they are static rather than dynamic. Hunt (1970) criticizes traditional career programs because they focus on telling children about the world of work rather than providing them the opportunities to engage in it. Thus the programs concentrate on "dispensing information" instead of "developing competencies." Their apparent failings are due to the absence of a rationale derived from the body of literature and research on career development and supported by a knowledge of child growth and development.

THEORY AND RATIONALE

Since the beginning of the modern era of career guidance in the early fifties, the body of literature and research related to vocational behavior has multiplied exponentially. The search for unifying constructs and principles of vocational behavior has been accompanied by a surge in the area of theory building. The present status of career development theory has received extensive treatment in many recent publications. Osipow's *Theories of Career Development* (1968), Krill, Dinklage, Lee, Morley, and Wilson's *Career Development: Growth and Crisis* (1970), Zaccaria's *Theories of Occupational Choice and Vocational Development* (1970) and collections of readings by Roth, Hershenson, and Hillard (1970) and Zytowski (1968) are current examples.

As theoretical orientations and models of career development have come to be better understood, researchers and practitioners have sought to validate theory and implement career guidance practices derived from theory. The most up-to-date review and synthesis of research on vocational behavior is Crites's book entitled *Vocational Psychology* (1969). Additional closely related reviews have been completed by Perrone (1966), Tennyson (1968), and Holland and Whitney (1969).

Clearly, no shortage of concepts and principles for career development exists. However, if a hard criterion is used, that is, replicated studies whose results have been proven in the field over a period of years, then one would have to conclude that very little about career development that is systematic in nature is really known (osipow, 1969).

Herr (1970) points out, however, that while no one approach yields the comprehensiveness of explanation one might wish, collectively there exists a conceptual frame of reference which views vocational development and decision-making through the lenses of many disciplines. There is emerging a set of constructs and propositions, some tested and some not, which serve to explain differential decision behavior and trends in the vocational aspects of development. Using a realistic criterion, certain heuristic statements can be made regarding the nature of career development:

1. Career development is considered to be one aspect of the individual's total development. It is most profitably viewed as longitudinal in nature and based on principles of developmental psychology. Vocational behavior develops over time through processes of growth and learning.

2. The theories of career development acknowledge a wide range of factors which determine or at least influence the process of human development (Zaccaria, 1970). Career development is integrated to the total fabric of personality development and is the result of the synthesis of many personal, social, and vocational factors as one matures (Herr, 1970).

3. The unfolding of an individual's career development beginning in early childhood is seen as relatively continuous and long term, but divided into stages or life periods for purposes of description and presentation (Zaccaria, 1970).

4. Each vocational life stage involves meeting and learning to cope with critical developmental tasks. Many of these developmental tasks center on the acquisition of coping mechanisms and mastery behavior which subsume career related choices and adjustments. The choices which an individual makes and the manner in which he enacts the resultant roles form a life sequence known as his career pattern. (Ashcraft et al., 1966).

5. Vocational behavior and career selection develop from less effective behavior and unrealistic or fantasy choice to more complex behavior and more realistic choosing. Career selection becomes increasingly reality-oriented and more realistic as one moves toward the choice itself (Herr, 1970).

6. An individual's striving to arrive at an appropriate vocational goal may be interpreted as a search for a work role that is harmonious with the need structures resulting from the gratification and frustration of early life, as a search for the new ego identity that marks the adolescent stage, or as an attempt to implement an already emerging self-concept (Ashcraft et al., 1966).

7. Vocational development theories support the existence and causal role of inner, tensional states, which, depending on the focus of the theory, are variously described as interests, needs, values, personality characteristics, or life styles (Zytowski, 1965).

49

The research and commentary on career development indicates, beyond any reasonable doubt, that systematic career planning must begin at the elementary school level. Elementary age youth need the opportunity to continuously and systematically explore, from an internal frame of reference, their values, attitudes, and interests in relation to the wide range of educational and career opportunities which may be available to them so that they will avoid premature educational and occupational foreclosure (Gysbers, 1969).

The kindergarten to sixth-grade level is the most reasonable place to begin examining the career development process. Children show an interest in the world of work at a remarkably early age. Even before their explicit interest in the world of work, children are exposed to events which shape aspects of their personal development related to work (Osipow, 1969).

Herr (1969, 1970), also concurs that intervention in facilitating career development must begin during the first decade of life. This is the nursery of human nature and the time when the attitudes are formed which later become manifest in vocational commitment or rejection. Youngsters in elementary schools must be exposed to experiences which are meaningful in terms of their individual characteristics and to information which is accurate if they are not to carry residuals of exaggeration and overromanticized occupational stereotypes into later decision-processing.

The timing for prevocational orientation may be crucial. According to Sherman (1967), once students get involved in the junior high school milieu their own social and physical maturation and the existing organizational structures and the rewards offered from these environments in which they live all influence them. If students are helped to focus on career development *prior* to becoming a part of this milieu, it could help them to build a kind of core attitude toward their personal future which might provide a slightly different perspective on the many other concerns of this age.

Bottoms and Matheny (1969), indicate that concern for career development cannot be a one-shot approach that takes place at the junior or senior high level. It is too late when the student reaches the point of making the transition from school to work. Career development should be conceived as a pyramid offering a broad base of exploratory experiences at the elementary and junior high school levels and gradually narrowing to a decision point as the student acquires appropriate preparation for his next step beyond school. Such a vocational development theme could serve as a common thread to unify the educational effort at all levels.

Career development programs initiated at the elementary school level must be systematically organized; the core of which is a sound conceptual model derived from career development theory that provides for specific vocational developmental tasks. A series of well-planned exposures such as gaming and simulation, role playing, and vocational exploratory experiences can then be implemented to assist students in coping with the demands of each vocational developmental task. Specifically designed and articulated activities can help to provide children and youth with a realistic understanding of self which can be translated into the intermediate goal of educational-vocational choice and the ultimate goal of vocational maturity. Career development programs thus conceived have the potential for providing a core of experiences around, which all future educational and occupational goals revolve.

FACILITATING CAREER DEVELOPMENT

In response to the need to assist youth in career planning and decision-making, a research project was begun in March 1970 at Southern Illinois University in cooperation with the Illinois State Board of Vocational Education and Rehabilitation. Entitled the *Career Development for Children Project* (CDCP) the goal of the project is to develop an exemplary career guidance program for elementary and junior high school students. This will be accomplished through a series of carefully articulated developmental experiences beginning in grade one.

The curriculum is divided into three stages. The AWARENESS STAGE, for grades one through three, provides various introductory experiences to help the child become aware of "self" and the "world of work". The AC-COMODATION STAGE, for grades 4-6, relates growing knowledge of self and the world of work, to the process of career development. The EX-PLORATION STAGE, for grades 7-8 provides students with concrete work-related activities and decision-making exercises which will facilitate career planning.*

There are two main aspects of the curriculum. One is to increase self-knowledge; for the child to understand his uniqueness, his abilities his interests. It is clear that self-understanding must be an integral part of the career development process. Career development theorists are virtually unanimous in viewing the formulation of an occupational preference as an implementation of the self-concept. A second aspect is to increase the child's understanding of the working world, not through a study of specific jobs, but through examination of occupational families, interest-area families, and a study of broad economic concepts. The interrelationship between these two aspects is a major theme of the program.

From an operational standpoint, CDCP is designing curriculum activities to provide direct, concrete experiences rather than only vicarious ones. Techniques such as role playing, gaming, and simulation will be emphasized in conjunction with individual and group guidance activities. Rather than merely read about service occupations, for example, students will simulate a health

---

* A comprehensive description of the curriculum outline may be found in Bailey, L.J. A curriculum model for facilitating career development. Career Development for Children Project, March 1971, 25 pp.

care enterprise in which they perform various worker functions. The sophistication and complexity of these activities will vary greatly between grade levels. An important feature of the program is that the curriculum is designed to allow the child to "try on" various occupational roles so that he will have, on a personal level, an idea of what certain kinds of work are like and will be able to understand how different kinds of work roles fit with his emerging concept of himself.

REFERENCES

Ashcraft, K.B. *et al. A report of the invitational conference on implementing career development theory and research through the curriculum,* Washington, D.C.: National Vocational Guidance Association, 1966.

Bailey, L.J. Facilitating career development at the elementary school level. Research Proposal Submitted to the Board of Vocational Education and Rehabilitation, October 1969.

Bailey, L.J. (Ed) *Facilitating career development: An annotated bibliography.* Springfield, Illinois: Board of Vocational Education and Rehabilitation, 1970.

Bottoms, G. and Matheny, K.B. *A guide for the development, implementation, and administration of exemplary programs and projects in vocational education.* Grant No. OEG-O-9-207008-2779 (085), Office of Education, September, 1969.

Crites, J. O. *Vocational Psychology.* New York: McGraw-Hill, 1969.

Gysbers, N.C. Elements of a model for promoting career development in elementary and junior high school. Paper presented at the National Conference on Exemplary Programs and Projects, Atlanta, Georgia, March 1969.

Herr, E.L., Unifying an entire system of education around a career development theme. Paper presented at the National Conference on Exemplary Programs and Projects, Atlanta, Georgia, March, 1969.

Herr, E.L. *Decision Making and Vocational Development.* Boston: Houghton Mifflin, 1970.

Holland, J.L., and Whitney, D.R. Career Development. *Review of Educational Research,* 1969, 30, 227-238.

Hunt, E.E. Career development K-6. Paper presented at the Conference on Developing a Career Oriented Curriculum in Cobb County, Marietta, Georgia, January 1970.

Kroll, M. *et al. Career development: Growth and crisis.* New York: John Wiley and Sons, 1970.

Osipow, S.H., *Theories of career development.* New York: Appleton-Century-Crofts, 1968.

Osipow, S.H., What do we really know about career development. In Gysbers, N.G., and Pritchard, D.H. (Eds.), *Proceedings National Conference on*

Guidance, Counseling, and Placement in Career Development and Educational-Occupational Decision Making, Contract No. OEG-O-9-644-008-4734 (399). Office of Education, October, 1969.

Perrone, PA. Vocational development, *Review of Educational Research,* 1966, 36, 298-307.

Roth, M. *et al. The psychology of vocational development.* Boston: Allyn and Bacon, 1970.

Sherman, V.S., Trial and testing of an experimental guidance curriculum. Palo Alto, California: American Institute for Research, Grant No. OEG-1-7-078091-3022, Office of Education, December 1967.

Tennyson, W.W., Career development. *Review of Educational Research,* 1968, 38, 346-366.

Zaccaria, J., *Theories of occupational choice and vocational development.* Boston: Houghton Mifflin, 1970.

Zytowski, D.G., Avoidance behavior in vocational motivation, *Personnel and Guidance Journal,* 1965, 43, 746-750.

Zytowski, D.G., *Vocational behavior: Readings in theory and research.* New York: Holt, Rinehart and Winston, 1968.

American schools are producing too many youngsters who qualify neither for a job nor for college. Many high school graduates go on to college only because they haven't the vaguest idea of what else to do.

Sidney P. Marland, Jr. U.S. Commissioner of Education. A speech delivered before Thirty-third Session of the International Conference on Education, Geneva, Switzerland, September 15-23, 1971.

Central to the belief that career decisions must be made through sensible choice rather than be haphazard chance—and that actual preparation for entry into careers in an organized, purposeful manner is a self-evident requisite—is the proposition that public education, from preschool through continuing education, must set about making arrangements of organization and instruction that will meet such needs.

Position Paper on Career Education. Formulated and adopted by the 50 State Directors of Vocational Education during their meeting the week of September 13, 1971, Las Vegas, Nevada.

Career education is needed by and intended for all people. It is a people-oriented concept which is responsive to public demand for both relevance and accountability. It is a lifelong process which extends from early childhood through adulthood. Career education is based upon the premise that all honest work and purposeful study is respectable. All types of occupations and all levels of occupational endeavor are contained within its parameters.

Report of the American Vocational Association Task Force on Career Education. Portland, Oregon, December 3, 1971

Occupational Education in Career Development

ALBERT J. PAUTLER

𝐀 WELL developed occupational preparation program is something each student should be exposed to during his 13 years of public education. The saying, "vocational education is nice for someone else's child," must be changed to "occupational education is of value to all children." This change will not occur unless the curriculum planners at the local level exert an honest effort to develop some form of awareness of occupational education in Board of Education members, administrators, parents, and, most important, the teachers in the local school system.

A logical first step at the local level would be to answer the basic questions: (a) How well are we meeting the occupational goals indicated in our statement of philosophy and/or objectives? (b) How well are our graduates, who do not go on to post-secondary education, doing in the world of work? (c) If we release a statement to the press regarding the number of graduates who

54

are accepted into college, do we do likewise for the students who enter the world of work immediately after graduation?

The members of a school district seriously concerned about developing a total program of occupational education for all the children of the district must first review what is presently available for the children. After this review, the next step will be to develop a model program of occupational education suitable to the characteristics of the district and the needs of the children. Well spelled-out objectives should be included as a part of the model. The total curriculum development leadership for such a project must come from the person responsible for curriculum development for the district. A piecemeal fragmentation, with each level going its own way, will not result in a total program of occupational education.

Planning should also involve representatives from the "area" vocational school and the community college or colleges so that a total program of occupational education might result. The model program would involve objectives and appropriate curriculum content starting with kindergarten and continuing through grade 12, with articulation with the programs of grades 13 and 14 in the community colleges. A logical division would be as follows: Kindergarten to grade 5; grades 6 to 9; grades 10 to 12; grades 13 and 14 in the community colleges. The model would reflect articulation between and among the various levels. Modification of the model would be necessary based upon the organizational structure at the local level.

Why?

Most people will work for a living at some time during their life span. Gainful employment is essential for most people in order to provide the basics of food, clothing, and shelter. The U.S. Department of Labor, in *U.S. Manpower in the 1970's,* reports the following:

Labor force participation of married women with children has increased sharply— even for those with very young children.

White-collar workers will continue to out-number blue-collar by more than 50 percent in 1980. However, 31 million workers will be employed in blue-collar jobs, an increase of more than 2 million over 1970.

The number of service workers will continue to increase in the 70's. The number of farm workers will decline still further.

Jobs in craft skills are increasingly well rewarded financially, reflecting a continuing need for highly skilled workers in the economy.[1]

What are the implications, if any, of these projections for your local educational program?

Some form of occupational education is necessary for all children in the public schools. The form does not have to be the traditional hands-on type of experience for all children. One aspect of occupational education should be to develop an awareness in children of the contemporary and future world of work. Such a task falls to all the professionals in teaching and not just the small groups of educators in home economics, business and office occupations, industrial arts, trade and technical, agricultural, and the distributive education specializations. The total staff or a cross section of staff members must be involved in the planning if a meaningful program is to result.

When?

The curriculum coordinator, superintendent, principal, teacher, or board member really concerned with a total program of

[1] U.S. Department of Labor. *U.S. Manpower in the 1970's.* Washington, D.C.: Superintendent of Documents, U.S. Government Printing Office, 1970.

occupational education should attempt to develop a program starting in kindergarten and continuing through grade 12, with close articulation with the community colleges in the area. Such a program might stress *awareness* of the world of work in grades K to 5. One simple unit dealing with the world of work might be included during each of the six years.

In grades 6 to 9 or 10, the program might stress the theme of *introduction* to the world of work. At this level, a good amount of input would be expected from the guidance staff of the school. The introduction to the world of work might involve a study of occupations as well as the tools, processes, and materials associated with the various occupations. Such a program might be patterned after the Introduction to Vocations program which has been operational in New Jersey for a number of years.

The problem area remains the program at the upper secondary level. Specializations such as those available in the area vocational schools in New York State are perhaps suited to the needs of many students. Yet the problem of career decision at the end of grade 9 or 10 remains a serious concern. Any occupational or vocational program that blocks a student from post-secondary education at the community college or college level should be of serious concern to all educators. The greatest degree of caution must be taken in planning a meaningful program of occupational education at this level.

Specialization for many students might take place in high school, but for others the most appropriate place may be the programs in the community colleges. Communication and articulation must exist between the public school and the local community college or colleges in regard to the occupational education program.

The school staff really concerned about

occupational education will attempt to develop a model program to best serve the students in the district. To be most effective, it should be a K-12 effort and not something left to the high school staff alone.

How? and Where?

The "how" and "where" questions might best be answered by those designing the program at the local level. What follows is an attempt to present a number of operational programs with some of their respective characteristics which may be of value in planning a program for your school district. Many other types of program organization are also in operation in various school districts. Additional research on the local level would be desirable before a decision is made on the "model" for the local program.

KINDERGARTEN TO GRADE 6

Technology for Children. There exists in New Jersey a new curriculum called Technology for Children, which is designed for the best interest of the child. In four short years it has caught the attention of New Jersey educators and received widespread acceptance. Sponsored by the Division of Vocational Education, New Jersey State Department of Education, and co-funded by the Ford Foundation, its adoption by educators is mushrooming because the child is given "prime time." The supporters, who commend the assistance of the staff of Technology for Children Project, are teachers who have long sought ways to make school interesting, knowing that learning can actually be entertaining and should be pleasant and intriguing.[2]

For more information, contact: Fred Dreves, Director, Technology for Children, Vocational Division, New Jersey Department of Education, Trenton, New Jersey.

Elementary School Industrial Arts Center. The primary function of this program at the

[2] Fred J. Dreves. "Emphasis on the Child." *Man/Society/Technology* 30: 116-19; January 1971.

McDonald School is to "provide a richness of experience" for the children. The Industrial Arts Center is considered a laboratory where students are given an opportunity to explore and experiment with the technological and esthetic aspects of their experiences in the classroom. The interrelationships among the various materials, processes, and crafts in every phase of industrial production can be adapted to the endeavors of the elementary school child.

Contact: Donald Hoffman, Centennial School District, Warminster, Pennsylvania.

Georgia Plan. This plan is an organizational structure for a kindergarten through grade 12 program of providing occupational education. At the elementary grades level, industrial arts is an important part of the program. The concern at this level is with occupations and the products of industry. Informal construction activities and a study of the world of work occur. Students are involved in reading, writing, and speaking about people and the work that they do.

Contact: Donald Hackett, Georgia Southern College, Statesboro, Georgia.

Grades 6 to 9

Introduction to Vocations. This program was started in 1965 by the Division of Vocational Education of the New Jersey Department of Education. The program is designed to aid the student in gaining occupational awareness. It is a year-long program divided into cycles — periods of two or three weeks' duration based upon one period per day. Time allotments are flexible, and vary with the needs of the individual, the group, and the available facilities. Cycling units include a minimum of four areas, such as home economics, industrial arts, business education, and science.

Contact: Margaret Blair, Director, Introduction to Vocations, Vocational Division, New Jersey Department of Education, Trenton, New Jersey.

Maryland Plan. This is a program of Industrial Arts developed by Donald Maley in cooperation with the Montgomery County

(Maryland) School System. The plan is operational and functional in grades 7, 8, and 9. In the seventh grade, an *anthropological* approach to the study of certain basic elements common to all civilized mankind makes use of the unit method of instruction. At the eighth grade level, the *contemporary* approach to the study of American industry uses the group process, group project, and line product technique. At the ninth grade level, the program is an elective and is of a *personal nature.* The content emphasis is on ʾontemporary units of study.

Contact: Donald Maley, Department of Industrial Education, College of Education, University of Maryland, College Park, Maryland.

Industrial Arts Curriculum Project. The IACP is a two-year industrial program in industrial technology for junior high school age students. The first year of the two-year course is called "The World of Construction," and is a study of man's managed production system which produces society's constructed projects. The second year's course is a study of man's managed production system which produces society's manufactured products.

Contact: Donald Lux, College of Education, Ohio State University, Columbus, Ohio.

GRADES 10 TO 12

New York State—BOCES. Boards of Cooperative Educational Services (BOCES) have become an integral part of the public education structure of New York State. Each of some 60 BOCES in the state helps to serve areas encompassing a group of school districts. Most BOCES sponsor a center designed to provide entry level employment to the students in attendance. The student spends about one-half of his school day in his home school and the other half in the "area" vocational center.

Contact: Division of Occupational Education, State Department of Education, Albany, New York.

Project "ABLE." The principal goal of Project ABLE is to demonstrate increased effectiveness of instruction whose content is explicitly derived from analysis of desired behavior

60

after graduation and which in addition attempts to apply newly developed educational technology to the design and evaluation of vocational education. The plan is implemented through a curriculum which includes 11 broad occupational families.

Contact: Quincy Public Schools, Quincy, Massachusetts.

Occupational Skills. This is a short-term/ after-school, noncredit program in occupational skills. A number of short-term courses are offered each semester during the school term. All students are encouraged to take as many of the courses as they desire and have time for. Classes meet usually for seven or eight weeks, one afternoon per week, from 3:30 p.m. to 5:30 p.m. It is a very flexible type of arrangement and worthy of consideration.

Contact: Robert Moscato, Maryvale High School, Cheektowaga, New York.

As a part of the curriculum planning effort to develop a model occupational education program for the local school district, investigate, visit, and gather as much information as possible from programs already operational. It is doubtful whether one would be able to find in operation a K-12 program which would be operational and suitable to the needs of his own community. Yet one should find many interesting and valuable programs from a number of different areas which, when put together into a model, would form the bases of a total program.

Preparation for and knowledge about the world of work for our students is too important a consideration to be left to chance alone. Occupational education should be a concern of all those associated with the public school. Occupational education should be a part of the program of each student. Do not confuse a K-12 occupational education program with the traditional type of vocational education of the past.

Someone in each school district must show a serious concern for occupational education if a really valuable program is to result. If such an idea and program "turns on" the curriculum coordinator in your school district, great. If not, the leadership and pressure will have to start at the classroom level, with those teachers who believe that some form of occupational education is essential for all children.

Vocational Guidance

Vocational Education
Is Service . . .

Gordon F. Law

Guidance has had a profound influence on American secondary education, especially during the past 20 years. Many practices that are now commonly employed in junior and senior high schools were first introduced by way of the guidance program. The widespread use of standardized tests, and their application in the classification, grouping, and counseling of students, are several typical examples.

Although it may be said that the guidance movement has brought many improvements to secondary education, it must also be admitted that its value to a large segment of the school population has been less than sensational. According to some recent studies, many students, especially those who were not preparing for college entrance, indicated that the guidance office had given them little or no significant counseling service.

Now, in a period when a full measure of guidance that is appropriate for all persons in all circumstances has been recognized among the imperatives in education, it is likely that a drastic change in form and emphasis will have to follow.

Early in the guidance movement, three basic objectives were established: the development of educational, personal and vocational competen-

cy. These fundamental goals have been sustained in theory. In practice, however, the major concern of guidance has been for college preparation and admission. Little time has been given to either the personal or vocational aspects of counseling. This college domination of the high school curriculum, which has had adverse effects on all levels of instruction and guidance, appears to be finally giving way to a more enlightened concern for individuals.

There are several publications, other than the Office of Education studies reported in this issue, which relate to guidance. These include the proceedings of the *First National Conference on Student Personnel Services in Area Vocational Schools*, available through the Georgia State Department of Education; the January 1968 *Bulletin* of the National Association of Secondary School Principals, and the publication of the University of Wisconsin Center for Studies in Vocational and Technical Education, *Guidance Bibliography No. IV, Addendum No. 4.*

The January 1968 NASSP *Bulletin* is exclusively devoted to "Progress in Pupil Personnel." The 10 articles, prepared by some of the national leaders in guidance work, are sources of insight and information, and at least 5 of them are concerned with topics that are closely related to vocational education.

For persons interested in studying a plan for career development in a major city, the Philadelphia public schools have prepared a publication, *Career Development*, which describes a program leading toward universal continuing education.

TOPIC ONE: Systems Technology in Guidance

Computer-Based Technology

7:1 "EXPLORATORY STUDY OF INFORMATION-PROCESSING PROCEDURES AND COMPUTER-BASED TECHNOLOGY IN VOCATIONAL COUNSELING" BY J. F. COGSWELL. SYSTEMS DEVELOPMENT CORPORATION, SANTA MONICA, CALIF. (PROJECT # 5-0141) 1967. (VT # 004-528) 256 PAGES.

The purpose of the Systems Development Corporation study was to design and implement a man-machine system for vocational guidance.

Five major steps were planned for the design phase. These were to: survey vocational guidance operations in the field; conduct a detailed system analysis of the counseling procedures employed at a selected field site; design a man-machine system by the counselors at the field site and the Systems Development Corporation research team; formulate and develop computer programs in the SDC laboratory, and collect initial evaluation data.

The survey of current counselor practices was conducted at a sample of 12 schools having vocational offerings. The basic instrument used to collect data on counselor activities was a card sort version of the Q-technique.

Counselors were given a brief overview of the project. They were then interviewed by members of the SDC research team. Following the interview, a card sort test was administered. Counselors were instructed to look through the 48 cards and sort them into three piles, in terms of the effort they spent on the counseling activities: "most effort," "some effort" and "no effort." A total of 87 counselors, 56 from post-secondary vocational institutions and 31 employed in comprehensive or vocational high schools, took part in the program.

Analysis of the card sort data indicated that a marked difference existed between what counselors are doing and what they would like to do. The findings from the survey supported the investigators' belief that counselors are forced to spend too much time with information-processing chores, "that ideally, they would like to change their activities in the humanistic direction of working more with students, and that they would like to alter the system to better meet the needs of students."

When looking for conditions that would assure a humanistic orientation, the researchers asked the counselors the question: "Is it possible to design a computer program system that is humanistically oriented?" The answer, based on logical and philosophical analysis, rather than hard empirical data, was a qualified 'yes.' The study proposed two primary rules for humanism in man-machine systems: the system shall exist for the convenience of—and to fulfill the needs of—the system, and the system must be respectful of the humanity of those who are processed by the system.

Speaking about the dangers of non-humanistic use of computer systems for guidance work, the report identifies three of the more serious problems: *privacy of personal data; misuse of prediction systems,* and *alienation of humans subjected to computer processing.*

65

When discussing the fact that an individual has a right to privacy of personal data, the report recommends four conditions that should be observed: *right of access; right of knowledge of source; right of review, refutation and appeal,* and *right of approval of dissemination.*

"If a dossier or information file is to be kept on any person, that person should be notified of its existence and be allowed access to it at will; the subject of a dossier has the right to know the source of any information included in his file, and that such sources be recorded with the information; the person who is the subject of a dossier should be permitted to review and refute any information in the dossier, and that his refutation be included as an integral part of the dossier; and the subject of a dossier has the right to approve (or veto) the transfer of information from his file to other agencies, persons or files."

Two principal dangers are reported in the use of computer systems to generate predictions about students. These have to do with statistical prediction and the direction of students to follow courses of action. "Counselors often use statistical predictions to *direct* students to follow courses of action that lead to the fulfillment of the predictions. In such cases, false prediction models can become valid with the passage of time. The automation of such procedures is not an improvement."

The report also includes sections describing the design of the computer software systems, an ethical and moral analysis of the design for a man-machine counseling system and plans for the implementation phase of the program. An appendix of more than 100 pages gives a detailed accounting of the processes taken in the development of this study.

The SDC exploratory study of information-processing procedures and computer-based technology in voca-tional counseling should be required reading for any person with interests in guidance or systems in education. It is a disturbing and provocative report that poses some fundamental questions about the entire guidance process. In the summary statement of the report, the concerns of the investigators speak for themselves:

"As the study progressed, it became increasingly apparent that the introduction of the computer into the counseling operation could accelerate the already present trends toward alienation and depersonalization. Despite our efforts to focus the design on the functions that both the men and the machine would play in the new system, we found the major ideas that were developed in the design meetings were for the computer. Very little attention was given to what the counselor's role would be in the new system.

"This observation paralleled past experiences in the design of military man-machine systems. The counseling system was becoming more like a machine than either a man, or a system with functions equitably distributed to men and machine.

"Our concern for the role of the human became more acute when we analyzed some of our data on counselor attitudes. These data suggested that actual experience working as a guidance counselor in schools tends to increase the positive value placed on data manipulation. This observation caused us to fear that once the computer is installed the counselors will use the extra time that would be gained to become more involved with data than with students."

Systems Under Development

7:2 "SYSTEMS UNDER DEVELOPMENT FOR VOCATIONAL GUIDANCE" BY ROBERT E. CAMPBELL, OHIO STATE UNIVERSITY, COLUMBUS, OHIO. (PROJECT # 7-0158) 1966. ERIC # ED 011 039. MF $0.50 HC $2.80. 70 PAGES.

The Ohio State Research exchange conference on systems under development for vocational education was reported to be an unique experiment in research stimulation and coordination. The purposes of the conference were:

To review experiences, problems and insights developed by the individual participants through research and use of these new technologies.

—To review the relation of these technologies to vocational education, vocational counseling and guidance.

—To arrange for continued communication among participants as they apply systems analysis and technology in vocational guidance, research and practice.

A group of 21 researchers met informally for two days to share problems and ideas in the development of new technologies and innovations for vocational guidance. Before the conference, each investigator had been involved in a research project relating to vocational guidance. These projects were classified into three groups: those devoted to the study of careers; projects for the development and presentation of materials for aiding career decisions, but not involving the use of computers; and, those concerned with the development of materials for the enhancement of career decisions with the assistance of time-shared computers.

Conference participants agreed that exchange during the conference was excellent: there was a sincere willingness for mutual exploration of problems and reciprocal assistance. They concurred that continued communication through a second conference would allow investigators to pursue difficult questions more deeply.

It was reported that systems development for guidance related activities was the topic participants wished to explore further. Special interest was expressed in systems to assist the individual in self-evaluation, support counselor activities, especially routine tasks and data storage, and survey the world of work in its many facets and complexities.

Participants felt they had just scratched the surface in identifying and discussing problems and issues in guidance related systems research. However, they did raise a number of important questions.

Model of Counseling Functioning. "As the building of a system progresses, theoretical decisions have to be met as to how people make vocational choices, the role of diagnosis, amount of self-direction. In building a model, does the researcher operationally simulate observed counselor activities, or does he develop a new model?"

Data Base Construction. "What kinds of information will a system need in order to accomplish its goals? For example, in providing information about vocational training opportunities, how should these be grouped, how much detail should be included, and at what points within a system's sequence should the material be introduced?"

Battery of Measurement Instruments. "What kinds of information should be obtained through tests and which tests are most appropriate to measure the appropriate traits . . . can systems be designed with enough flexibility to handle the complexities of test interpretation not only for singular tests but tests in combination?"

Taxonomy of Occupations and Descriptions. "This is basically a problem of how to classify and present educational and occupational information, e.g., nature of training, requirements for admission, job opportunities . . . To provide this exploration, a complex well-organized occupational classification system is needed . . . There are also problems relating to storing local, geographic or national trends and the continual difficulty of maintaining up-to-date information."

Other concerns expressed by conference participants related to the monitoring of systems by counselors and teachers; the influence that variations in educational settings and student populations would have, and the fundamental differences that exist between a taxonomy of occupations and a comprehensive examination of the world of work.

TOPIC TWO: Career Development Theory and Practice

Career Planning Curriculum

7:3 "GUIDANCE CURRICULUM FOR INCREASED SELF-UNDERSTANDING AND MOTIVATION FOR CAREER PLANNING" BY VIVIAN S. SHERMAN. AMERICAN INSTITUTES FOR RESEARCH, PALO ALTO, CALIF. (PROJECT # 5-0047) 1966. ERIC # ED 010 625. MF $0.25 HC $0.72. 18 PAGES.

The question of what vocational guidance curriculum experiences are appropriate for junior high school students was a major concern of this American Institutes for Research study. How the problem was pursued, what conclusions about curriculum needs were reached and what was proposed and developed comprised the content of this report.

The report acknowledges the considerable individual variation among young persons' self-understanding and motivation toward career exploration. This suggests that guidance programs have not always been able to bring about adequate self development, so crucial to orientation toward and establishment in a career.

This study views guidance as "a structuring of situations conducive to internal reorganization of knowledge, understandings, attitudes and values" that would further growth within the individual. "If youngsters were given opportunity to project their own thoughts, feelings or experiences against those of others, perhaps with support and acceptance of a group whose members have problems similar to their own, they might gain insight into self."

The first step in curriculum design was the development of questionnaire items on the basis of the following six areas which relate to students' personal values:

1. Students' Perspectives of Purposes of Education and Key Problems Facing Them.

2. Status of Career Planning: individual students' planning, areas of interest, degree of specificity and careers considered.

3. Developmental Perspective of Self: individual variation due to heredity, influence of people and events, early interests.

4. Self Concept: important dimensions of self, influencing environmental-situational factors, self perceptions.

5. Relationship of Personality Characteristics to Occupations: occupational stereotypes, job requirements and opportunities.

6. Planning for Career Exploration: locus of responsibility, clarification of values and goals, clarification of plans.

It was reported that the statement of educational objectives in behavioral terms should be a basic concern of educators. "Specifying desired behavioral changes can clarify both the nature of learning experiences and procedures for evaluating the extent to which these changes occur."

Since attitudes involving the total individual was the realm for investigation, Krathwohl's taxonomy of affective objectives was used as a guide. "This classification system has not yet been widely used and needs practical application in order to evaluate its usefulness as an educational tool. It seemed especially suited to development of the social-emotional dimension of self. It rests upon the process of internalization and includes major categories of receiving or attending, responding, valuing, organization, and characterization by a value or value complex."

The result of this project is a completed set of vocational guidance curriculum materials developed to bring about increased self-understanding and career motivation in junior high school students. These materials, contained in a separate Appendix, are sequentially organized through daily lesson plans. Each lesson includes a statement of Objectives, Means of Eliciting Response and Evaluative Devices.

The Objectives outline specific behavioral responses, possible student attitudinal responses and cognitive processes demanded. Under Means of Eliciting Response are methodological considerations by the teacher, specific practices, plans, materials, verbal directions and statements, and relationship to developmental tasks or growth needs of the learner. The Evaluative Devices for each day are in the form of questionnaires, verbalized responses, comment sheets or observations.

The study suggests that these materials be used flexibly, since they are adaptable to different age and grade levels. However, they seem to be based on an inherently flawed premise. Attitudinal changes and self development for career orientation are vital objectives that may be better realized through a program of loosely designed units rather than daily lesson plans which presume to weigh and credit students' immediate behavioral "changes." Conducted by a directive teacher, this linear curriculum imposes a method of self realization which is fundamentally conformist, non-organic and not actually determined by the variety and involvement of the students.

Life Career Game

7:4 "CAREER SIMULATION FOR SIXTH GRADE PUPILS" BY R. GARRY SHIRTS. DEPARTMENT OF EDUCATION, SAN DIEGO, CALIF. (PROJECT # 5-0123) 1966. ERIC # ED 010 076. MF $0.25 HC $1.64. 41 PAGES.

In considering the career development of younger pupils the principal investigator, R. Garry Shirts, speculated that the Life Career Game might prepare students to gain a better view of the career decisions they would face in the future. It might also help them to realize how their decisions would relate to their forthcoming school program. Consequently, Shirts and others developed and conducted a two-part pilot project which involved sixth grade pupils.

During the developmental part of the project, the Hopkins version of the Life Career Game was modified and simplified. The adaptation seemed more appropriate for sixth graders.

The second or research phase of the study was designed to determine if the modified game would change sixth grade pupils' attitudes toward education and the world of work and/or increase their knowledge about the career process. The Vocational Development Inventory (VDI), developed by John Crites of Iowa, and the Vocational Information Achievement Test (VIAT), developed as part of the project, were used as measures of attitudinal change and information acquisition.

The experimental design included a treatment group of three classes selected randomly from 56 sixth grade classes in the Cajon Valley Union and Santee School Districts of California, and a control group of three classes selected from the same population. The treatment group played the modified version of the Life Career Game for 15 hours over the period of a month. During the same period the control group was taught the regular sixth grade curriculum which did not involve a systematic study of career development.

The final field study was conducted in four classrooms. Two of the classes played the game twice, using different profiles, while the other two completed only one profile game. The two classes which were able to complete two profiles played once with the scoring procedures and once without them.

Information and ideas about the game during the field test were obtained through interviews of pupils and teachers and visits to classes. Teachers kept records of all questions asked by pupils. At the conclusion of the field test, teachers participated in a half-day critique. Following are some of the comments derived from the field testing:

The interviews with pupils were not very productive. However, some things were learned, including the following: The slower pupils felt somewhat frustrated because they could not understand parts of the game. All pupils felt that the game was "a lot of fun" and that they were "learning a lot." Several suggestions on how to improve technical aspects of the game were made.

The teacher interviews revealed a strong liking for the game. Several suggestions were made for improving the game's technical quality. Observers were impressed that pupils were able to work by themselves with little control or direction. Some doubts were expressed about the readiness of sixth grade pupils for instruction on vocations and career decisions.

It was reported that the experimentation failed to obtain significant differences between the control and experimental groups on the pre-treatment and post-treatment scores. In the opinion of the investigator, the most likely explanation for the non-appearance of significant differences is attributable to the age and maturity of sixth grade pupils. "Although the need for and value of some sort of vocational education in the elementary school has been pointed out many times, it is possible that such experiences, to be meaningful to sixth grade pupils, cannot project as far into the future as the career game attempted to do."

TOPIC THREE: Counselor Training Programs and Institutes

Counselor Training Program

7:5 "A TRAINING PROGRAM FOR VOCATIONAL COUNSELORS" BY DONALD L. FRICK. COLORADO STATE UNIVERSITY, FORT COLLINS, COLO. (PROJECT # 5-0054) 1966. (VT # 004-203) 26 PAGES.

The Colorado State training program for vocational counselors was held for four weeks during the summer of 1965. Thirty secondary school counselors were selected on the basis of needed vocational counseling in the communities they represented. Major emphasis of the program centered around the philosophy and content of vocational education.

The threefold purpose of the training program was to develop in each

trainee the ability to make practical application of vocational counseling techniques in his local community; inform trainees concerning the provisions and implications of federal legislation dealing with vocational training of youth and adults, and provide trainees with the information they need to give intelligent counseling for individuals at various levels of educational attainment.

A large portion of the program was devoted to counseling interview sessions in which the trainees gained experience counseling youths and adults faced with vocational selection and training problems. The instruction also included classes relating to federal legislation for vocational education,

70

visits to vocational training programs in operation, and presentations by resource persons from business, labor, community groups, and industry.

The culminating activity was an individual project in which each trainee developed a community action plan to meet the needs of his home situation.

Second Training Program

7:10 "A TRAINING PROGRAM FOR VOCATIONAL COUNSELORS" BY DONALD L. FRICK. COLORADO STATE UNIVERSITY, FORT COLLINS, COLO. (PROJECT # 6-1592) 1967. (VT # 002-871) 45 PAGES.

The second Colorado State training program for vocational counselors, conducted during a five-week summer session in 1966, had a similar format to the program that was held during the previous summer.

Twenty-one school counselors from four states were selected on the basis of type of community, nature of present assignment and the need for training to perform this assignment.

During the first two weeks on the campus of the University, intensive formal presentations were made by staff and resource personnel on the philosophy and structure of vocational education and occupational information services. Formal instruction was supplemented with group discussions, demonstration interviews and further study of personality factors and counseling theory and practices.

The third and fourth weeks were held at the Emily Griffith Opportunity School in Denver, a public vocational-technical school for youths and adults of all ages. During this period most time was spent in counseling interviews with students of the school. This core experience was supplemented by field trips to business and industry.

The counselors reported that the training program had indeed been a significant experience. They stated that their background orientation to the world of work and aspects of vocation-

al development had been inadequate and that, prior to their participation in the program, they had not been aware of the possibilities for vocational training.

The main value of the two Colorado State guidance training programs is that they have approached the problem of counselors' lack of knowledge about vocational education directly and practically. The testimony of participants reveals that guidance counselors who have had neither special preparation nor first hand experience in vocational counseling and teaching need basic instruction.

The field experience at Denver's Emily Griffith Opportunity School was an important phase of both programs. Trainees thus gained experience in testing, interviewing and counseling in life situations with young people and adults from a broad range of educational backgrounds and varied occupational aspirations. Another significant benefit of this experience was that counselors enrolled in the training programs had the opportunity to observe a quality vocational program in operation.

Counseling the Disadvantaged

7:6 "COUNSELOR INSTITUTE AND FOLLOW-UP WORKSHOPS" BY HOWARD E. MITCHELL. UNIVERSITY OF PENNSYLVANIA, PHILADELPHIA, PA. (PROJECT # 5-0112) 1965. ERIC # ED 010 281. MF $0.50 HC $4.92. 123 PAGES.

This report deals with a program to improve the effectiveness of high school counselors in their vocational guidance work with low-income youth. Citing the comments from business, industry, labor, government, and education, the report states that "our presently inadequate vocational guidance program for low-income youth has two major deficiencies.

"1. The school counselors, as a group, often lack essential knowledge about low-income, disadvantaged youth.

"2. The limited rapport between the business-industrial complex and the school vocational guidance program has partially resulted in a potential labor force with 'improper' attitudes about employment and its relationship to education. Furthermore, it is apparent that industrial leadership has limited knowledge concerning the role of the school counselor."

The counselor training program, conducted as part of the Human Resource Program (HRP), University of Pennsylvania, consisted of a three-week summer institute and a follow-up and program evaluation.

The objectives were to:

—Enhance counselors' understanding of the attitudes which culturally deprived youth have toward matters such as employment, education, family life, and the world beyond their experience.

—Increase counselors' knowledge about changing employment conditions and opportunities.

—Assist in the development of an improved liaison between school guidance counselors and industrial personnel.

A total of 50 guidance counselors, 44 of whom were from the Philadelphia public school system, participated in the summer session. The Institute was comprised of four main activities: lectures by visiting specialists and HRP staff members; panel discussions involving counselors, high school students, industry representatives, government personnel, and academicians; field trips to 14 Philadelphia area industries, and unit group discussions in which participants conversed about the lectures and field trips.

During the next school year, two workshop sessions were held (November and March). At the first workshop, attention was given to guidance programs for the culturally deprived in other urban communities. At the later session, new approaches for improving the competence of guidance personnel were discussed.

A newsletter, *Focus-On-Progress*, was published as part of the University of Pennsylvania project. Distributed five times during the year, it contained materials to acquaint counselors with new trends in guidance and counseling which would be of interest to urban school counselors serving low-income families. Although the actual editing and publishing of *Focus-On-Progress* was done by the HRP staff, counselors were actively engaged in collecting material and deciding what should be published.

Vocational Guidance Conference

7:7 "NEW DIRECTIONS IN VOCATIONAL GUIDANCE" BY PHYLLIS C. WILSON. QUEENS COLLEGE OF THE CITY UNIVERSITY OF NEW YORK, NEW YORK, N. Y. (PROJECT # 5-0184) 1965. ERIC # ED 003 099. MF $0.50 HC $4.68. 117 PAGES.

"In the present rapid advance of automation, urban concentration and general industrial change, counselor educators are severely challenged in providing school guidance trainees with pertinent courses in vocational counseling. Forward-looking courses must evolve from up-to-date knowledge and enlightened point of view on the part of the faculty." So urged Dr. Phyllis C. Wilson, coordinator, guidance and school counseling, Queens College, when introducing the purpose for the counselor educator's institute.

The report of this six-day institute contains the papers of six principal speakers and the summary address by Dr. Pierson, dean and director of student personnel, Queens College. The program outline and rosters of registrants, guests and other participants are also included.

In the first address, "Project People or Project Program," given by Hubert Houghton of the U.S. Office of Education, the importance of assisting each person in developing his maximum potential is stressed. "Counselors must assist youth to develop sound self-appraisal techniques that can be used throughout life—indirect and informal ones in the early school years, increasingly direct and comprehensive ones later."

Also contained in this address is an operational definition of vocational guidance, extracted from the March 1965 issue of the National Vocational Guidance Association Newsletter:

> Vocational guidance includes use of the teaching and counseling processes by which a professionally trained individual works with another person or group of persons, irrespective of age or employment setting, to: (a) broaden his knowledge and understanding of the place of work in the socio-economic pattern of societal and cultural development; (b) aid and assist him in obtaining factual data and in gaining realistic insight and knowledges, abilities, skills, attitudes, interests and characteristics, and the relationship of these to job election, satisfaction and performance, and, (c) help plan a future course of action.

Other presentations recorded in this report relate to employment trends, labor's view, problems of increased urbanization, effects of rapid change on personality, and the technological impact on society.

In his summary remarks, Dean Pierson states that counselor training should be interdisciplinary in character. "Greater emphasis must be placed upon the behavioral and social sciences and upon philosophy, theory and research. Techniques of counseling, testing and job analysis are not enough."

This report calls attention to the fact that occupational orientation is becoming a major topic among many persons involved in the preparation of school guidance counselors. The array of participants who are prominent in guidance education circles, as well as the group of distinguished guests and observers, is testimony to the growing stature of vocational guidance. Of particular significance in this and other related reports is the concept that all young people need instruction relating directly to the world of work.

Short Course for Counselors

7:8 "SHORT COURSE FOR COUNSELORS ON VOCATIONAL-TECHNICAL TRAINING AND OPPORTUNITIES" BY FRED D. HOLT. UNIVERSITY OF GEORGIA, ATHENS, GA. (PROJECT # 5-0875) 1965. ERIC # ED 003 108. MF $0.18 HC $3.88. 97 PAGES.

The three-week course on vocational and technical training and opportunities, conducted by the University of Georgia for 25 counselors, had four main objectives:

1. To develop an increased awareness of the diversity of the vocational and technical world of work.

2. To develop an understanding and recognition of the value and potential contribution of the vocational and technical schools.

3. To develop familiarity with the demands of both large and small industries and businesses in terms of desirable employee characteristics and become more cognizant of the situations in which new employees find themselves.

4. To develop a more comprehensive understanding of the interaction of the social and psychological forces which affect man and his work.

The basic instructional program involved large and small group discussions, lectures, field trips, and group meetings. Considerable attention was given to theoretical aspects of vocational development, with particular emphasis directed toward the sociological and psychological factors which affect man in the world of work.

The instructional staff of 4 was augmented by 10 consultants and 6 off-campus personnel. Participants were taught by specialists in sociology, psychology, social work, and counselor education. Representatives from the U. S. Office of Education, a labor union, the U. S. Department of Labor, and other organizations also took part in the program.

Approximately one-third of the total time was devoted to field trips to vocational-technical schools, large and small industries and businesses. Prior to all trips, preparations were made to help determine the intended value of the experience.

Seven findings, together with a tabulation of participants' comments, are contained in the summary section of this report. The findings were concerned with the role of the counselor, relationship between schools and business and industry, training facilities and opportunities available, automation, and prevalent attitudes toward blue collar work.

In addition, the report includes transcripts of reports compiled by groups of participants. These presentations deal mainly with theories of vocational development and dissemination of vocational-technical information. Each report contains a digest of the topics considered in group activity and a bibliography of related references.

Statements in the section on dissemination of occupational and education information advise that the student should leave high school with personal skills in the informal evaluation of ideas, concepts and information.

"He should possess an objective viewpoint which will allow him to survey collected data about himself, his attributes and his talents, and the ability to use this in all decision-making processes. This skill should serve him throughout his life and permit him to relate growing self knowledge to new and complex situations.

"In the occupational information course, the counseling process should be supplemented by *role playing, dramatizations, work experiences, situational workshops, personal interviews,* and the *collection of related data* from many available sources."

Counselor Education

7:9 "VOCATIONAL ASPECTS OF COUNSELOR EDUCATION" BY CARL MC-

DANIELS. THE GEORGE--WASHINGTON UNIVERSITY, WASHINGTON, D. C. (PROJECT # 5-1208) 1965. ERIC # ED 010 016. MF $1.00 HC $8.00. 200 PAGES.

The George Washington University conference on the vocational aspects of counselor education brought 31 leading educators together for a three-day session. The report contains transcripts of five papers presented during the conference and the summations of three work group sessions.

The report states that the background papers represent the views of the writers on previously selected topics. There is a wealth of information contained in these papers—much food for thought and ample material for numerous studies which can be pursued at various educational levels.

Kenneth B. Hoyt, The University of Iowa, presented a paper, "Needed Counselor Competencies in Vocational Aspects of Counseling and Guidance," dealing with skills, knowledge and attitude which should apply to a *majority* of counselors in a *majority* of school settings.

When speaking of the importance of counselor attitude in vocational counseling of all students, Hoyt states that counselors need to recognize the necessity of devoting concentrated attention to students who choose to do something other than attend college. "Counselors cannot become effective change agents in our society if they accept general societal biases as they presently exist. The current popular notion that the 'best' thing a student could do would be to attend college is one that counselors should be actively seeking to change."

Another important point made by Hoyt is the idea that counselors must recognize the kinds of personal values necessary for those individuals who could profit from vocational guidance.

A status report of current training approaches, format materials and curriculum content by R. Wray Strowig

and Philip A. Perrone of the University of Wisconsin is based on a nationwide questionnaire which had been sent to counselor educators, state guidance supervisors and city guidance directors. This survey revealed that there is considerable room for improvement in total programs and in their component details. Suggestions for better field experiences of guidance trainees and for a closer integration of learning, research and service, are among the recommendations.

Henry Borow of the University of Minnesota delivered a report on research in vocational development which alludes to the growing dissatisfaction with the classical trait-measurement approach to vocational guidance, and it traces the development of subsequent models. The discussion treats the concepts of psychological life stages, career pattern, vocational development tasks, self identification and occupational role models, and some of the benchmark studies from which the concepts were developed.

Borow states that no simple, clearly discernable relationship may be claimed to exist between research discovery in the field of vocational development and the need for curriculum revision and new training methods in counselor education. "Nonetheless, one can hardly dispute the claim that our expanding views of occupational behavior call for a searching reappraisal of counselor education programs with a view toward effecting substantial modification both in content and method."

The report concludes with nine specific recommendations, mainly dealing with the improvement of counselor education.

University of Oregon educator, John Loughary, in proposing new developments in vocational aspects of counselor education, stresses the importance of counselor behavior in the process of vocational development.

While recognizing the potential value of computer-based systems for the processing of occupational information, Loughary places them in proper perspective in his concluding statement. "It must be noted that the one most significant determining factor regarding new developments in vocational aspects of counselor education is the counselor educator."

The fifth paper, "Manpower Legislation of the Sixties: A Threat and a Promise," was prepared by Theodore J. Cote, director of professional services, Division of Vocational Education, New Jersey State Department of Education. In this, the major provisions of federal legislation relating to manpower employment and vocational education are discussed in the light of their implications to counselor education.

In his summarizing remarks, the author states that manpower legislation of the sixties proposes to improve the conditions of people through the combined efforts of counseling and training. "In so doing, it redirects the emphasis of the counseling program to the vocational aspects of guidance and the efforts of counselors to the so-called average and below-average or otherwise disadvantaged student."

The conference report contains a number of interesting topics and positions. Materials presented should have value for vocational counselors and their instructors. At a time when preoccupation in Systems approaches to teaching and counseling often seems to subordinate the importance of persons who do the job, it is encouraging to find a series of presentations and discussions which concentrate on strengthening the qualities and qualifications of counselors.

Rural Guidance Workers

7:11 "VOCATIONAL-EDUCATIONAL INFORMATION WORKSHOP FOR RURAL GUIDANCE WORKERS" BY K. NORMAN SEVERINSEN. WESTERN ILLINOIS UNI-

VERSITY, MACOMB, ILL. (PROJECT
6-2203) 1967. (VT # 004-178)
103 PAGES.

The demand for farmers and farm
workers has steadily decreased. Consequently, rural students need to know
about other job opportunities and the
environment of urban communities.
However, as the report indicates,
only a small proportion of school
counselors are equipped to advise students in rural areas of urban employment possibilities.

The chief emphasis of this project
was placed on giving counselors information about jobs and employment
certificate requirements in Illinois,
Iowa and Missouri. Specialists in these
areas were brought to the campus, and
counselors were encouraged to develop new approaches in the dissemination of information to their students. The main objectives of the project, then, were to attack the problem
of inadequate knowledge of vocational
and educational information among
rural guidance workers and to assess
the method to be used.

The project consisted of three
phases: the *training* phase where
counselors were exposed to concrete
vocational information and encouraged to plan new activities; the *implementation* phase where counselors
were encouraged in their plans
through four "drive-in" conferences
conducted throughout the school year,
and the *evaluation* phase when participants and staff opinions were surveyed, and the effects of the new services on students were measured.

After the two-week workshop was
publicized through mailings, 23 applicants were accepted in the program.
Specialists, particularly those in trade
and technical occupations, were selected as speakers. Participants in the
workshop, extending from Aug. 15 to
26, 1966, were expected to evaluate
each session. They were also asked to
assist in the development of a vocational information test and a career

questionnaire for students.

These 50-minute Vocational Knowledge Tests were objective multiple
choice instruments, having two forms
for pre- and post--testing. A career
questionnaire, designed for machine
scoring, was developed to evaluate vocational attitudes of the students. The
tests were administered to students at
the schools of the participants and at
two high schools serving as controls.

The subjective evaluation by the
counselors revealed that the goals of
the project were accomplished, since
the counselors were generally favorable to the workshop.

The Vocational Knowledge Test revealed that students, especially in
grades 11 and 12, benefited significantly from increased informational
services. However, evidence showed no
measured effect of these services on
students' attitudes. Changes in attitude
seemed to be due to variables other
than increased counselor efforts.

Since the workshop stimulated
counselors, and increased their knowledge, the report stated that such workshops, scheduled just prior to the
school year, can be quite influential in
stepping up guidance activities in rural schools. The study recommends
similar inservice projects for counselors and the use of consultants in these
programs.

The study further recommends that
tests of vocational knowledge should
be refined to determine the value of
such testing in research and guidance.
Since the measurement of vocational
attitudes has not been actively explored, the report suggests that future
inservice workshops might be devoted
to this problem.

Health Career Institute

7:12 "GUIDANCE COUNSELOR INSTI-
TUTE FOR HEALTH CAREERS" BY PHILIP
W. MORGAN. UNITED HOSPITAL FUND
OF NEW YORK, NEW YORK, N. Y.
(PROJECT # 6-2209) 1966. ERIC #
ED 012 342. MF $1.00 HC $8.92. 223
PAGES.

The perennial manpower shortage in the health field has been compounded in recent years by the proliferation of jobs arising from new treatment techniques and fields of knowledge, and by increasing public demands for expanded health services.

Recognizing that high school guidance counselors are in a strategic position to stimulate interest and circulate information on health careers, the Advisory Committee of the United Hospital Fund of New York initiated a 12-day counselor institute on career opportunities that are found in the health field.

The Institute gave attention to the full range of health occupations, including professional and ancillary categories. The program was comprised of a series of major addresses, visits to a variety of health facilities, classroom and small group discussions, and the distribution of literature. Altogether, 48 high school and employment service counselors from New York City participated.

In an attempt to gain prior insight into the knowledge of health careers possessed by city vocational guidance counselors, a questionnaire was sent to 800 secondary school counselors. Responses showed the greatest deficiency of materials and knowledge to be in the area of ancillary or paramedic careers. It was further noted that none of the respondents felt he had sufficient information about any of the 38 careers listed. As a consequence, the Institute focused attention on the full range of health occupations.

The agenda included 19 major addresses, given mainly by administrative officers and professors from hospitals and professional schools and organizations. Two full days were spent visiting New York Hospital, where staff members from different departments spoke on various hospital careers.

Edward Linzer, executive director, Mental Health Center, discussed the scope of new developments in the mental health field and the variety of emerging career opportunities associated with them. He explained that the seven major categories of persons who work in the mental health field function as psychiatrists, psychiatric social workers, clinical psychologists, occupational therapists, recreational specialists, psychiatric nurses, and psychiatric aides.

A visit to the Columbia University School of Dental and Oral Surgery included a tour of the facilities and two film showings, "The Challenge of Dentistry" and "Opportunities in Dentistry." Visitors were given papers describing career opportunities in dental hygiene, dentistry and related fields.

Duties of the trained dental assistant were described in a presentation by Dr. George O'Grady, assistant professor of dentistry. He stated that the formal training of dental assistants is a recent development. "In the past, a dental assistant received on-the-job training from her employer. This system was known as the blind leading the blind. He didn't know what to teach her, and she didn't know what to do."

Participants in the health careers program also visited the Institute of Physical Medicine and Rehabilitation in New York City and Squibb Pharmaceutical Laboratories, New Brunswick, N. J.

The Guidance Counselor Institute for Health Careers revealed to the United Hospital Fund, through its various phases of preliminary discussions and questionnaires, that there are severe shortcomings in the guidance services as they currently exist. "There is a critical need for programs designed to give guidance counselors more information on health careers. It is also obvious that there is a need for better occupational material to be presented to counselors in a variety of ways."

Counselor Training Program

7:13 "TRAINING INSTITUTE FOR VOCATIONAL GUIDANCE AND COUNSELING

PERSONNEL" BY FRANK E. WELLMAN,
UNIVERSITY OF MISSOURI, COLUMBIA,
MO. (PROJECT # 6-2212) 1966. ERIC
ED 011 614. MF $0.18 HC $4.28.
107 PAGES.

This four-week training institute for
vocational guidance personnel, conducted by the University of Missouri,
provided instruction for 40 trainees
from 12 North Central states. The
general purpose of the project was to
develop understandings, knowledge
and professional materials with respect to:

1. Economic factors influencing the
need for vocational and technical education, and the vocational decision-
making process among youth and
adults.

2. Social and cultural factors
related to the vocational counseling of
youth and adults.

3. Psychological factors related to
the career development and vocational
choices of noncollege-bound students.

4. Administrative considerations in
the evaluation of economic, social, cultural, and psychological factors in
program organization, as well as in
the coordination of vocational counseling activities of the various local,
state and federal agencies.

The Institute provided 30 hours of
scheduled activities each week. Half of
the time was devoted to lectures and
discussion of vocational counseling in
the areas of economics, sociology, psychology, and administration. The remaining time was spent in small group
sessions where papers were prepared
on assigned topics.

The basic instructional staff was
comprised of faculty from the University of Missouri Departments of
Economics, Education and Sociology.
Representatives of the U. S. Office of
Education, the U. S. Department of
Labor, local school systems, and other
college personnel served as special
consultants.

The report contains outlines of the
various instructional phases of the
program—economic, social, psychological and administrative dimensions of
vocational counseling. The content and
structure of the Institute was said to
be unique as an approach to training
vocational guidance and counseling
personnel. "The inclusions of multi-
disciplinary content within one concentrated training period has seldom
been attempted, and the indirect approach to the improvement of the
work of vocational counselors through
supervisory training has not been exploited in the field of guidance and
counseling."

Trainees and staff favorably evaluated this new approach. It was reported that the major strengths were the
high quality of trainees, appropriateness of curriculum content, program format, and the stature of instructional staff members.

TOPIC FOUR: Regional Resources

Job Information Center

7:14 "REGIONAL CENTER FOR COL-
LECTION, SYNTHESIS AND DISSEMINA-
TION OF CAREER INFORMATION FOR USE
BY SCHOOLS OF SAN DIEGO COUNTY"
BY EDWIN A. WHITFIELD AND RICHARD
HOOVER. DEPARTMENT OF EDUCATION,
SAN DIEGO, CALIF. (PROJECT # 6-
1620) 1967. (VT # 004-123) 153
PAGES.

The developmental phase of the San
Diego County Career Information
Center, conducted from July 1, 1966,
through June 30, 1967, is the substance of this report. During this period, career information was produced
for all occupations requiring less than
a baccalaureate degree for which
training within the County was available. This resulted in approximately

200 eight-page descriptions. This material was distributed to 12 participating schools, and an evaluation of the materials and dissemination procedures was obtained from students, counselors and school officials.

The dissemination vehicle used was a system based on the microfilm aperture card. A two-card format was chosen for each occupation. The first card contained four pages of general information; the second card, local information. Each school was supplied a microfilm reader and a reader-printer which enabled students to project microfilm copy on a screen and, if desired, print out hard copy. In addition, parameters pertinent to the occupation, such as aptitudes, length of training and restrictions, were key-punched into each aperture card.

The main body of information for each occupation was prepared in a standardized format suitable for conversion into microfilm form. Each brief was referred to as a VIEW script (VIEW standing for Vocational Information for Education and Work). Each pair of briefs for an occupation was put on microfilm.

The evaluation of the VIEW materials and their use in the pilot schools involved several phases, each utilizing a different evaluation instrument. The reactions of participating students, pilot school counselors and summer counselors were obtained through a questionnaire and group meetings. Each school counselor in San Diego County was also asked to evaluate the document known as "VIEWPOINT, Entry Employment in San Diego."

Students who had used VIEW materials, as well as other types of occupational information, reported that VIEW materials were more helpful, understandable, realistic, interesting, complete, and up-to-date. A later evaluation by high school students generally supported the reactions obtained in the first instance.

The 21 counselors queried indicated that, in their estimation, student reaction to VIEW scripts had been either "favorable" or "very favorable." It was further reported that there was increased use of other vocational materials and that there appeared to be more interest in vocational guidance by the total school staff.

Among the specific needs revealed through this study is one for more counseling and guidance for students who do not plan to attend a four-year college. "This was emphasized by the large percentage of students who received jobs unrelated to their training, who changed majors after once entering the junior college, who felt they were not using their ability to their best advantage on the job they held, or who changed jobs within one year after their junior college training."

It was generally concluded that occupational information disseminated via aperture cards proved to be valuable and useful to both students and counselors. With a concentrated effort on the part of guidance personnel working with students, this system can be utilized to provide an even more effective vocational service in the schools.

TOPIC FIVE: Experiments and Developmental Studies

Tests for Creativity

7:15 "A STUDY OF THE CONCURRENT VALIDITY OF THE MINNESOTA TESTS OF CREATIVE THINKING, ABBR. FORM VII, FOR EIGHTH GRADE INDUSTRIAL ARTS STUDENTS" BY LESTER G. DUENK, UNIVERSITY OF MINNESOTA, MINNEAPOLIS, MINN. (PROJECT # 5-0113) 1966. (VT # 002-740) 230 PAGES.

The primary concern of this study

was to establish the concurrent validity of the Minnesota Tests of Creative Thinking, Abbr. Form VII, by determining the relationships between its scores and criteria measures based upon industrial arts oriented, creative performance tests developed by the investigator. A secondary objective was to determine the relationships between measures of creative abilities based upon accumulated teacher ratings of observed student behaviors as they occurred in typical industrial arts classes and those acquired through the use of the investigator's instruments.

Other purposes of the study were to estimate the relationships among measures of creative abilities in industrial arts as determined by: teacher ratings of typical performance in industrial arts; the investigator's specialized performance test approach, and the Minnesota Tests of Creative Thinking, Abbr. Form VII.

The population sample included 129 eighth grade boys who were receiving industrial arts instruction in two suburban junior high schools at St. Paul, Minn.

A specialized performance test of creativity abilities, developed by Jerome Moss, had previously been used in an investigation in which typical classroom performance measures were employed as the criteria of creativity. This test was constructed by the investigator and administered to the sample. The Minnesota Tests of Creative Thinking were also administered at approximately the same time. Descriptive data gathered from cumulative records included intelligence scores, average grades in seventh grade English, social studies, mathematics, industrial arts, and art, and achievement test scores in reading, social studies, writing, mathematics, and science. Personality rating scales were also obtained.

Pearson product-moment correlational techniques were used to estimate the concurrent validity of the Minnesota Tests as well as the rela

tionships between measures of creative abilities, I.Q., achievement, and personality.

The findings of this study revealed that few significant relationships were established between MTCT and industrial arts test scores. It was speculated that "creative thinking" involving specific industrial arts related subject matter may be tapping different or additional characteristics than the "creative thinking" involved in responding to the non-specialized content of paper and pencil tests.

The study states that industrial educators may be wise to use the word "creativity" with caution, for without proper qualification, reference to creative production becomes quite ambiguous. "The artistic student who can express creative talent in an article of esthetic beauty may not necessarily be capable of planning a creative approach to a machine production problem or to a situation which calls for unusual interpersonal relationships."

Motivating Students

7:16 "MOTIVES INFLUENCING NEEDS TO ACHIEVE IN VOCATIONAL EDUCATION" BY FRANCES B. HELTZEL. CORNELL UNIVERSITY, ITHACA, N. Y. (PROJECT # 5-0157) 1966. ERIC # ED 010 295. MF $0.20 HC $1.88. 47 PAGES.

Forces affecting the motivation of high school students are numerous, varied, complex, and extremely difficult to measure. Continued study into this all-important aspect of learning should lead to improvements in teaching effectiveness. And for guidance counselors, constantly assisting students to make educational choices, a better understanding of relationships between motivation and school achievement is desirable.

The Cornell University study of motives influencing needs to achieve in vocational education, although failing to obtain conclusive findings, should serve as an important step in the accumulation of knowledge about this subject.

Objectives were: to construct an instrument to elicit basic motives as categorized by Maslow and measure their strength, using Krathwohl's taxonomy of affect levels; and, to measure experimentally induced motivation in terms of affect, level of aspiration and effort criteria.

Two hypotheses were tested. A task perceived as highly relevant for one's vocational preference and for which one correctly perceives oneself as competent, will elicit a higher level of affect.

The relationship of affect and its antecedents—career-relevance of task, self concept and observed ability—will vary with different subgroups of sex, SES and grade level when grade point average is controlled.

Parallel instruments of 42 items were constructed to measure motives for striving, based on Maslow's hierarchy of needs for security, belongingness, esteem, and self-actualization. The strength of each motive was measured according to Krathwohl's taxonomic levels of responding, valuing, organization of values, and characterization by a value. Subsequent to pretesting procedures, a 20-item test was devised.

Experimentation was designed to provide a validation of the instrument by creating different motivation levels through the manipulation of specific variables: performance score, self concept and task relevance. A total of 214 tenth and twelfth graders in Elmira, N.Y., were tested. An item analysis based on low- and high-scoring students showed that items written at seven of the nine Krathwohl levels discriminated satisfactorily.

It was reported that only pretest results can be given as the research had to be terminated at that stage. "The final pretest results indicated that items written to measure different levels of affect did discriminate satisfactorily; they did not fall into the predicted difficulty levels hypothesized by Krathwohl's hierarchy. However,...

efforts to continue the research beyond the pretest phase proved abortive.

"Further attempts to validate the affect instrument through concurrent administration of Finger's Personal Values Inventory, yielding a persistent score, and French's Test of Insight, measuring need-achievement, likewise proved futile."

Research and Practice Guidelines

7:17 "GUIDANCE IN VOCATIONAL EDUCATION: GUIDELINES FOR RESEARCH AND PRACTICE" BY ROBERT E. CAMPBELL. OHIO STATE UNIVERSITY, COLUMBUS, OHIO. (PROJECT # 5-0212) 1966. ERIC # ED 011 922. MF $0.75 HC $7.60. 190 PAGES.

The Ohio State Center for Research and Leadership Development in Vocational and Technical Education, responding to the growing need for effective programs of vocational guidance, invited nationally recognized leaders from several disciplines throughout the country to develop guidelines for initiating and improving such programs.

The stated major purpose of the three-day seminar was to provide an opportunity for leaders in vocational education, guidance and related disciplines to pool their resources and thinking in formulating plans for initiating and improving programs of research and practice. Among the overall goals were those to stimulate interdisciplinary research and interest, evaluate the status of vocational guidance and identify specific problem areas, and reduce the time lag between research, theory and practice.

The report contains transcripts of the major presentations made at the seminar, together with the comments of reaction speakers. Also included is a directory of 37 consultants and 190 participants, and the schedule of group discussions.

In the summary section are listed 7 guidelines for guidance practice and 14 guidelines for areas of needed research on guidance in vocational education.

Guidelines for Practice

• Guidance is a process of helping the individual to examine his life experiences to the end that he may know and choose himself and his actions more clearly and purposefully.

• Both teachers and counselors have roles to play in guidance, but the counselor should make a unique contribution to the vocational program.

• The educational-vocational framework provides the most logical rationale for pursuing discovery of self.

• The criterion to be employed in defining the role and functions of the counselor in vocational education is psychological consistency.

• There is a job for both vocational educator and counselor in providing experiences which enable the student to identify suitable social work-roles.

• The myth of the individual with a single occupational value can no longer be supported as a basis for vocational guidance practice.

• Guidance in vocational education cannot escape its responsibility to develop the abilities and talents of *all* individuals.

Identifying Areas of Needed Research on Guidance in Vocational Education

• Since many of the attributes learned in early childhood, such as concepts of mastery, coping behavior and achievement motivation, bear upon later vocational planning and adjustment, more research is needed on younger children so that we may discover the conditions under which these traits are learned.

• **The values** that people hold **about occupations** are culturally acquired. However, we do not yet understand very much about the psychological processes by which this acquisition occurs. Research needs to be designed that will reveal how children, for example, develop their occupational valuing system as well as their generalized vocational motives.

• As new fields emerge and the nature of the industrial order becomes increasingly complex, it becomes more important that those responsible for vocational curriculum construction, training and counseling have access to improved systems for the classification of occupations.

• A larger percentage of secondary school and post-secondary school students hold part-time jobs than at any time previously. Experience with such work is logically expected to assist youths with problems of realistic vocational planning, but we suspect that this expectation is not generally borne out by the facts. Research is needed to compare the vocational maturity status of youth who have had outside work experience with those who lack such experience.

• While research has emphasized chiefly the influence of trained counselors upon the vocational plans of students, investigations are needed which will study the impact of other adults and authority figures on the vocational thinking of youth.

• Curriculum research is needed that will begin to furnish some answers to the question of what kinds of formal course experiences are most likely to lead to the specified goals or behavioral outcomes of vocational education. Despite all the discussion about needed curricular changes, very few studies have yet been designed with this sort of cause-effect relationship in mind.

• The average working life expectancy for American high school girls today is approximately 25 years. Yet many of these young women have seriously underdeveloped work motivation. There is an urgent need for research on cultural variables, both within and outside the school setting, that may be utilized to accelerate vocational readiness in girls.

• The quality of commitment that a vocational education student may have to vocational planning, and the attitude that he shelters toward work in general and his vocational curriculum in particular, will depend upon a variety of life history and background factors that are frequently unclear to his teachers and which, indeed, may not yet be well understood by occupational research workers.

Studies are needed, therefore, which investigate the comparative effects of selective life experiences, such as history of parental unemployment, parents' occupation, values held by the peer group, etc., upon such indicators of vocational development as level of occupational aspiration, accuracy of occupational knowledge, and strength of career planning motivation.

• We continue to assume in normal economic life that the intellectual traits of the individual, such as his aptitudes and trained skills, are the only important personal variables that contribute to occupational success or failure. However, research has long shown that personality and character traits are at least as important in occupational success and advancement as the cognitive traits.

• A good deal of pressure exists to encourage culturally disadvantaged youths to enter vocational education programs inasmuch as they often seem not to prosper in purely academic or college preparatory programs. Yet such disadvantaged youths have often been exposed to background variables which are serious deterrents to success in any type of formal training program, including a vocational education program. Through research we need to identify those factors related to restricted socioeconomic status which limit the youth's promise as a trainee.

• New types of post-secondary but sub-collegiate occupational specialties have recently been emerging, such as computer programmer, computer technician, social worker aide, and psychiatric aide, on which very little empirical research has yet been done and about which little is known. If vocational training programs in such new fields are to avoid some of the pitfalls experienced in older fields of vocational training, systematic and intensive research will need to be designed to identify important worker trait requirements so that curriculum development and vocational counseling can proceed on a sounder and better informed basis.

• Guidance within vocational education has not prospered in the past for many reasons, notably for the reason that relations and communication between vocational educators and counselors have hardly been ideal. Research is now needed that will focus on a study of interpersonal relations and attitudes between the members of these two fields. What, for example, is the vocational educator's concept of the counselor? Who is he? What does he do? Conversely, what is the counselor's stereotyped impression of the vocational educator?

• It is unfortunately true that the typical training of the counselor does not equip him to work effectively in the setting of the vocational, or technical school. In fact, his training may often bias him unwittingly against the values of vocational education programs. Research can and should be done on the relation of the counselor's socioeconomic background and professional training to his occupational attitudes and values.

• Since some students who enter vocational education curricula do not readily think in terms of long-range goals, the strategy of instruction should include the scheduling of frequent, short-term recognitions and rewards. In this connection the current work in reinforcement counseling, growing out of behavior modification theory, seems most promising.

Important Information Source

This report on the national seminar on guidance in vocational education is

83

an important source of information that should have value to all vocational guidance workers. The report contains a wealth of material, much of it prepared by nationally known authorities in various academic disciplines and governmental offices. As it would be difficult to quickly absorb all of the contents, permanent acquisition of the document is recommended.

The reader is sure to find some interesting and provocative commentaries and pronouncements among the presentations and discussion reports. The wide divergence of background among seminar participants and the many points of view expressed should help to precipitate feelings of identification or reaction among readers, which may in turn provoke further thought and action.

Social Readiness for Employment

7:18 "DEVELOPMENT OF A JUNIOR HIGH SCHOOL INSTRUMENT FOR APPRAISING SOCIAL READINESS FOR EMPLOYMENT" BY VIVIAN E. TODD AND ZELPHA BATES. CALIFORNIA STATE COLLEGE AT LONG BEACH, LONG BEACH, CALIF. (PROJECT # 5-8462) 1967. (VT # 003-235) 84 PAGES.

What are the attitudes or beliefs that stand in the way of job getting and job holding? Is it possible to identify some of those that are critical? Can an instrument be devised to appraise the presence or absence of such beliefs? These are the basic questions asked in this developmental study.

The two-fold concerns of this project were: (a) an exploration of the critical factors in the development of an appraisal device for schools serving disadvantaged communities, and (b) the development of an instrument for appraising or teaching groups of students regarding social readiness for employment.

The general design of the project was developed in accordance with the following methodological organization:

—Identify areas of social readiness for employment through interviews with selected personnel managers and on the basis of related literature.

—Work with junior high school personnel, identifying the level of indices appropriate for junior high students.

—Develop an appraisal form suitable for evaluating readiness for employment.

—Devise appropriate items for two forms of the instrument and arrange them using random numbers.

—Administer the instruments to groups of junior high school girls in each of two schools.

—Conduct statistical analyses and, through interviews, study validity of responses to the instrument.

On the basis of interviews of selected people in business, industry and schools and the *Handbook for Young Workers* published by the U. S. Department of Labor, a two-part instrument was devised ("Where Is It Done?" and "What To Do?"). The project reported that student responses obtained in junior high schools serving disadvantaged communities showed the items were appropriate in differentiating among such student groups. It was concluded that the instrument developed is useful for describing the current status of a group of junior high school students in its social readiness for employment.

"Thus, it is an aid to a teacher taking students from where they are to a greater understanding of the social aspects of employment."

Junior College Study

7:19 "SELECTED CHARACTERISTICS, SOCIOECONOMIC STATUS AND LEVELS OF ATTAINMENT OF STUDENTS IN PUBLIC JUNIOR COLLEGE OCCUPATION-CENTERED EDUCATION" BY JOHN W. HAKANSON. UNIVERSITY OF CALIFORNIA, BERKELEY, CALIF. (PROJECT # 6-8420) 1967. (VT # 003-958) 47 PAGES.

"The public junior college has moved far indeed from the original concept of an institution offering the first two years of undergraduate study. . . . Where fully developed it is no longer a junior or 'beginning' college but an institution responsive to many needs of the people in its locale, truly a community college." With these introductory statements, the report identifies the need for studying the backgrounds, qualities and qualifications of people taking occupation-level courses.

Three purposes are given for the University of California study:

1. To determine whether the relationship between low socioeconomic status and low educational attainment holds when the criterion of achievement is completion of a two-year occupation-centered curriculum in a public college.

2. To examine the extent of shifting of occupational and educational goals and to compare students who enroll directly from high school in two year, occupation-centered programs with those who first enroll in college credit transfer programs and then later change their programs.

3. To describe students in two-year occupation-centered curricula in public junior colleges in terms of selected variables: socioeconomic status scholastic aptitude, course of study pursued in high school, and sex.

Institutional Settings

Six public junior colleges were selected for the investigation. Four of these were located in Midwestern states of Missouri, Kansas, Illinois, and Michigan. The other two were in California.

Data from the High School Graduate Study, previously conducted by Leland Medsker and James Trent of the University of California, were used in this research. The Medsker and Trent study was designed to survey the general intellectual, psychological and social characteristics of some 10,000, 1959 high school graduates,

and to examine factors influencing attendance and persistence in college.

Data concerning personal and social characteristics and educational background were collected by questionnaire in 1959 while these students were still in high school. Information obtained for the follow-up of those in the original survey group consisted of records of performance and retention in post-secondary education as well as employment status.

Treatment of Data

Nine specific questions were framed to satisfy the first objective of this study, which is to describe students in terms of certain characteristics and attributes. These questions are:

—What proportion of these students originate from each of several socioeconomic levels?

—What is the mean and range of their scholastic aptitude scores?

—What proportion of these students falls into each of several levels of scholastic aptitude?

—What is the distribution of these students among different courses of study followed in high school?

—How do men and women differ according to these variables?

—How do students in each of a number of major categories of occupational centered curricula differ in terms of socioeconomic status, scholastic aptitude, course of study in high school, and sex?

—To what extent do students in two-year occupation-centered curricula in public junior colleges differ from graduating high school seniors in terms of these variables?

—How do those who complete a two-year occupation-centered curriculum differ from those who start but do not finish, in terms of socioeconomic status, scholastic aptitude, course of study followed in high school and sex?

—How do those who enter a two-year occupation-centered curriculum directly from high school as a first choice differ from those who enter as a second choice, in terms of the above variables?

The basic method of analysis was to make a series of comparisons of groups of students, each one in terms of a number of selected variables, testing each comparison for significance. Further analysis consisted of percentage comparisons of subgroups in an attempt to discover different relationships between variables. Where the data permitted, cross-classification of three variables was also carried out.

The results of the investigation are treated in considerable detail. From a discussion of the extent of basic shifts in program, a conclusion drawn is that the study points to potentially serious trouble for the junior college movement.

"First, it is apparent that the junior college may well fail to meet society's need for really large numbers of technicians unless it can: (a) entice more high school graduates directly into occupation-centered curricula, or (b) succeed in getting much larger proportions of potential academic program dropouts to switch to terminal programs rather than withdraw.

"Second, unless public junior college enrollees can be brought to a better understanding of their own responsibility for the degree to which they commit themselves to success in their chosen courses of study, they and their parents may hold the college rather than themselves responsible for failure."

"PLAIN TALK"

RESEARCH AND DEVELOPMENT PROJECTS reported in this issue focus attention on three general categories: computer-assisted systems of information gathering and counseling; career development theory and practice, and college and university institutes and instructional programs designed to prepare or upgrade counselors in the vocational aspects of guidance.
Other important themes treated are the national seminar for developing guidelines, and the University of California investigation of the status, characteristics and levels of attainment of students taking occupational-level courses in junior colleges.

The systems approach to guidance was the main theme of two projects headed by Campbell and Cogswell. All of the other studies had sections dealing with one or more aspects of computer-assisted guidance work: job information retrieval, analysis of personal and educational qualities in students, and computerized teaching and man-machine counseling.

There was a consensus that school guidance programs would be strengthened through the judicious use of data processing methods for the collection and organization of job and student information, and for the reduction of clerical activities by counselors. However, some deep concerns were expressed about the projected role of the computer in the total guidance function. It was feared that heavy reliance on man-machine systems would cause some counselors to lose their ability to relate with students.

Questions were raised about the value of using the computer to match people to jobs, which has been suggested in some circles. Both the occupational information retrieved and the taxonomy of personal traits and abilities that could be attributed toward predicting job success would always be limited in scope and depth. They would be far too general and incomplete for making individual prescriptions.

Dangers to Students

In Cogswell's investigation of "Information-Processing Procedures and Computer-Based Technology in Vocational Education," there are a series of statements which warn the reader about the "nonhumanistic" effects the computer may have on guidance. Commenting that man-machine systems are intended to provide more counselor time with students, the investigators state that they may lead only to more counselor time with data. Three specific dangers to students who are counseled by computer are cited in this study: possible invasion of privacy; the misuse of predictive systems, and the alienation of people.

Career development, or vocational development as it is sometimes called, is rapidly becoming an instrument for change in guidance and curriculum. After a period in which career development was mainly a theoretical concept, it is now becoming an integral part of the curriculum plan for many schools and districts.

The implications of career development theory and practice to vocational education are tremendous. Not only will this student-centered approach to guidance and education help insure that many more young people develop realistic concepts and goals, but it should also help to eliminate the gulf that has existed between the so-called fields of preparatory and terminal education.

The term *career development* has been defined as a series of experiences, decisions and interactions which, taken cumulatively, result in the formulation of a self-concept and provide the means by which that self-concept can be implemented through vocation and avocation. Common elements associated with career development are: self and community awareness; experience in simulated and real situations; the capacity for planning and decision making, and willingness to take purposeful action.

Common Elements

Although a good share of career development theory has emanated from the behavioral sciences, it is interesting to note that many of the principles and goals are closely related to those of vocational education. These include the development of self-concept, experience in real life situations, realistic planning and decision-making, the individualization of instruction, all intrinsic elements of any good program of vocational education. There may be some semantic differences, but the overall purpose is virtually identical.

If the vocational or practical arts teacher has missed the opportunity to become acquainted with the theoretical rationale for career development, or with some of the plans for its implementation that are now taking shape, this is the time to correct the deficiency. As the person best equipped through background and experience to effectively apply the principles of career development into the shop and classroom, the teacher of practical subjects should be actively involved in the whole process, and not be a sideline observer.

Many college and university programs to prepare guidance counselors are currently in a process of reconstruction. There is increased emphasis upon the behavioral studies and a corresponding reduction in the number of courses on counseling methods and techniques. The trend is toward the provision for a more extensive theoretical base, capped off by an extended period of supervised internship.

Another new development in the preparation of guidance counselors, one that has received considerable attention in the studies reported here, is the movement toward a multi-disciplinary team approach to guidance. The theory supporting this move is that guidance work handled exclusively by former teachers tends to inhibit and stereotype the process. Innovative practices, it is contended, may more likely be developed by group interaction of persons with diverse experiences and points of view. The fields of sociology, psychology, government service, and commercial personnel work are frequently mentioned as additional sources for the

88

pupil personnel team.

Missing Ingredient

When the U.S. Office of Education sponsored studies are viewed in retrospect, it is apparent that a most important phase of vocational guidance has not been treated. This is job placement.

The placement of prepared and qualified persons in productive employment is a rewarding climax to the whole process of vocational orientation and education. It is so pivotal to the ultimate career success of individuals that the position of the placement counselor should be thoroughly studied. It would be good to know, for example, what the placement counselor needs to know about such things as the job market, labor laws, employment practices, and job-seeking techniques.

The process of placement also needs attention. What are the most effective techniques for establishing and maintaining an effective job placement and follow-up program to best help students make the great transition from school to work?

Careers Unlimited

IONE T. BAAL

THE REAL KEY to successful vocational training is cooperation between education and industry. This is true on every level—national, state and local. Probably the most vital area is the local level.

A persistent problem associated with secondary-school guidance programs is the difficulty faced by schools and teachers in acquiring adequate information about local and regional career opportunities. Conversely, it is also difficult for school officials to apprise business and industry of school training and counseling programs relevant to career opportunities in their firms. Yet it goes without saying that industry and business have a large stake and a sincere interest in secondary-school students. Stated another way, both groups—schools and industry—tend to operate with a minimum of communication although their ultimate interest in the student is mutual.

If one of the purposes of the secondary school is to enable the individual to function in the economic activities of society, then the activities and orientation of schools must be directed toward preparing each individual with salable skills and attitudes necessary for partial or complete employment compatible with his needs at various ages. A variety of school personnel are involved in reaching this goal, but a knowledgeable counselor is of prime importance.

In order to be knowledgeable in their advice-giving roles, guidance counselors cannot limit themselves to students who will take college training. They must also be able to advise young people concerning future vocations. Thoroughly knowledgeable guidance in this respect comes only from actual experience in the working world and first-hand knowledge of what opportunities are available. Thus, whatever experience a counselor has in the world of work becomes invaluable, if not a prerequisite, to the counseling of all youth.

Out of Proportion. Counselors are generally in agreement that they are "over exposed" to academic experiences and limited in industrial or business background. Consequently, it can be concluded that it would definitely benefit counselors and their students if there could be a mutual exchange of problems and experiences between the world of work and the educational enterprise.

An active step toward this premise was taken in Des Moines, Iowa, in the fall of 1967. A series of meetings involved people from the Greater Des Moines Merit Employment Council, public and private school personnel, and civic organizations including the Des Moines Chamber of Commerce and organized labor. The focus of these meetings was to develop a structure that would facilitate direct communication between school counselors and business, industry and labor.

Out of this initial exchange developed a project called "Careers Unlimited." The title itself is significant, since the underlying philosophy of the project de-emphasized classification of students by what they "ought to do." On the contrary, the project would provide an increased amount of career information, visitation to area industry, seminars for counselors, employment offices, and other related activities.

Striving for Equity. One of several "Careers Unlimited" programs developed was the Annual Summer Vocational Guidance Institute aimed at bringing together tomorrow's jobs and job-seekers. These summer Institutes are joint projects of the Merit Employers Council (National Alliance of Businessmen), Des Moines Junior Chamber of Commerce, Des Moines Public Schools, nearby Drake University, and Plans for Progress, the national voluntary equal-employment-opportunity program of American business and industry.

The overall goal of the Institute was encapsuled by Richard Marshall, administrative coordinator of Plans for progress, when he said in his keynote address to the second Institute: "People who have 'equity' will have a different attitude."

To achieve this equity, the Institute strove to improve the effectiveness of junior and senior high school guidance personnel in their vocational counseling of disadvantaged youth; to enhance educators' understanding of the world of work and disadvantaged youngsters; to increase employers' understanding of the educational enterprise; and to translate these understandings into meaningful action in schools and the business community.

On Campus & On the Job. Nineteen Des Moines business and industrial establishments served as host companies for the first Institute conducted in 1968. Stuart Tiedeman, head of Guidance and Counseling, Drake University, acted as academic director.

The Institute consisted of a four-week workshop for 25 counselors, combining on-campus academic activity at Drake University with on-the-job experience in Des Moines business and industrial establishments. Each counselor received graduate credit from Drake University in addition to a regular salary from the company by which he was employed.

During the first week, the counselors attended lectures, panels, discussions, and films on the Drake campus; visited 12 business and industrial firms in the Greater Des Moines area; and, with work-experience coordinators from host companies, engaged in seminar discussions of various topics and problems.

The last three weeks constituted the work-experience phase of the Institute. Except for one day each week spent on the Drake campus, the counselors were employed by the host companies in a variety of jobs. Group conferences, interviews with employees and management, and other experiences designed to better acquaint them with the world of work, were part of the work-experience program.

The last day of the Institute was reserved for reporting. Each of five counselor report groups presented criticisms, suggestions and recommendations to representatives of the schools, business and industry.

Pre-Institute and follow-up data obtained during the first two Institutes was used to analyze changes in such areas as (1) attitudes toward the disadvantaged; (2) attitudes reflecting optimism, realism, and commitment; (3) perception of the counselor's role in working with minority youths; and (4) general knowledge of the world of work. The results indicated that participants found the Institute helpful and informative, and that the Institute did, in fact, affect both attitudes and behavior.

Impressed by Industry Support.
The factor which most impressed counselors was industry's willingness to cooperate in the initiation and support of these Institutes. The evaluations made it clear that all participants appreciated this interest and initiative, as well as the opportunity for increased communication between industrial and school personnel. Guidance personnel indicated that they wished to nourish further development of this cooperative

spirit.

Participants were impressed with institute programs in general. They indicated that field trips, seminars and work experience were especially beneficial. The greatest value of the field trips was that they gave counselors an overview of business and industry and a greater awareness of the variety of entry jobs available in Des Moines. Counselors also felt they benefited from personal contacts made with business and industrial personnel.

Counselors were generally enthusiastic about the seminars. The informal setting permitted an easy exchange of ideas that made the seminars a useful forum for discussing problems of common concern to business, industry and education. Counselors felt, however, that the meetings would have been even more valuable if more business and industry people had been involved.

Work experience was rated higher than any other feature of the Institute. The greatest value attributed to it was the opportunity afforded counselors to become at least slightly business-oriented and to develop some understanding of "how it feels" to work in a non-educational environment. Of particular value was the opportunity counselors had to gain some understanding and appreciation of entry-level jobs. Some counselor comments were:

"Increased understanding of various jobs available"

"Found out how it feels to punch a time clock"

"Bankers' hours aren't what I expected"

"Learned about 'ladders of progress' "

"Found that business and industry do a lot of counseling with employ-ecs and do it well"

"Discovered that employers have problems, too"

Overall Benefits. Among benefits cited by counselors for the Institute as a whole were the excellent resource people they met and a better understanding of vocational counseling.

One counselor said the Institute had increased his awareness of the need to fit minority groups into the mainstream of employment; another said it had given him better ideas on how to solve the problems of the disadvantaged; and a third remarked on the need for labor unions to become more involved in helping the disadvantaged.

Several counselors expressed a new sensitivity to the non-college bound. "White-collar workers in business are created through merit," said one, "not merely by college degrees." Another saw a need for counselors to spend more time with non-college bound students to help them improve their work habits, increase their knowledge of available job opportunities, and show them how to go about getting a job.

One counselor summed up the benefits of the four-week experience this way: "A better understanding of the work and workers in our city and of the manner in which people start on a job and advance because of their interest and effort—and my responsibility in explaining this to my counselees."

Industry's Assessment. Business and industry representatives evaluated the Institute as worthwhile because it provided an opportunity to inform counselors of their personnel needs, to engage in a meaningful dialogue with counselors about mutual problems, and to learn what the counselor's job really is and what the guidance program is all about.

Most companies expressed the feeling that they would like to continue to maintain a close working relationship with counselors and schools. They planned to continue to make their personnel available as speakers and consultants, as well as conduct business and plant tours throughout the year.

The first Institute served as a motivator for more direct contact between business, industry and school personnel.

During the 1968-69 school year, the 25 counselors who participated in the first Institute implemented many of the ideas generated. This increased their effectiveness in counseling disadvantaged as well as other students.

New Ideas Implemented. A follow-up questionnaire asked counselors to indicate some activities they had adopted as a result of the Institute. Here are the activities they listed.

• Using personnel from business and industry in small-group guidance programs to provide information on how to apply for jobs.

• Organizing a "vocationally oriented" faculty meeting.

• Incorporating more of the needs of business into the curriculum.

• Relating instruction more closely to actual work situations.

• Using more group guidance activities to develop self-understanding.

• Spending more time counseling students who are participating in the Neighborhood Youth Corps.

• Spending more time in vocational counseling for non-college bound students.

• Taking more students to visit business and industry.

• Arranging a Business-Industry-Education day for juniors. (Students were assigned to an employer for an entire day.)

• Inviting business people to speak at student meetings and inservice sessions for teachers and counselors.

• Enlarging the vocational unit in group guidance and encouraging teachers to emphasize vocational opportunities in their specialties.

• Inviting gainfully employed members of minority groups to speak to counselees.

Help in Several Forms. A definite aid to counselors came from firms that provided junior and senior high school students with descriptions of entry jobs in the Des Moines area. Many companies classified and described individual jobs, and even though some descriptions were brief, they explained the purpose of the job, duties of the worker, knowledge and skills needed, and in most cases, stated what working conditions were like. Having these entry-job descriptions available helped students choose their school curriculum. In some instances, it even encouraged potential dropouts to stay in school.

A counselor recommendation became reality when a summer placement center was developed through the cooperative efforts of the Merit Council, Iowa Employment Security Commission and the Des Moines schools. A school counselor who had taken part in the first Institute worked during the second summer with State Employment counselors in the student placement center.

Prior to the close of school, counselors took applications of students interested in federal programs, summer jobs, and permanent employment after graduation. They also arranged job interviews and issued work permits.

Leaders in business and industry came to school to interview potential employees. It was no surprise that the students were more relaxed in their own environment and thus made better impressions than they would have otherwise. Many non-college bound seniors were placed in permanent jobs.

Second Institute. When counselors in the second Institute were asked what business and industry could do to help, the most frequent comments were these:

"Come see us at our schools—keep in touch"

"Furnish resource people to come and explain work opportunities in individual companies"

"Give us more job information, especially descriptions of entry-level jobs—hiring policies, openings, qualifications, flow charts"

"Help us arrange plant tours for students"

"Involve more small businesses in the Institute program"

"Provide us with visual aids telling about their companies"

"Support National Alliance of Businessmen"

"Educate second-level and lower supervisory personnel to work more effectively with disadvantaged workers"

"Re-evaluate the appropriateness of tests used for entry jobs"

Better understanding of each other's problems and increased rapport with the educational world were benefits frequently mentioned by participants from business and industry. One business representative mentioned the "direct involvement of business," adding that in some cases, it might be the company's first contact with the schools. Another said that as a result of the Institutes, he found more young people who knew what to expect from business and who were better prepared to work.

Next Year, Teams. Since the majority of counselors in Des Moines have now attended one Institute, plans next year are to invite teams— a principal, teacher and counselor from each participating school. They will come from schools heavily populated with disadvantaged students.

To be effective in working with youth, one must recognize and develop positive attitudes toward the employment world. One must acquire an understanding of socioeconomic classes and the vocational expectations and problems of different racial, religious and minority groups. Thus, Institute participants plan to increase their effectiveness as counselors in relationship to disadvantaged youth by spending more time discussing jobs and opportunities with them; listening to them; becoming more sensitive to their needs; trying to make schedules truly flexible to fit their needs; and making work more meaningful to them through the use of visual aids such as films, tapes, slides, and other materials.

The Vocational Guidance Institute has opened many doors toward greater vocational understanding for counselors. Now the task is to follow Ralph Waldo Emerson's advice to "Put your creed into your deed." ∎

THE CENTOUR METHODOLOGY APPLIED TO VOCATIONAL STUDENT COUNSELING AND ADMISSION

by David J. Pucel

The Problem

Can vocational counseling instruments be developed which are valid for guidance and admission purposes? If they can, can the data obtained through them be simplified so that the information yielded is readily usable by typical counseling and admissions personnel? These questions have been asked since Parsons began the vocational guidance movement in 1909. Many persons have assumed that such data gathering instruments can be developed in the same fashion that Strong developed the *Strong Interest Inventory*. Instruments would be administered to persons who were successful at different occupations and persons successful at different occupations would have different patterns of scores on the instruments.

Assuming such differences can be found, how can knowledge of these differences be summarized for vocational counseling purposes? Usually, no one instrument is capable of detecting large enough differences between successful persons in different occupations to enable it to stand alone as an effective counseling aid. People are complex and the personal factors which contribute to success in different occupations are varied. Therefore, data has to be gathered on many variables, and these data must be synthesized into some easily interpretable form. Profiles have been the principle method of summarizing data on many variables, but it is difficult to know how to interpret variations in profiles as the number of the variables in the profiles increases. The following example illustrates some of the interpretation problems. Data has been gathered on seven aptitudes and nine interest factors on persons successful in one of two different occupations. On the basis of this information, a profile is developed for each occupation. Students asking for vocational counseling in relation to these two occupations are tested and profiles are plotted for each student. The task is to compare and interpret each student's profile in terms of each of the occupational profiles. The process to this point is relatively mechanical and simple, but the process of interpretation is extremely difficult. Persons can be classified into four categories; those who would be successful in occupation one, those who would be successful in occupation two, those who would be successful in both occupation one and occupation two, and those who would not be successful in either occupation one or occupation two. How can cut-off points be established in order to operationalize the above four categories when sixteen different scores must be considered? One could eliminate some of the variates even though all might be important. Or, one could arbitrarily establish a rule that if a person got a score more extreme than 80 per cent of a successful group on more than five variates, he would be classified as unsuccessful in that occupation.

Such decisions are typical of decisions that are made in an effort to simplify data so they can be managed and interpreted. In many cases, much of the ability of the variables to explain differences between successful persons in different occupations is lost in the process of simplification.

(Rulon, et al, 1967) in their book *Multivariate Statistics for Personnel Classification*, have elaborated on a method of reporting one score that summarizes the similarity of a person's score pattern to the score patterns of successful persons in different occupations using any number of *normally* distributed variables. It is called the "Centour Method". The *logic* of the Centour Method and an example of its application are summarized briefly below; no attempt is made to elaborate upon the statistical calculations.

The method is based on the assumption that persons who have the highest probability of success in a given occupation are those who are most similar to the average successful person in that occupation. Therefore, one will predict which persons will be successful in a given occupation correctly most often if one predicts on the basis of the "average" or most "typical" person who is actually successful in that occupation. Such an assumption implies that if an individual possesses more of a given trait than a group of persons successful in the occupation he will be just as unlikely to be successful in the occupation as an individual who has too little of that trait. It is important to define the success criterion because the validity of the above assumption appears to change dependent upon the criterion of success.

Criteria Consistent With the Method

The Centour Method *would not* be consistent with defining success in terms of course grades. In most cases, course grades are directly proportional to increased ability. Therefore, the more ability the higher the course grades. With this success criterion, one would probably establish minimum cut-off points and not be greatly concerned with how high the scores are above these points. Although such a criterion has been used frequently in the past, its relevance to judging vocational training success is questionable.

The Centour methodology appears to be most consistent with the criteria that success in an occupation should be judged by how satisfied and satisfactory a person is in the occupation. In other words, how happy is the person in the occupation and how happy is his employer with him? Using these criteria, it is logical that one might have *too much* ability or a strong need for security to be happy in a given occupation which requires less ability and provides little security even though he could perform the job tasks very well. Such criteria are becoming increasingly accepted, for it is not enough to say that a person received a high grade in the training program. The ultimate question is: What type of employment did he obtain, and is he satisfied and satisfactory?

If one assumes that the appropriate criteria to evaluate whether a person is successful in a given occupation are whether or not he is satisfied and satisfactory, and that satisfaction and satisfactoriness can be adversely affected by too much of a given trait as well as too little of the trait, then the Centour methodology appears appropriate for vocational counseling.

Gathering the Necessary Data

The problem of identifying appropriate variables to measure is the same when using Centours as profiles. However, when using Centour methodology one need not be greatly concerned with the number of variables being measured. The only limitation on the number of variates used is the number of relatively independent variables that can be identified which relate to the criterion. In the case of vocational counseling, one would have to determine those variables which could be assumed to relate to whether or not a person would be satisfied and satisfactory in the specific occupations to be studied.

The methodology will not be seriously affected if non-independent variables are included or if variables which do not separate groups are included. The Centour score reflects those variables which actually differentiate the groups which are being investigated. For instance, if carpenters and electricians had the same score distributions on numerical aptitude, numerical aptitude would not differentiate carpenters from electricians. The inclusion of such a variate, using the Centour methodology, would have no affect on the Centour score, but would represent a waste of resources to gather the data. The same reasoning applies to non-independent measures.

Groups of successful workers have to be defined in each of the occupations studied. These groups would consist of persons who are defined as satisfied and satisfactory in their respective occupations. Relevant measures would be taken on each person in each of the defined groups and score matrices would be constructed with the aid of a computer for each occupation. Although each matrix will have as many dimensions as variables, the example below will be in terms of two variables and, therefore, two dimensions for ease of discussion.

Think of an individual as being represented by a small building block. His block is placed at the point which represents his combination of scores. (See Figure I).

FIGURE I

Individual Carpentry Student
Scores in Two Dimensional Test Space

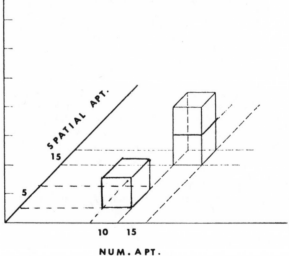

As an example, successful carpenters and electricians are measured with two instruments, a measure of numerical aptitude and a measure of spatial aptitude. John, Joe and Jim are three successful carpenters. John has a score of 15 on numerical and 15 on spatial. Joe has a score of 10 on numerical and 5 on spatial. Jim has the same combination of scores as John. Their scores are represented on Figure I. When two or more people have the same combination of scores, their blocks are piled on top of each other. The result is a three dimensional histogram. When all of the score combinations of the carpenter group are represented, the figure begins to look like Figure II.

FIGURE II

Example Bivariate Histogram of
Scores on a Population of Carpenters

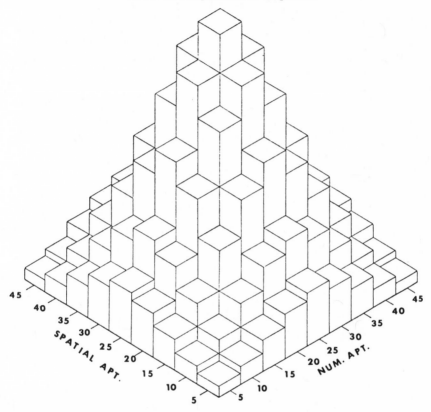

The "average" or "typical" successful carpenter has a score combination near the center of the total distribution as indicated by the height of the columns. The further a person's combination of scores is from the center of the distribution, the smaller the number of successful carpenters who have that combination of scores. Therefore, persons who have combinations of scores more similar to the majority of successful carpenters will have higher probabilities of being successful carpenters than persons who have combinations of scores farther away from the center or majority of the group.

An examination of the numerical aptitude axis of Figure II shows that as numerical aptitude increases to a point (score of 25), more and more successful carpenters have those scores; but as numerical aptitude continues to increase, the number of successful carpenters with such levels of numerical aptitude decrease. The same is true of the spatial axis. One can also see that many different combinations of numerical and spatial aptitude can represent persons equally distant from the center of the successful group.

If Figure II is smoothed out so both the numerical and spatial dimensions are normally distributed, we have a figure similar to Figure III. If Figure III were sliced parallel to its base at frequency A, the score combinations which correspond to the dotted line would all be equally distant from the center of the distribution. The dotted lines can be viewed in much the same way elevations are represented on geographical contour maps. All of the points on a given contour line are at the same elevation. All of the points or score combinations represented on the dotted line in Figure III have an equal frequency and are, therefore, on a given contour relative to the center of the distribution. People with any score combination represented by the dotted line would have the same probability of being a member of the successful group. A score at the apex of the distribution would have a Centour score of 100 because such a combination of scores would represent the "average" or "typical" successful carpenter. The farther a combination of scores is in any direction from the center of the distribution, the lower the score. A person with a combination of scores which no one in the successful carpenter group had would have a score combination which would have a Centour score of zero when scored against the carpentry matrix.

FIGURE III

Centours Represented on a Normalized
Bivariate Distribution of Carpentry Scores

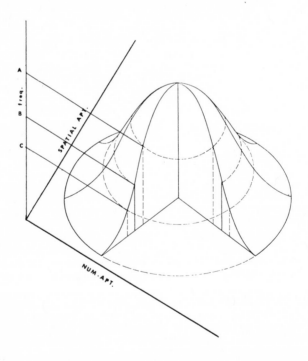

Although the above explanation was in terms of two variables (numerical and spatial aptitudes), the logic can be generalized to any number of variates. However, it becomes almost impossible to diagram more than two variates.

An Application of the Centour Method

The following example drawn from Project MINI-SCORE data will attempt to show the effectiveness and efficiency of using the Centour Method. Project MINI-SCORE (Minnesota Student Characteristics and Occupationally Related Education), funded by the U.S.O.E., is attempting to investigate and develop aids which can be used in vocational counseling and admission.

The population used in the following example was persons who applied to six different Minnesota post-high school vocational curriculums during the period from September 1, 1966, through December 31, 1967, and were accepted to the curriculums and who eventually graduated from them. The six curriculum areas were power and home electricity, carpentry, automotive, mechanical drafting and design, machine shop, and welding. Data were gathered on each individual at the time of application using the seven General Aptitude Test Battery written aptitudes and the nine Minnesota Vocational Interest Inventory homogeneous scales. The criterion used to define the successful group in each occupation was whether or not persons graduated from the program. (On-the-job success criteria data are now being gathered to determine how satisfied and satisfactory these individuals are, but these data were not available at the time of this study.)

With the aid of the computer, the matrix of score combinations was developed and stored for each curriculum. Persons successful in each occupation were then scored against their own matrix as well as each of the other five matrices.

The computer output for each individual consisted of his sixteen raw scores as well as his Centour score relative to each occupation (See Table I). The asterisk indicates the curriculum group of which the individual was a member.

TABLE I

Sample Computer Output for an Individual

NAME Doe, John   DATE 9/30/67

Raw Scores	GATB								MVII								
	G	V	N	S	P	Q	K		H-1	H-2	H-3	H-4	H-5	H-6	H-7	H-8	H-9
	107	95	105	120	113	107	97		16	3	3	7	4	11	2	4	10

CURRICULUM	CENTOUR SCORE
Power and Home Electricity	1
*Carpentry	92
Automotives	41
Mechanical Drafting and Design	34
Machine Shop	31
Welding	40

The data presented in Table I is in a form usable by vocational counselors and persons in charge of admissions to vocational programs. The raw scores are available to interpret scores using traditional methods. The Centour scores can be used by counselors to give persons an indication of how similar their score patterns are to successful persons in different occupations. Admissions officers can establish Centour cut-off scores for different training programs based on persons successful in different occupations.

John Doe took the tests prior to entering the vocational school, enrolled in the carpentry program and was later successfully graduated. When he was scored against successful persons in each of six occupations, he achieved the Centour scores in Table I. The table indicates that John actually got a higher Centour score in carpentry than in any of the other five areas.

If successful persons in each of the six occupations were *not* different on some of the 16 variables being measured, one would expect that one-sixth of the carpenters would fall into each of the six occupations. In other words, only one-sixth of the people in each of the six areas would have their highest Centour score in the area from which they graduated.

Table II shows, however, that successful persons in each of the occupational areas are differentiated. Using the highest Centour obtained as the basis for classification, Table II indicates that the percentage of correct classifications range from 73% for power and home electricity to 37% for machine shop, with most areas around 60%.

TABLE II

Percentage of Graduates Classified
Correctly Using the Highest
Centour Score

	Total No. of Grads.	Actual Per Cent	Expected Per Cent
Power and Home Electricity	71	73%	16.7%
Carpentry	69	55%	16.7%
Automotives	171	58%	16.7%
Mechanical Drafting & Design	91	65%	16.7%
Machine Shop	71	37%	16.7%
Welding	91	61%	16.7%

Table III shows how drop-outs from the six areas would have been classified using Centours based on the matrices developed on successful graduates. More than half of the drop-outs received a higher Centour score in an area *other than the one* in which they were enrolled and eventually dropped out of. In other words, not only would most of the vocational graduates have been counseled toward the program they graduated from, but most of the drop-outs would have been counseled away from the programs they dropped out of.

TABLE III

Percentage of Drops Who
Would Have Been Classified
Differently Based on the
Highest Centour Score

	Total No. of Drops	
Power and Home Electricity	45	60%
Carpentry	31	94%
Automotives	136	60%
Mechanical Drafting and Design	68	51%
Machine Shop	61	66%
Welding	43	66%

Such high percentages of correct classifications are very unusual when attempting to classify in terms of six occupations. One must be cautioned, however, that in the above example no attempt has been made at cross-validation. Eventually, the findings presented here will be cross-validated on new samples.

The main advantages of using the Centour Method are obvious. Any number of normally distributed variables can be used as long as they are related to the criterion. The data from these variables can be synthesized by a computer to provide one score which reflects the similarity of an individual on the variables measured with members of a designated group or groups. The methodology, therefore, overcomes most of the problems of trying to interpret ambiguous profiles while providing an easily interpretable score.

Although the statistical calculations surrounding the generation of Centour scores are complex, they are easily overcome with the aid of a computer. Data could be supplied to one central source by many schools so scoring could be done on a mass basis. As the tests were scored and returned to the schools, the data could be stored at the central source so the matrices could be periodically up-dated to always provide current criterion groups. Such a system using Centours would greatly increase the efficiency of present vocational counseling procedures and help make such counseling more objective and reliable.

REFERENCES

Rulon, P.J., et al, *Multivariate Statistics for Personnel Classification*. New York: John Wiley & Sons, Inc., 1967.

THE COUNSELOR'S

MOST LOGICAL HELPER

THEODORE J. COTE

THERE APPEARS TO BE some reluctance on the part of many teachers to accept guidance as anything other than a frilly appendage of the public school, permitted by an affluent society and capable of instant removal with little effect on the going organization. The counselor is frequently viewed as conducting extensive therapy when all the student needs is a couple of aspirins.

The teacher dimly perceives that both he and the counselor are concerned with the student but somehow fails to appreciate the significance of the interrelationship of their respective roles. Moreover, closer understanding tends to be inhibited by a number of petty grievances.

Counselors do not have to teach. They do not have papers to grade or marks to turn in. They do not have to meet a class schedule and are frequently paid on a higher scale.

It is an unfortunate fact that for many teachers, the counselor and his program are in another world. But if this situation is typical among teachers, it is compounded in the case of the vocational teacher. His fancied grievances pick up where the others leave off.

Dim View. To many vocational teachers, the counselor is a Latin teacher who could not cut the mustard and entered guidance with the express purpose of creating more mediocre Latin teachers by influencing mechanically apt students to go to college.

When students appear in their shops with something less than the desired level of intelligence or something more than the desired level of nonconformity, they are likely to lay the blame directly on the doorstep of the counselor. The fact that the law of averages plays a part, and that similar distributions invariably occur in academic classes, tends to be ignored.

Most of the barriers that exist are

based, however, on a lack of understanding not so much of the goals of guidance but of its operation. Few teachers would dispute the point that each student has unique needs largely unmet through the group processes of the instructional program and that if the student is to develop to the maximum of his potential, the school must offer a service where he can express himself and be served as an individual. The guidance program is education's answer to this need and the counselor is its agent.

To deal with the individual needs of students, the counselor must deal with students as individuals and it is on this crucial premise that guidance faces its greatest difficulty. Congress has expressed its strong belief in the guidance program through financial support under provisions of the National Defense Education Act and school boards throughout the country have expressed their confidence by responding with expanded programs.

Overburdened. Despite the resulting dramatic increase in the number of guidance personnel, the average counselor is still responsible for approximately 450 students. If we assume a six-hour day and a 180-day year, this means that he has less than 1,100 hours for counseling—if all his time were available for this service, which it is not. At best, he has approximately a little more than two hours per student per year to assay the student's strong and weak points, to solve all of his problems, and to suggest to him the type of occupation in which he might expect to find the greatest satisfaction and success.

Consider this task against the amount of related mathematics a teacher can teach, or the maximum number of typing skills that can be developed, or to what extent a student can learn a single complex operation of a milling machine—in less than three hours a year.

Recall also the heavy demands made on the counselor's time by affluent and vocal parents who have the influence to bring pressure to bear not only on the counselor but also on the school administrator to assure that their children will be accepted in the best colleges of the country.

Even if the vocational program is offered in an area vocational school where preoccupation with college placement is not a factor, little is gained. The time that might be used for counseling must be expended in the extensive process of student recruitment and selection.

In addition, the counselor is expected to be an expert in psychology, sociology, college placement, remedial techniques, referral methods, and other disciplines too numerous to mention. To what extent is it reasonable to expect that he also be intimately aware of all the ramifications of the 20,000-odd occupations that comprise our current world of work, to say nothing of the almost daily changes in each of these occupations brought about by technological and other developments?

Scapegoat? Is it possible that we may expect too much of the counselors in our schools? Is it possible that we are expecting a perfectly mortal individual, prone to the problems that beset us all and committed to his own set of values (as we all are), to be all things to all people? Is it possible that we are pulling together the accumulated failures of parents, society, the economy, and our own brand of education, and laying them on the doorstep of what appears to be the ideal patsy?

The above questions will probably never be answered to anyone's satisfaction but one point emerges in bold relief and is perfectly clear. Counselors at the present time in our public schools need assistance—all the assistance that we teachers are able to muster.

The petty animosities referred to earlier in this paper must be recognized as such and treated accordingly. The nature of the relationship between guidance and education, and more specifically, between the counselor and the teacher, must be studied dispassionately in terms of the common goal—the continued progress of the student toward a life rewarding to himself and meaningful to society.

Such studies as have been conducted within this area have produced a second point: teachers must work more closely with guidance personnel.

Fallacy. At this juncture the vocational teacher tends to seek an "out" in the fact that guidance is largely an academic process and hence his involvement must of necessity be minor, if in fact he should be involved at all. Such a viewpoint reveals a complete lack of appreciation of the situation. In actual fact, the role which can and should be played by the vocational teacher in the guidance program is a major one; greater perhaps than that of any other person in the school with the possible exception of the counselor.

Willey and Dunn state in their *Role of the Teacher in the Guidance Program* that the teacher who is with the pupil most of the school day "must effectively serve as the pivot of the group to assist him." And what teacher does a student spend more time with than the vocational teacher?

Academic teachers meet their students in large classes and have little contact with the individual. Unless Joe distinguishes himself as an outstanding exponent of either English or mischief, he is likely to be doomed to an existence as "the blond kid in the second row" with about as much personality as (and much less attention than) the philodendron plant that sits on the corner of the teacher's desk. This is not an indictment of academic teachers as parties indifferent to the individual nature of their charges; it describes an unfortunate situation which limits their value as aides to the counselor.

Such, however, is not the case with the vocational teacher. The very nature of his instructional duties brings him face to face with the individual student throughout the period that he is in the shop. Nor are the contacts fleeting ones. In a class of 15 students meeting three hours a day during a school year, the teacher can be with a typical student an average of 40 hours—with more time available if he needs it. Contrast this with less than three.

Mutual Affinity. The vocational teacher has a close affinity for the student and the student for him— more so than in the case of the average teacher or counselor. Since employment is the objective of the program, the performance of the student on his first and subsequent jobs is a direct reflection of the vocational teacher who taught him his occupational skills. As a result most vocational teachers get to know their students as people as well as pupils and spend much time in reaching them in ways that other teachers, and even the counselor, can only dream about.

In working with his students, the vocational teacher has the added advantage of continuity, since he usually sees his students daily. His ability to sample the behavior of the student is without equal; he sees him at his highest and lowest and at all points between.

Rapport, the quality so important to successful counseling wherein each party accepts the other, can be taken for granted in the vocational instruction setting. What vocational teacher has not sat through the painful account of family problems by a student from the other side of the tracks or offered a note of encouragement to a student struggling with the mysteries of his first love?

And what vocational teacher fails to recognize that satisfactory resolution of these problems is as important to the full development of the student as his learning of occupational skills and, in fact, is prerequisite to his optimum learning?

If the vocational teacher is in such a promising setting for counseling and frequently finds himself in "counseling" situations, does it not follow that a tremendous potential exists for him to be of immeasurable assistance to the counselor and the student in this crucial aspect of the guidance program? The answer, of course, is obvious.

But before the full potential of this hidden resource can be realized, teachers must do three things:

• learn more about the counseling process

• involve themselves in the guidance program

• overcome any negative bias towards guidance.

One of the greatest blocks to a vocational teacher's learning more about counseling is a rather widespread feeling that this skill is sacrosanct and the private reserve of the professional guidance counselor. In reality this is true only in a relative sense. While some students have serious problems that can be coped with only from a broad psychological background, many student problems are vocationally oriented or at least such as can be dealt with by any well-informed educator with the time to listen and the inclination to work with the student.

Information Sources. Most vocational teachers could be said to have both the time and inclination and have only to become well-informed. For a beginning, vocational teachers are likely to already have a course in Individual Development, which is a basic requirement in most states. Teachers who would assist in counseling should supplement this with an understanding of the processes of guidance which can be gained through survey courses available in most universities.

In the writer's institution, as in many others, such a course designed specifically for vocational teachers is available as an elective in the teacher certification program. In addition to acquainting the teacher with the mysteries of the field, the course identifies the types of counseling problems from which the teacher should "back off" and refer the student to the counselor for more professional attention. Such courses also suggest areas of further study.

At this point the teacher should not overlook the value of consulting with his vocational teacher-educator who is frequently able to work these courses into the teacher's ongoing certification or upgrading program.

As a last resort, several excellent texts are available to acquaint the vocational teacher with ways in which he can be of assistance to the guidance program and help youth to maximize their school experiences. The book mentioned earlier by Willey and Dunn is a good example, as is *The Role of the Teacher in Guidance* by Johnston and others.

Ways To Help. As vocational teachers are very much aware, most counselors are understandably weak in their knowledge of occupational information as it relates to nonprofessional pursuits, and at least half of their charges (and perhaps more) are in need of precisely this type of information. The brief and frequently out-of-date occupational monograph and the once-a-year Career Day are inadequate to meet the voracious needs of the inquiring adolescent mind.

The required information, localized and up to date, exists in boundless quantity within the school's vocational education program and could be made available if teachers would simply visit the counselor and volunteer to meet with any students he might refer to them. Or they could offer the services of their students who are members of vocational youth organizations, for this purpose.

Submitting flattering statistics to the school administrator makes the counselor look good, and other than college placement figures, he usually has little to show. The vocational teacher can go far in creating a good relationship by making available to the counselor the graduate follow-up data he routinely collects for his state reports.

Other ways of cooperating will readily suggest themselves to the imaginative teacher who is willing to help. It might be added parenthetically that to provide these services is an excellent way to acquaint the counselor with the characteristics required of potential students in the occupations taught in the vocational program

Simplest Hurdle. It has been noted earlier that the last thing that vocational teachers must do to release the full potential of vocational education's resources for guidance is to overcome any negative bias they might have toward that field. It may be argued that this should have been listed first, as a prerequisite to other tasks. Actually, it has been placed last because it is the simplest task. Simple, that is, if the others have been accomplished.

It is the strong conviction of the writer that no vocational teacher who studies guidance to any significant degree and who conscientiously devotes a part of his energies to assisting the counselor can long maintain a negative bias toward that program, the success of which means so much to every student.

Hundreds of thousands of dollars in federal and state funds have been expended over the past few years in workshops, conferences, and seminars to acquaint guidance people with vocational education in order to establish better relationships.

It is interesting to conjecture how much more effective would be the results, at no expense, if twenty thousand vocational teachers were to ask the counselors in their schools: "Can I be of any help?"

Career Guidance:

Program Content &

Staff Responsibilities

NORMAN C. GYSBERS & EARL J. MOORE

GUIDANCE has traditionally been regarded as a collection of related services provided to a person before he enters training, selects an occupation, or begins to work. Guidance programs operating on this principle rely heavily on individual interviews, testing, and occupational information.

The focus tends to be on diagnosis and prescription at a point in time.

To meet current and future challenges, however, the traditional focus on a single educational/occupational choice at a given point in time must give way to a more comprehensive view of the student and his career development. Developmental guidance programs and activities must be derived from the needs and goals of the people and institution to be served rather than from a tradition-based collection of related services.

This means that the roles of school counselors, teachers and others, as well as the nature and content of guidance programs, will be determined partly by the population and conditions in the communities the programs serve.

It means that those who plan and implement the programs must be able to assess individual and institutional needs, determine goals, state performance objectives, decide on appropriate activities, and devise appropriate evaluation procedures.

Good for Counselors. The needs-assessment, goal-setting approach to the development and implementation of guidance programs is particularly salubrious for school counselors who have tended to become process-oriented and reactive in the traditional pattern of services. The new approach will require them to expand their base of operation, choice of activities and techniques,

109

TABLE I: CAREER GUIDANCE RESPONSIBILITY ASSIGNMENT: SOME EXAMPLES

	Counselors	Teachers
Indirect Functions	Career guidance curriculum planning Teacher and parent consultation Inservice training programs	Career curriculum for basic education Parent-teacher conferences Development of instructional materials
Shared Functions	Joint vocational education instructor-counselor-student planning/contracting Joint employer-vocational education instructor-counselor planning Testing and evaluation	Joint teacher-counselor-student planning/contracting Team teaching of career concepts/units Joint teacher-parent-student planning/contracting
Direct Functions	Individual counseling Group instruction/orientation Group counseling	Individualized instruction Classroom and group instruction Student organization and club advisement

110

and sense of mission. It will get them actively involved in the educational mainstream at all levels.

The first step in establishing a career guidance program along those lines is to assess individual and institutional needs. It can be accomplished in several ways; by using the current program as a base, by going to authoritative sources outside, or by getting the opinion of persons in the school and community to be served. Generally, need statements are derived from a combination of these three procedures.

The next step is to use the collected need statements to establish the goals to be accomplished. At this point goal priorities are determined; those that can be attained with reasonable expectation are rank ordered.

The third step is to make the goals operational by stating program and student performance objectives. These objectives are written to indicate the type of outcome to be expected so that evaluation can be made. Finally, activities to accomplish the performance objectives are carefully matched with those objectives.

Content Derivation. One of the bodies of knowledge from which the content of career guidance programs is being derived is career development theory, research and commentary. Statements of student needs, goals, objectives, activities and outcomes are being drawn from this literature, and along with input from other sources, are being brought together in comprehensive career education programs—kindergarten through adult.

The possible outcomes of career guidance programs are also receiving careful attention. A question being asked is: What would persons who experience such programs be like?

In an article in the 1971 AVA Yearbook, the authors offered the concept of the "career conscious individual" as a possible answer.

We suggested that all students at all educational levels are capable of career consciousness and that it develops throughout the life span as a result of a continual process of internalization of knowledge and skill in four domains: (1) self knowledge, (2) work and leisure knowledge, (3) career planning knowledge and skill, and (4) career preparation knowledge and skill.

We are suggesting here that career guidance content can be developed directly from the knowledge and skill derived from the first three domains and indirectly from the last one. The last, and the largest in terms of content, forms the basis for basic and vocational education programs.

Fixing Responsibility. Once program goals, objectives and activities have been delineated, the next step is to assign responsibilities to the school staff and to parents and others as appropriate.

To assure program quality, consistency and sequence, we strongly urge that one department or person be assigned responsibility for coordination of the school's career guidance program. We would recommend that the guidance department assume this responsibility along with its other functions.

The assignment of specific functions to members of the school staff and others should be done by team-

TABLE II: DIRECT CAREER GUIDANCE PROGRAM CONTACTS: SCHOOL COUNSELORS

	Student Objectives	Student Outcomes	Direct Counselor Functions
Elementary School	To develop an awareness of their own characteristics.	Given a picture of himself, a child will be able to describe aloud his appearance using accurate descriptions.	Counselor conducts weekly group activities using puppets, stories, pictures, audio recordings, self-drawings and snap shots.
Junior High School	To understand their capabilities in educational areas.	Given a list of school subject areas, the student will rank the areas according to his relative strengths.	Counselor holds individual sessions with assigned students to consider past achievements and current abilities.
Senior High School	To develop an awareness of personal characteristics and behaviors that are viewed as desirable for employment.	Placed in simulated job situations, students will be rated as employable.	Counselor holds group counseling and role playing sessions regarding elements of employability.

TABLE III: SHARED CAREER GUIDANCE PROGRAM CONTACTS: SCHOOL COUNSELORS

	Student Objectives	Student Outcomes	Shared Counselor Functions
Elementary School	To recognize that varied personal satisfactions are derived from working.	Given a work role, students will be able to describe one personal satisfying aspect of it.	Counselors, teachers and students plan a structured interview for use with parents and other work role models.
Junior High School	To recognize the interdependency of workers in the work setting.	Given a potential business enterprise, students will list ways workers depend upon one another.	Vocational education instructor, principal, counselor and students plan junior achievement projects to be implemented in the community.
Senior High School	To formulate tentative career plans consistent with knowledge of self.	Individual will select and be placed in a work-study setting consistent with measured ability and achievements, expressed and measured interests and values, and physical capabilities.	Vocational education instructor, counselor and student discuss and arrange for placement; later, they discuss adjustment aspects of work.

TABLE IV: INDIRECT CAREER GUIDANCE PROGRAM CONTACTS: SCHOOL COUNSELORS

	Student Objectives	Student Outcomes	Indirect Counselor Functions
Elementary School	To differentiate job responsibilities in occupational clusters.	Given specific jobs in an occupational cluster, students will be able to name a unique aspect and a similar aspect of the workers' responsibilities.	Counselor will consult the teacher regarding media and arrange for a field trip for students to observe occupational cluster models.
Junior High School	To understand the importance of effective communication skills in career settings.	Students will describe in a written essay the daily work situations wherein precise and accurate communication is necessary.	Counselor conducts an inservice program for teachers (e.g. English) on relating subject matter to relevant work world situations; also consults with them individually.
Senior High School	To possess the ability to identify alternatives in career planning.	Students will rank alternative careers for which personal characteristics and training requirements are sufficiently similar to the preferred career to serve as alternative plans.	Counselor constructs system and develops programs for an interactive computer-based self-directed guidance system.

work and should focus on the types of contacts they may have with students: direct contacts, contacts shared with others, or indirect contacts. Table I presents several examples to illustrate this assignment procedure.

We suggested above that the guidance staff be given responsibility for overall coordination. Tables II, III, and IV illustrate aspects of their role in more detail. All have the same structure, but each treats a single type of counselor-student contact: Table II, direct; Table III, shared; and Table IV, indirect.

Team Work Needed Now. To take advantage of the current emphasis on career development as a way to restructure education in general and guidance in particular, we need to begin now.

Counselors, teachers, vocational educators, administrators, and lay personnel from the community, together, should examine their guidance practices and responsibilities from a career development perspective. That is the first step. ∎

A REGULAR PLACE FOR GUIDANCE

Gordon F. Law

No DISCUSSION of the vocational education curriculum could be complete without giving consideration to vocational guidance. Certainly, the function of guidance in public schools, vocational and otherwise, has an important influence on the overall program. And when the vocational aspects of the typical guidance operation are examined, it seems fair to ask why there is so little actual counseling that has to do with occupations, and why such a small proportion of the student body is involved.

When critics of vocational education complain that it has not penetrated the main ranks of the school population, the associated failure of guidance to provide appropriate occupational orientation is often overlooked. To what extent can the relatively low numbers of students engaged in vocational education programs be attributed to a guidance system which consistently gives major attention to the exigencies of college placement? This in spite of the fact that only 20 percent of the school population can expect to receive a baccalaureate degree, and notwithstanding a situation where youth unemployment is three to six times that of the adult average.

Segregated Counseling. Along with documented evidence that any systematic program of vocational guidance does not exist in many schools are the general low status, structural flaws and other limitations of those in operation. The most damaging weakness in vocational guidance, as it is handled in many schools that I have observed, comes from the guidance worker's penchant for classification and grouping of students. A consequence of the tracking syndrome is that vocational guidance is prescribed for a limited, selected, and segregated portion of the school's population—the people typically designated *non-college, non-academic, slow-learners, low-achievers, vocational,* or by some other appropriate euphemism.

In addition to the fact that vocational counseling is segregated, and reaches only a fraction of the school population where it is available at all, is the problem associated with

116

the budgeting of counselor time. All too often the student-counselor load is between 400 and 500 students.

The guidance counselor sits in his office and meets with these people one at a time. A grim joke about this situation is that counselors get to know three groups of students: outstanding leaders, athletes, and recipients of academic honors who bring glory to the school; persistent trouble makers who are potential sources of embarrassment to school officials; and students who have ambitious and vocal parents.

All the rest of the student body remain merely names and faces, people who are called into the guidance office one or two times a year for a cursory review of "the schedule," "credits needed for graduation," or "future plans."

Three Propositions. Rather than give any more attention to what is wrong with guidance—an indoor sport with many participants—I would like to present some thoughts of a more positive nature. In this regard I have three propositions to make, namely:

1. *Career guidance and orientation is needed by everyone.*

2. *Vocational guidance needs a regular place in the school curriculum.*

3. *There can be no satisfactory program of career guidance without vocational education.*

Let us look at these three concepts one at a time.

First, vocational guidance is needed by all. The obsessive preoccupation with college counseling and the proliferation of testing, classification and grouping of high school students over the last 20 years have produced a stratified structure of education.

Along with the classification of students and their assignment into groups has been an insidious byproduct, the generalization of individual traits, interests and capacities into group stereotypes.

The worst feature of the grouping system in vocational guidance is that it immediately imposes a negative social connotation on all who would be involved. It should be readily apparent that when teachers, students and parents look on any section of the school's operation as having a low level of social acceptance, there is a strong tendency to shun any association with it. In this situation the only students likely to volunteer for vocational guidance—vocational education too for that matter—are the ones who have given up on further education and who don't care too much what others in the school and community think about them.

Delusion. To be blunt, any program of vocational guidance planned exclusively for a limited section of the school population, a group that might be designated "in special need of vocational guidance," is little more than a cheat and a delusion. For any such program badly serves the persons involved, and by its nature excludes a significant number of young people who fear to be labeled in the vocational classification.

What about the population of students who do not elect to take part in a vocational counseling program, or who are not chosen by the guidance department as likely recipients of such exposure? Are there not many here who profess college aspirations only because of the social pressure to do so?

117

Is it not reasonable to assume that all of these people will eventually go to work? Do counselors really believe that college is an end in itself? What happens to those who drift through college with no real concept of occupational goal? What of the two and four-year college dropouts, how well-prepared are they for facing the realities of adult employment?

If vocational counseling were available to all, and all were required to participate in the program, the false dichotomy between various forms of education would soon disappear. But if only students who are classified as vocational as a result of low school achievement are channeled toward vocational counseling, then the stigma associated with this realm of the educational process will persist, and by design or inadvertence, large proportions of students who are in need of guidance about the working world will be excluded.

The program I envision would take in all students, regardless of their ultimate college or career aspirations. There would be no grouping into educational categories, such as general, vocational, or academic. Rather, the assignment of students into group guidance classes would be made on a random basis, thus allowing for group interaction between individuals who otherwise would have little contact with one another.

If the vocational guidance program were longitudinal, a continuing process, as it has often been described in career development theory, there would be ample opportunity for an individualized program. From a common core of group activity, individual students would move toward the development of occupational knowledge, concept of self, and vocational competence in any variety of ways, largely determined by each person's qualities and drives.

Needs Regular Place. This brings us to our second proposition: vocational guidance needs a regular place in the school curriculum. In my estimation, career orientation and guidance have become too important to leave to chance.

The one-shot career day, which has become so popular in some schools, and the week-long unit on occupations, which is typically given as part of junior high social studies, can no longer be accepted. They fail to provide the depth and intensity, the total commitment needed. They are mere palliatives. What is really required is a new emphasis on vocational guidance that is measured by a regular place in the school's curriculum.

Time was when the young person was readily acceptable in the work force, and mere youth, lack of education or specific job skills was no serious disadvantage. The shift from childhood and school to work in the adult world, whether on the farm, factory, office or store, was only too easy and too early. But today, the entry jobs that beginning workers used to find no longer exist, and young people face a formidable array of closing doors.

In addition to the threat of technological unemployment are other barriers to the ready employment of youth—child labor restrictions, quotas imposed by some sections of organized labor, management hiring policies that call for education and maturity standards that often exceed the requirements of the job.

The whole process of preparing for and finding productive employment is rapidly gaining in complexity and sophistication; the number of persons, especially young ones, who are hired off the street is steadily diminishing. All of this means only one thing: all schools must begin to do something they have not bothered to do in the past—take an active part in helping each young person make a satisfactory transition from school to work, from childhood to adult life.

Needs Vocational Education. My third position is based on the contention that vocational guidance without vocational education is at best incomplete and tentative. For guidance in itself, without the opportunity for career-related education, would have little relevance for many students; it would lack purpose, meaning and direction, and be merely an academic exercise.

And when I talk about vocational education, I mean the real thing, not some form of simulation.

The vocational way of instruction is gaining recognition today for its intrinsic values, its unique success in bringing meaning to schoolwork. Recently discovered by economists, sociologists and social psychologists, the vocational approach to teaching, with its heavy emphasis on behavioral goals, individualization of curriculum content, and evaluation of success in straightforward utilitarian terms, has been proposed as the appropriate vehicle for regenerating the secondary curriculum, especially for that great mass of unfortunate students who now flounder in the general program. But as the form and style of vocational instruction are infused into the flaccid body of this general program, there are dangers that its vital juices will be lost in the process.

Certainly the typical general curriculum has been a dismal failure. Its students have been subjected to a collection of uncoordinated courses that too often are weak imitations of academic subjects, taught by persons who would rather give their attention to the academically talented, the self-motivated, and the well-adjusted.

There is no question here that a much greater penetration of vocational education into the public schools will improve those schools. But there is concern about the expedient adoption of vocational method, without meaning. For vocational-type structure without commitment toward vocational goals, will prove to have limited value.

Even as the watered down college prep courses have badly served the educational needs of many students by giving them a poor imitation of someone else's prescription, so also would quasi-vocational offerings, lacking in spirit and substance, prove to be an exercise in futility.

Universal Program. The existence of a substantial and varied vocational education program, not just a token offering in auto mechanics and beauty culture, should serve as a prime resource for a universal vocational guidance program.

First of all, to those students who would logically take part in some aspect of the vocational program, and this group should certainly represent a substantial part of the school population, the vocational courses readily available in the community should be a major source of motivation. Through field trips to vocational education facilities, extended individual visits, and through periods of exploratory participation (for some, on a rotating basis), students would gain first-hand knowl-

119

edge with respect to the conditions and requirements in various occupations.

For those who planned to defer occupational choice until later or who definitely expected to attend college, there should be exploratory cooperative education programs, especially during the summer months. Through supervised employment experience prior to college, the prospective engineer, teacher, pathologist, or attorney could gain valuable insights into his anticipated career.

The vocational cooperative program also has many as yet untapped possibilities for the greatest educational problem of all, the unmotivated and uncommitted students. Using the group guidance class as a home base, a sanctuary where concern for the individual is paramount, the skillful vocational guidance counselor, with the close cooperation of vocational shop teachers, co-op coordinators, and community leaders, could be a key factor in effecting a weaning process whereby potential losers would gain a secure foothold in adult society.

How Realistic? In conclusion, it may be fair to ask just how practical is this three-fold proposition. Is it at all realistic to believe that the schools will ever adopt a universal program of career guidance? Will it find a regular place in the curriculum? Will every region of the country also have a complete and comprehensive program of vocational education available?

When one thinks of the inertia in public education, it does sound like an implausible dream, doesn't it?

But strong new currents are running. The vocational educator, the person who logically should be involved in these important changes, should know that there is a groundswell of sentiment for scrapping the traditional guidance program and for vitalizing the general curriculum.

The American Association of School Administrators' publication, *Imperatives in Education*; the U.S. Chamber of Commerce bulletin, *What is the Responsibility of Business in Modernizing Education;* the *Riot Commission Report of* 1968; the 1967 and 1968 Manpower Reports of the U.S. Department of Labor; Donald Super's *Theory of Career Development*—these and other recent publications relating to career guidance, vocational development, and the "organic curriculum," all point to new directions in career-oriented guidance and education.

The Guidance-

Administration Team

ELEANORE FISHER
JAMES B. VAN HOVEN

IT IS very common in the educational parlance of 1971 to speak of teaming. One reads of team teaching, team planning, teaming by subject area, and so on. The concept, while worthwhile and educationally sound, is hardly new. One makes a determination to organize a staff into teams, and proceeds in an orderly fashion from there.

Not so in our case. We did not know we were going to be a team. We knew as we started to work together that we were thinking alike. We recognized that we had the same philosophical goals for our students. We began to sense that we frequently heard the same drummer. But we did not really know we were a team until the students began arriving in school in September.

It was then, after two summer months of planning and discussing and theorizing and trying to create a new school environment for our 350 middle school students, that we realized if we were going to put some of our ideas into practice, the principal and the guidance counselor were going to have to function as a team.

We agreed on certain fundamentals: The young adolescent is in search of his identity. He is plagued by the fear of subjection by his parents, his peer group, his school. His feelings of self-worth are shaky. His self-image is frequently vastly different from his actual appearance.

He needs help in developing values. He needs exposure to multiple life styles. He needs to recognize the universality of his fears and his feelings. He needs a comfortable place where the significant adults in his life are concerned with promoting his personal growth as well as furthering his academic excellence. We wanted our school to be that kind of place.

We started even before the first day of school. Late in August, we sent a letter and small handbook to each of our students. These included the kind of information they would need to know—class assignments, schedules, etc. The content was not original, but the tone was. There were no negatives, no "don't's." There were invitations to do things together, some pictures (done by students), lots of references to the good year ahead. For the new students entering our school, there were arrangements for student guides to act as "buddies" and a preschool orientation including an informal picnic on the lawn with the principal.

We borrowed from the McLuhan concept that the medium is the message. In this case the environment was the message. Through appeals to local residents and inexpensive purchases on our own, we refurbished the guidance office. We decorated it as a living room. Sofas, soft chairs, a bright orange rug, "groovy" posters, colorful paper flowers, live fish, lamps, mobiles, and books. The message was loud and clear and received immediately. Kids flocked (and flopped) into the office from the first day. Some offered to add favorite posters, some took immediate charge of the aquarium, some even offered to dust.

To Reduce Tension

Traditional school practice dictates that the principal is the "captain of the ship" and that his primary function is to maintain the operation of the institution. In our case, the principal viewed his primary role as providing an atmosphere which recognized that learning takes place through one's feelings, emotions, and affect as well as through one's intellect. We felt that it would benefit the children if together we could offer a supportive atmosphere in which all students in the school felt at home, and were free to use their energy and enthusiasm to pursue their education with as little anxiety as possible.

Within the framework we reexamined our daily schedule, we revised school rules to a few important ones (and then insisted that these be obeyed), we eliminated study halls and detention. We tried to talk to students without an exclamation point in our voices. For example, one teacher dealt effectively with the problem of chronic tardiness when she said, "We have so much to accomplish in our 40 minutes together it would really be helpful if everyone could try to get here on time," rather than, "You are to go to the office for a blue pass before I admit you late into my class!" We moved from class to class without bells ringing.

In all, we tried to reduce the institutional atmosphere. Whenever possible we would eat lunch with the students, greet them by name, be available during break times. Although we frequently had regular appointments with students and staff, we more often had drop-in conferences. The open-door policy meant that a troubled child could seek the open door of the principal or the open door of the guidance counselor and perhaps find satisfaction before he went home that day.

We experimented with an unassigned block of time for 90 minutes in the middle of the day. Students were free to have lunch, join a club (there were 31 manned by the school psychologist, the nurse, teachers, and parents), watch a movie (selected and shown by fellow students), go to the gym or the game room (where the student might challenge the principal or a teacher to a fast game of ping-pong), or the library or a quiet room to study or meet with the student council, or join a rap session in the guidance office or a jam session in the music room, or you name it.

Another departure from the customary was the way in which we handled scheduling.

We both felt we could play a role here, and in doing so those traditional lines between "administration" and "guidance" got blurred again. First, the principal felt that the counselor would be unnecessarily burdened by assuming primary responsibility for student scheduling. This activity was turned over to the teachers themselves, and the principal and counselor contributed their perceptions on individual students after most of the detailed effort was done. This freed the principal to be more of an instructional leader and freed the counselor to devote much more energy to coordinating group counseling activities and to individual conferencing.

Probably the most dramatic example of our rewriting of our job descriptions became apparent in the area of discipline.

How did this process work? Some examples of how problems common to most schools were handled in ours should illustrate the team concept in operation.

Dealing with school discipline is one of the most important and most distasteful parts of the principal's job. In most school settings at least once a day he sits as judge and jury over a child's actions in school. Teachers and parents expect both consistency and fairness. Yet in accepting our premises, we found that you cannot have both; consistency in disciplinary action is impossible if you truly believe in treating each child as an individual. Accepting this idea also implies that the principal cannot act alone, since he is of necessity not as fully aware as the counselor of each child's problems and attitudes.

As we worked together on disciplinary matters, we found that similar problems required widely varying responses. Sometimes a "hard-line" approach would work best, given the student's own and his parents' backgrounds. Most times our assessment of the problem would result in a different approach, involving a lot of talk, with the counselor and the student, perhaps group discussions, and slow progress toward a behavior change. In a few rare instances we knew that nothing we tried would work (usually after we had tried everything). Then our job became one of educating the staff to this fact and finding ways of minimizing the problem.

It is our contention that the guidance program and attitude should permeate the school and that each staff member is involved with the whole process of education. With this in mind we set certain specific goals. We felt it was our duty: (a) to help students identify their true interests, develop decision-making techniques, and develop a capacity to live with and deal with change and diversity; (b) to counsel students, to help them realistically appraise their achievement and potential (through tests, grades, conferences, etc.); (c) to refer students to specialists both in and out of the school system; and (d) to plan to increase a student's sensitivity, creativity, and feelings of self-worth.

Both of us felt we could contribute in

our own ways to providing this kind of guidance to individual students. Much time was spent by the principal in discussing with students their problems and seeking solutions. In some cases he was better able to reach a student than the counselor, and vice versa. In such cases we agreed beforehand on our strategies and shared together in planning further steps.

Privacy and Commitment

The counselor also used the technique of group discussions. Generally this method was employed to introduce a new idea, to clear the air, or to handle a problem. The results of these sessions were shared with the principal, and further actions were decided jointly. Sometimes the sessions resulted in the group's airing a concern with the principal; often he became the "heavy" in saying no to demands or recommendations. This was often accepted as part of an overall continuing program to develop an awareness of social constraints on individual or group behavior.

Group counseling and individual counseling in which confidentiality is an inherent factor presented a challenge to our team approach. Students needed to feel secure that their personal affairs remained private. Particularly in group counseling, a technique we used with much success, the participants rely on a sense of privacy and commitment to the group.

Knowing this, we agreed that the counselor would not share content material. Whenever possible, the counselor shared a sort of progress report on the counselees with the principal and the teachers who had originally identified the students to be in the group.

Whenever possible, the principal also joined the weekly meeting of the pupil personnel team. During those sessions, case conferences were presented about individual children, plans for placement, guidance, testing, etc. In this way, the principal was constantly apprised of the decisions being made about the children.

These modes of operation are both difficult and frustrating to the team as well as to teachers and parents (students are less uncomfortable). There is constant ambiguity, regarding both the principal's and counselor's roles, and regarding appropriate courses of action. In dealing with students' feelings, attitudes, and behavior on an individual basis, one quickly becomes aware that there are no "pat" answers, and that the possibility of error looms large. Sometimes only the conviction that past practices have not worked provides the impetus to proceed. Yet the rewards from success are exhilarating.

A Lot of Hard Work

The principal must swallow hard and let go, or slide, some of that authority that he traditionally possesses in the minds of parents, teachers, and students. Oftentimes the strict authoritarian stance is the worst to take. Almost always decisions about individual students are better made jointly. We must be prepared on occasion to be wrong; at times dead wrong and in public exposure as well!

The whole process requires a lot of plain hard work. Almost constant discussions occur among the team members about individual students and parents. This informal and constant communication is absolutely essential to keep abreast of developments. The stream of students to be seen is endless, and even a walk through the corridors may produce four or five vitally important interchanges with students. The need for voluminous record keeping also becomes quickly apparent. Each contact should be written up (this year most were not) in order to improve decision making and follow through regarding each child.

Ironically, the program was too popular. That is, there were always so many students in the guidance office, there was such constant and frequent interchange, that some few, shy, introverted students were discouraged. We must be more vigilant in seeking out those quiet, retiring students. The school must help and encourage them to seek their own maximum self-fulfillment. We are now discussing procedures whereby we can reach each other.

This mode of operation, particularly in the case of the principal, departs so radically from traditional community and staff expectations that misunderstandings can often arise. In the case of staff, increased communication on courses of action taken and more involvement in these processes themselves are necessary. The concept of inconsistency is not lightly accepted, nor is the increased attention required to focus on the humane as well as academic purpose of the school.

In the case of the community, the task is even more difficult. Schools are thought of as orderly, efficient places where rules and regulations are obeyed. Social reality dictates that schools remain so for the good of all. However, the approaches we have enumerated often can be misinterpreted as overly permissive and as reducing standards. The only way to rectify these misconceptions is through constant discussion with the community about the broad purposes of education and a clear translation of the reasons for particular courses of action consistent with those purposes.

The guidance-administrative team we have described must overcome these difficulties for the simple reason that such a team approach is more humane, more sensitive, more functional than past arrangements— and it seems to work!

What Can a Counselor Do?

BETTY TESH

☐ **"If the faculty only understood my role," sighs the** counselor, gazing wearily into the depths of her coffee cup. "If only they realized what I'm trained to do."

Ah, Dear Counselor, if only they did . . . what then?

I am a counselor in possession of a rare commodity, an understanding faculty, and I find it a most trying experience. How I long to be one of those counselors who must struggle with discipline, attendance, clerical, and scheduling problems dumped at the Guidance Office door like foundlings—a counselor who can cry out into the earless halls, "Doesn't anybody know what I'm here for?"

While such a position is both common and deplorable, it does have its rewards. Who can deny the romantic appeal of being a martyr—a misunderstood martyr at that? But what reward is to be found in starting each day knowing that there are 32 people waiting for you who know exactly what you are expected to know and to do and who expect just that from you?

Let's begin with something simple—the referral, to the counselor, of students who are experiencing difficulties. In many schools this process is crisis- or provocation-oriented. Suppose, for example, that Harvey Ledbetter arrives in class without a book, paper, or pencil for the twenty-third straight day, walks by the aquarium to deposit his chewing gum, and falls asleep during roll call. Some teachers might tap Harvey gently on the shoulder and announce, "Friend, your attitude is intolerable. Please go to the guidance office and get it straightened out."

I would count myself lucky to have a teacher like that on my faculty. With such a one, what more is required of me than a startled look when Harvey appears at my office door? I may then invite him in for a 30-minute interview, spending 17 of those minutes discovering whence he has come. After being assured by Harvey that he "didn't do nothing" and that **Mr. Culpepper "loses his cool all the time," I might elicit an agreement from him that he would try hard not to do whatever it was he was doing. As Harvey disappears into the class-change throng, I could then pat myself on the back and be proud that I had made the best of what came my way.**

My faculty, however, affords me little opportunity to back pat. When an unexpected shadow falls across my threshold, more than likely it's a teacher saying, "Let's talk about Harvey Ledbetter. How are his reading skills? What's his home situation? You're the counselor—give me some facts that will help me help him."

Think what this does to my ego. Rather than being regarded as the psychiatrist-in-residence, I am viewed as the encyclopedia-in-residence—a reference source rather than a source of solutions.

Of course, if my faculty believed counselors to be first-aiders, I might keep a stock of simple cure-all speeches on hand, administer them on demand, and feel quite competent. Instead, our teaching team sees me as a consulting specialist, with a knowledge of students (individually and collectively) and of reliable sources of information.

My faculty considers the *process* of referral as important as the *result* of referral and handles the matter as professionally as a surgeon handles his scalpel. Unlike the teachers at another school I know of who use the phrases "Go to the Guidance Office" and "I want you to see the counselor" as if they were synonymous with "No supper tonight" and "Wait till your father gets home," my faculty has mastered the art of the semantic sell.

"Would you like to talk with the counselor about this?" "Do you think the Guidance Office might be of help?" and "Have you thought about sharing this with the counselor?" These are the referrals they make. They realize that suggestions often succeed when orders fail, and so they have become competent in the art of implanting impulses.

Now consider what their referral artistry does to my popularity rating. Experience bears out that the teacher who commands a student to present himself before the counselor also arms that student with one sure topic for discussion—the teacher who sent him. When a steaming, stewing sophomore slams into my office with an explosive, "Mrs. Miffle sent me to you," and I greet him warmly and acceptingly—even lovingly on my better days—I have a definite advantage in the "Nicest Teacher Over Here" derby. I need do nothing more than nod agreeably and say "Mmmm" to cement the friendship.

But can I win any "Best Teacher" awards in competition with a faculty that uses underhanded methods? The first to identify a referral situation, they are also the first to stimulate friendly feelings by developing a partnership with the student. The teacher and the student begin discussing options, and the teacher tosses me into the conversation like a fish into the bucket, to be weighed and measured and determined to be a "keep" or a "throw back."

Now, my sophomore enters with, "Mrs. Miffle and I were talking and she said you could have some ideas to help me. And I thought, well, so long as you're up here with nobody much to talk to. . . ." Because the idea to talk is his own original idea, a student who comes away from a counseling session with any degree of satisfaction either compliments himself on making a wise move or admires Mrs. Miffle for reminding him of my availability.

Not only does my faculty usurp my birthright of student adoration, but they snatch from me the sweet cup of exoneration. How I would delight in saying, "I might have helped the girl if I had only known" or "I could have told him that school was not accredited if I'd known he was considering it." How can I help but know when our pack of professionals keep a stock of mimeographed forms in their desks which they send me by the thousands. The form announces, "——— needs to see you — immediately — this week — at your convenience (check one) for the following reason: (fill in the blank)." So, I must forfeit the protective cloak of ignorance. Even more cruel is the note that invariably accompanies the form: "Please look for the right opportunity."

Why do they have to be so understanding! If they were only less aware of the role of the counselor, I could have such a neat little book with appointments written in ink a week in advance. As it is, charged with their commission, I must go out of my carpeted office into the hassle of the halls, the lunacy of the lunchroom, the scramble of the stairwell, to seek those "right opportunities." Linwood, who would clam up when surrounded by filing cabinets and book shelves, burbles on as we sit on the auditorium steps during lunch just as his teacher knew he would when she ordered me out of my lair.

There is something close to sinister in the conduct of my faculty following a referral—an animosity that expresses itself in a total lack of interest in satisfying one of my deepest needs, the need to blab. Given the slightest encouragement I might merrily disclose how Sally's mother *did* run away with the gasman and what Price's father told his boss. Yet our faculty holds the confidentiality of the counselor in such high regard that not even a devious, "Is it true?" escapes their lips. They wait for me to report what should be reported. How can I betray a trust when there's no accomplice?

In terms of sheer physical labor, the testing pro-gram is the most strenuous. Handing out the answer sheets and watching the clock and taking up the pencils isn't the exhausting part; it's what happens when the scoring service sends back the results. How peaceful are the lives of those counselors who possess faculties content to have standardized test results recorded and forgotten.

The moment I take a big brown envelope from my mail, I am surrounded by a great hungry herd. Milling about me, they demand to know when I will bring a report on the math scores to the Math Department meeting and if I will prepare an item analysis of the English grammar section for the English Department. They ask if I will speak to a junior class about the meaning of percentile scores and determine how many freshmen who elected shop courses scored at, or below, the twenty-fifth percentile on the mechanical aptitude test.

The math teacher spends his planning period peppering me with questions. "This score says her math grade placement is 7.0. What was it last year? Did she miss questions about fractions? Decimals? Has she progressed at least one grade level each year?"

It might be worth all the time and energy if only those same faculty members who pester me most to know and understand the results of standarized testing would accept without question the numbers that appear on my test reports. They refuse obstinately to accept one standardized test score as a completely accurate picture of any student. Because they see test scores as indications, they continue to look for verifying data or opposing data, and they demand from me more and better means of assessment.

Let's imagine that I am accomplishing all the duties my faculty has set for me. I'm providing an information service, a testing service, a counseling service, and an orientation service. I change my bulletin board weekly, water my snake plant every Friday, and have volunteered to hem the junior varsity cheerleaders' skirts. Wouldn't you think I could face my faculty with, "Say, Group, don't you feel you have a whizbang counselor here?"

No, I keep very quiet for fear of provoking another reminder that a research report should be due any time now. The Business Education Department wants to know the area offices which use shorthand. The principal wants to know if I will determine a way to measure the amount and accuracy of student information regarding curriculum offerings. The librarian wants to know if the students feel the occupational materials are sufficient.

"Add that to your list of things to do, Miss Whiz-Bang Counselor," a teacher will chuckle. "And while you're about it, find someone in town who can tell my class the difference between a computer operator and a computer programmer and what training each one needs. You're supposed to be a resource person on occupations, aren't you?" Then they saunter on down the hall, mulling over an idea to have me sit in on a sociology class to answer questions about early marriage.

What can a counselor do with a faculty like mine? Admire them, that's what. Appreciate them for seeing that no counselor can be any better than the expectation of his faculty.

I appreciate mine. Whatever I am, I owe to my faculty, which stands ever behind me—pushing and shoving. ☐

VOCATIONAL GUIDANCE for ALL

Is Differentiated Staffing the Answer?

E. NIEL CAREY

"T HEY WERE the best of times. They were the worst of times." Dickens said it first in his *Tale of Two Cities*. It might also be said of guidance at the present time. Current demands for guidance services are probably unequaled.

The requests for career information, the number of people who seek career counseling, the number of individuals and organizations who turn to schools and to school counselors for services related to guidance and counseling, and the number of educational and training programs that specify a guidance and counseling component are unprecedented.

Yet the criticisms of school counselors and guidance programs are well known to anyone who reads professional or popular journals. Many studies, conferences, and Congressional hearings have pointed to the lack of appropriate guidance services for vocationally oriented students and to the lack of vocational guidance services for all students (6, 8). The dichotomy in the guidance field has been most obvious in federal education legislation. Title V-A of the National Defense Education Act, one of the important sources of funding for guidance programs for the past ten years, actually recommended reduced appropriations for guidance, counseling and testing. However, under the provisions of the Vocational Education Amendments of 1968, vocational guidance is now listed as one of the primary purposes for the expenditure of vocational education funds.

Traditional Route. Despite the criticisms, the uncertainties of federal appropriations, and the shortage of well-trained and qualified personnel, most state and local educational agencies are shouldering the responsibility of providing appropriate guidance services for all students. Many will try to improve services in traditional ways.

Some will try to decrease the student-counselor ratios, and some will try to add quality to the counselor training programs by requiring more course work for counselor certification. Others may try to have the counselor relieved of tasks such as keeping attendance records, monitoring the administration of tests, or handling routine data collection and survey procedures.

But even if these attempts are successful, there is little research to indicate that the overall quality of guidance programs will be improved. Perhaps what is needed is a new approach to providing guidance services.

New Pattern. One such approach would be to use a differentiated staffing pattern to provide a range of services such as those described by Bottoms and Hoyt (1, 5). This kind of organization would employ the services of individuals with different training, skill levels, and interests.

They might work together in providing the traditional guidance services or they might work in new guidance-curriculum models such as those suggested by Bottoms and Reynolds, Herr, and Law (2, 4, 7).

Four categories of personnel which appear to have the greatest potential for delivering guidance services are (1) paraprofessional, (2) guidance teacher, (3) school counselor, and (4) specialist coordinator. These certainly are not, however, the only categories that could be included in a differentiated staffing pattern.

Paraprofessional. It is conceivable that at least three kinds of paraprofessionals could make significant contributions to the guidance program in most school settings. The first is the secretary-clerk, who already plays an important role in most schools. The duties, training, and responsibilities of this person are too well-known to merit further comment here.

The second is the paid or volunteer aide who could perform a number of vital tasks in the school or community. Such aides would be recruited and trained for only one or two tasks or responsibilities. For example, students or out-of-school youth could be recruited to conduct community surveys or follow-up studies.

The third kind, the technician, would probably have completed a two-year post-secondary program enabling him to make contributions to the information, testing, placement, and follow-up services. He would likely be able also to handle data-processing and computer procedures and operate all kinds of audiovisual equipment.

(See references 3 and 9 for articles which outline the selection, training, and utilization of paraprofessional workers in education and guidance.)

Guidance Teacher. Each year our society seems to become more complex; each individual's options become more numerous and our population more mobile. Under these circumstances, our educational systems will have an increasing responsibility to help individuals understand the range of opportunities open to them and their potential for taking advantage of those opportunities.

At the present time this is done in many different ways, but often ineffectively. Among the many reasons are that teachers are not always adequately trained to do the job and that counselors are often indifferent to this aspect of their job.

Variously labelled career orientation, group guidance, or prevocational orientation, this important process could be accomplished most effectively by having guidance teachers teach the new guidance-curriculum models referred to earlier. This person would have to be a competent teacher with knowledge, understanding, and course background in vocational-technical education and guidance.

Ideally, the guidance teacher would find new and creative ways to combine school and community resources such as computerized information systems, simulation and gaming techniques, multimedia systems, field trips, and work experience.

School Counselor. In a differentiated staffing organization, the school counselor could be a more effective staff member. The routine, time-consuming tasks, which many counselors contend keep them from working with all students, would be left to paraprofessionals.

Counselors would thus have adequate time to work with other staff members to develop more relevant curricular offerings and career development activities; to conduct local research and follow-up studies; and to provide the traditional counseling, information, and placement services.

Specialist/Coordinator. The vocational guidance specialist/coordinator would work at the school or school-system level with other guidance workers, administrators, and teachers. He would work with them in at least two ways.

First, through inservice training he would demonstrate the vocational guidance programs that could appropriately be offered to all students. Second, he would be responsible for coordinating those facets of the guidance program which pertain to vocationally oriented students—such as the job placement program, for example.

The specialist/coordinator would obviously need a background of experience and coursework in the vocational aspects of guidance, in vocational education, and in the interrelationships among human development, education, and the world of work.

It should be noted that several state education departments, including those of California, Florida, New York, Pennsylvania, and New Jersey, are employing vocational guidance supervisors, specialists, and coordinators in a variety of organizational patterns. Several states—Ohio, California and Georgia—have such specialists or coordinators operating in many local districts. At least one of these states, Ohio, has prepared a job description for the vocational guidance coordinator.

Strengths. The differentiated staffing pattern offers several apparent advantages which might be listed as follows:

1. It should result in more guidance services, provided to more people more effectively, than can be expected of a traditional approach.

2. It should result in more efficient utilization of personnel and consequently reduce the per-student

137

cost of services.

3. It would provide a career ladder for guidance which would permit persons with a variety of backgrounds to enter at different points.

4. It should offer better opportunities for guidance personnel, vocational educators and community resource personnel to team up to create more relevant educational and career development programs.

5. It would lend itself to the kind of planning, evaluation, and accountability that is increasingly required in education.

Obviously, there are also certain disadvantages. They revolve around the changes that would be necessary in teacher and counselor education programs and in certification and financing procedures. However, the disadvantages would indeed be worth surmounting if differentiated staffing could produce guidance services suitable for vocationally oriented students and vocational guidance services for all students.

References

1. Bottoms, Gene. "Overview of Student Personnel Services in Georgia's Area Vocational-Technical Schools." Paper presented at the National Conference on Student Personnel Services, Atlanta, Ga., October 1967.
2. Bottoms, Gene and Reynolds, K. "Work Experience Programs for Behavior Modification." *American Vocational Journal,* (May 1969) 44:24-26.
3. Carlson, Jon; Cavins, D. and Dinkmeyer, D. "Guidance for All Through Support Personnel." *The School Counselor,* (May 1969) 16:360-366.
4. Herr, Edwin. "Unifying An Entire System of Education Around A Career Development Theme." Paper presented at the National Conference on Exemplary Programs. Atlanta, Ga., March 1969.
5. Hoyt, Kenneth B. "Guidance: A Constellation of Services." *The Personnel and Guidance Journal,* (April 1962) 40:690-697.
6. Industrial Relations Seminar, *The Transition from School to Work.* Princeton, N.J.: Princeton University, 1968.
7. Law, Gordon F. "A Regular Place for Guidance." *American Vocational Journal,* (March 1969) 44:27-28.
8. Rosen, Howard. "Vocational Guidance —Room for Improvement." *Manpower,* August, 1969.
9. Salim, Mitchell and Vogan, J. "Selection, Training, and Functions of Support Personnel in Guidance." *Counselor Education and Supervision.* (Spring 1968) 7:227-236.

138

VOCATIONAL GUIDANCE EUROPEAN STYLE

Less academic and more closely tied to the public employment services, the European model offers clues to those seeking to strengthen the vocational aspects of guidance in this country

THEODORE J. COTE

SOME TIME AGO a rather remarkable volume appeared in the book stalls in the crowded streets of London. It was entitled *The London Tradesman*, by R. E. Campbell, and described in detail all the trades, arts, and professions then existing in London and Westminster along with the qualifications required to learn and practice them.

It not only provided advice to parents on "how to study and improve the genius of their children before they bind themselves apprentices" but also advised potential learners on how to get along with the master and even how to avoid the temptations of the big city.

The book which was published in 1748 stands as a symbol to the uni-versality in time and place of society's concern for the vocational development of its youth.

Despite the precocity of Squire Campbell, little was done in Europe to develop formal programs of vocational guidance until the turn of the present century, or approximately the same period that marked the growth of the movement in this country. In contrast to the American model, developed largely in the public school, the European counterparts grew quite apart from the field of education, which explains many of the differences currently existing between the programs on the two sides of the Atlantic.

This article will examine some of these differences within the context

139

of the orientation, organization, and operation of the several programs.

People Oriented. The school orientation of the vocational guidance program in the United States has tended to isolate it from the people as a whole, who by and large fail to understand or appreciate its advantages and consequently fail also to provide strong support for program development. This has been true from the outset. It was the educational community that bought Parsons' program, not the general public.

In other words, in America the need for vocational guidance was originally felt and implemented by the professional, whereas in most of the European countries it was started by lay people who grouped together to provide assistance in meeting real problems of the moment.

For example, vocational guidance got its start in Germany in 1900, when feminist groups formed an occupational information service for members of their sex in an effort to broaden the vocational opportunities open to them. In Switzerland, it was employer groups in 1902 who, dissatisfied with apprentice turnover, formed committees to assist youth in making more informed choices of their life's work.

Parental Support. Significantly, parents have been involved in the vocational guidance process from the earliest days, and this condition has persisted to the present time. A review of foreign publications in the field invariably provides reference to the place of the parents in the process, and in France, for example, their role is written into the federal regulations which mandate the national program. As a result, the average European—more readily than

his American cousin—tends to subscribe to, if not demand, vocational guidance services and to provide grassroots support to the program.

Within the educational environment, the vocational guidance program in America has tended to develop as an academic discipline, the exclusive precinct of those who are professionally prepared and certified with impressive collections of credits in psychology, sociology and kindred fields.

In Europe on the other hand, the program is viewed in a much more pragmatic sense. It is generally felt that the practitioner has greater need for knowledge of occupations and training opportunities than for expertise in the dynamics of adolescent behavior. As a result, the average European vocational guidance worker probably has a more extensive understanding of the world of work than his counterpart in this country.

It must not be inferred that the European practitioner requires no special preparation for his work; he usually does, but it emphasizes the informational aspects of occupations rather than the theoretical concepts involved in the process of counseling. Indeed, the guidance worker in Europe is not generally regarded as a counselor. Such terms as "careers teacher," "careers master," or "vocational advisor" are much more common. The distinction goes beyond name only in that vocational guidance is not really viewed as involving counseling at all as we know it.

In describing the program in the Netherlands, a leading authority states that vocational guidance "in the Netherlands consists of an exchange of information [leading to] a reciprocal or two-some conclusion that is called for want of a better word, vocational advice." Another national expert notes that "vocational guidance in Sweden is of a purely informative character, i.e., information is given which refers to the situation of the individual. On the basis of this information, the individual himself makes his decision."

While they may be somewhat differently defined in other countries, the programs tend to be designed around what has been referred to as the classic "trait and factor" approach.

Organizational Patterns. Occupational information, the keystone of any vocational guidance program, tends to be treated in the abstract in the United States; that is, the major aim appears to be to encourage youth to learn the characteristics and requirements of as many occupations as possible as "nice-to-know" information. In Europe, with a lower school-leaving age, data on occupations are treated in a much more concrete way as "must-know" information closely related to the employment picture existing at a specific time in a specific country.

This condition necessarily requires a high degree of reliance on the employment services of the respective ministry of labor or similar national agency. On the other hand, it is becoming increasingly evident in the several countries that the schools have a major role to play in the vocational guidance of youth. Consequently, program organization usually involves widely varying degrees and types of responsibility on the part of both agencies which tend to distribute themselves in interesting patterns.

In Sweden for example, the vocational guidance program is conducted within the public school system for students under school-leaving age, with the services provided by a specially designated teacher. His salary is paid by his local school board for teaching his regular subject, usually civics, and by the National Labor Market Board for time devoted to vocational guidance. This arrangement not only permits guidance to be a school function but also places an obligation on the teacher to keep up-to-date on occupational and employment information. This plan is growing in popularity, with the number of involved teachers showing an increase of 25 percent from 1967 to 1970.

Coordinated Program. The pattern in England is somewhat different. Vocational guidance is available to young people to age 18 under the general direction of the Department of Employment and Productivity. In the schools, however, the program is coordinated by a part-time "careers teacher" who works closely with the appropriate "careers officer" who is a professional guidance worker trained by the DEP. In this case, the teacher is paid entirely by the local educational authority.

The careers officer is also paid by the local school system, with 75 percent of his salary reimbursed by the DEP. Accordingly, the careers officer has all the resources of the employment service behind him and, as an employee of the educational system, has easy access to the school's information on the student and can also conveniently arrange appropriate activities with the careers teacher.

Organizational patterns of vocational guidance programs in other countries vary widely between that of Germany, where the national employment service has a virtual monopoly on all vocational guidance, to that of France, where the major direction since 1922 has come from the Ministry of National Education despite persistent attempts to connect the service more closely with public employment exchanges maintained by the Ministry of Labor.

Paradoxically, while the French program is not aligned with employment exchanges, neither is it closely aligned with the schools. Rather it is organized on a *département* (county). basis through separate vocational guidance centers manned by counselors, social workers, physicians, and psychologists.

The relationship of the employment service to the schools in most other countries varies in degree and usually consists, as it does in this country, of providing occupational information and placement service.

Operational Difference. Generally speaking, the methods used in other countries to perform such vocational guidance functions as personal appraisal, provision of graphic occupational information, and occupational placement do not vary markedly from those employed in our own programs. As such, they do not warrant special mention beyond noting that, on the whole, the significance of aptitude testing is held to be much higher than it is here.

Compared to our own programs, the function within which widest differences in emphasis and performance are observed is that of occupational exploration or prevocational experiences. Interestingly enough, this is the very program area

within which the Vocational Education Act of 1963 and the subsequent 1968 Amendments are attempting to stimulate meaningful activity at the local level as a valuable, if not necessary, prerequisite to vocational education.

Czechoslovakia provides an example of extreme emphasis with its universal stress on the polytechnical aspect of *all* education. Within this context, all teachers perform a vocational guidance function by being required to relate whatever subject matter they are covering to the area of national productivity.

It is not unusual to find toddling young Czechs learning to read from books about workers in the morning and in the afternoon performing minor assembly tasks on actual mechanical components provided by a local branch of a state industry. An intelligent vocational choice is considered as a basic responsibility of the individual to the state. And no opportunity is overlooked—in schools or out—to impress this fact upon youth and to provide suitable experiences to assist him in making it.

More Benign. A similar conviction is held by the Swiss, but is more benignly implemented through the provision of *Berufswahlklassen*, special classes designed to provide opportunities for vocational exploration. The classes are compulsory in public and private schools for students who are not already vocationally committed and involve a series of half-day, on-the-job experiences throughout the year in several local enterprises.

Integration is accomplished through four hours per week of scheduled discussion with vocational advisors. In instances where a suitable choice is not forthcoming, the experience is extended into the summer months for potential school-leavers.

The program in Sweden is referred to as Pryo—prevocational practical orientation—and is compulsory for all eighth-grade students, who must therefore spend two periods of three weeks in different on-the-job work orientations. The teacher-counselor makes the necessary arrangements with employers to accommodate half the class while the other half attends school as usual. The experiences are preceded and followed up by appropriate lectures and discussions.

In 1966, some 90,000 students were placed in 170,000 jobs through this national program. Students who plan to leave school are referred to the vocational guidance office of the employment service for job placement.

In Denmark, basically the same program is offered in grade 7, and is popularly referred to as "Eight Days in Industry." As in the other countries, it is compulsory and is correlated with lectures and opportunities for individual conferences. Because of strong local autonomy, however, the manner in which the program is implemented is at the discretion of the individual school, and the quality varies widely from one community to another.

Offered as Elective. In contrast to other European countries, the prevocational program in the Netherlands is elective rather than compulsory, is offered in the *Lagere Technische School* rather than on the job, and is limited to industrial occupations.

In the first year, the student spends approximately half of his time in class work and the other half in the various shops being introduced to the several crafts and trades in which training is available. From these, with the assistance of his teachers, he chooses an occupation to study in his second year, during which time more specific exploration is provided. He may also change specialties in either the second or third year, before ultimately entering an apprenticeship or a higher vocational school.

Programs of prevocational education are conspicuous by their absence in the school systems of France and Germany, reflecting in both countries the void in school-based programs of vocational guidance. There is hope, however, that the situation may change in Germany, as trade unions and employers are becoming increasingly critical of the quality of guidance provided by the employment service and are now recommending closer cooperation with the public schools.

In France, a recent project involving a highly successful prevocational program for out-of-school youth in Caen has resulted in recommendations for broader programs which may eventually penetrate the hard shell of public education.

Generalizations. There are obvious dangers in generalizing with respect to *the* European vocational guidance program, or even for that matter, *the* vocational guidance program in any given country. If such a generalization were to be made, however, it might be said that the European program differs in its broad aspects from the U.S. program in the following ways.

First, the American counselor is prepared for and is expected to provide assistance to the student with reference to all aspects of his development including social, personal and vocational, while his foreign counterpart is merely concerned with the vocational. As a result, vocational guidance *is* guidance in Europe and available to and welcomed by a large proportion of the population, while in this country it is only a part, and in some cases, a small part of the guidance program.

Second, the client-centered vocational guidance of youth in America tends to be more abstract and academic than in Europe, where the wellspring is the public employment service which works much more closely with the schools than is true in our program. As a result, the connection between guidance and preparation for employment as well as ultimate employment itself is much clearer, and the program tends to be more meaningful to the student and his parents.

Third, despite the fact that such prevocational programs as industrial and the other practical arts have been integral parts of the American curriculum for decades, their potential as means of occupational exploration for guidance purposes has nev-er been fully exploited. Nor, for that matter, have the resources of the employment community in this country ever been fully harnessed for occupational exploration, as they have been routinely for years in European countries where the importance of such activities is emphasized by making them compulsory.

As the result, the European student who drops out of school at the minimum leaving-age is clearly better prepared for the task that faces him than is his American cousin.

Source of Clues. The foregoing is not meant to suggest that our guidance program should be abolished and rebuilt along the lines of the European model, for the latter has far to go to even approach the level of sophistication and general effectiveness that characterize the American one. It does suggest, however, that programs with traditions fully as long as our own, however unidimensional, might well provide fruitful sources of clues for those interested in improving our guidance program with respect to its vocational aspects. ∎

144

Vocational Development

VOCATIONAL MATURITY AND
VOCATIONAL TRAINING

by
David J. Pucel
Howard F. Nelson
Darrell Heitzman
David N. Wheeler

According to early trait-and-factor theory, vocational choice was a point in time event, occurring usually upon leaving high school. More recent research into vocational choice behavior has pointed out the developmental process of occupational choice and underlined the importance of the concept of vocational maturity over time (Carter, 1940; Super, 1942). Ginzberg and others (1951) proposed a vocational choice theory consisting of three major postulates:

1. Vocational choice is a process spanning the adolescent years.
2. The process is largely irreversible.
3. The process ends in a compromise between the individual's needs and the external realities.

Super (1957) has additionally emphasized the longitudinal nature of the choice phenomenon by suggesting the phrase ''vocational choice'' be replaced by that of ''vocational development.''

> The concept of vocational development leads logically to that of vocational maturity . . . . Vocational maturity is used to denote the degree of development, the place reached on the continuum of vocational development from exploration to decline. Vocational maturity may be thought of as vocational age, conceptually similar to mental age in early adolescence . . . (pp. 185-186)

Central to the idea of vocational development is the concept of vocational maturity. Crites (1965, 1969a, 1969b) has devised a standardized measuring instrument to assess an individual's vocational maturity at a point in time. His *Vocational Development Inventory* (VDI) consists of an Attitude Scale and a Competence Test, of which only the Attitude Scale has been fully developed. This 50 item scale, standardized on some 5,000 students from grades 5 through 12, deals with the concepts of: (a) involvement in the choice process, (b) orientation toward work, (c) independence in decision making, (d) preference for vocational choice factors, and (e) conceptions of the choice factors.

Most students who took the Project MINI-SCORE applicant test battery which included the Attitude Scale of the VDI, were 18 years of age. This places them toward the end of the exploratory or tentative stages of vocational choice—development as set forth by most theoreticians (Ginzberg, et al, 1951; Super, 1957; Miller and Form, 1951), with vocational "maturity" or the realistic stage of vocational choice several years away. Therefore, if retested at a later date, an increased level of vocational development should be expected. Further, if vocational education helps to increase an individual's vocational maturity as is often suggested by supporters of vocational education, those who persist in vocational education ought to reach a higher degree of vocational maturity over a given period of time than initially similar persons who do not attend a vocational school.

STATEMENT OF THE PROBLEM

This investigation, a sub-study of Project MINI-SCORE research, was designed to investiage (1) the utility of the *Vocational Development Inventory* (VDI) as a counseling aid to be used with post-high school students, and (2) the effect post-high school vocational training has on the vocational maturity of students as measured by the VDI.

THE UTILITY OF THE VDI AS A COUNSELING AID FOR POST-HIGH SCHOOL VOCATIONAL STUDENTS

Two measures of the utility of an instrument as a vocational counseling aid might be (1) whether or not it provides information in addition to information obtained from other instruments, and (2) whether or not the instrument provides information which can be used by individuals to make occupational choices. The VDI was investigated in regard to both of these criteria.

The Uniqueness of Information Obtained from the VDI

Population and Sample: In order to investigate the question of the uniqueness of data obtained from the VDI, the VDI scores for a sample of individuals were correlated with other scores on the individuals available in the Project MINI-SCORE data bank. The population consisted of 6061 students that made application for entrance into one of the 24 post-high school, Minnesota Area Vocational Technical schools taking part in Project MINI-SCORE during the period between January, 1968, and September, 1968. The intercorrelations were obtained from a sample of 1000 persons drawn randomly from the population. Intercorrelations were computed between the VDI and the following instrument scales: (1) the seven written *General Aptitude Test Battery* (GATB) aptitudes, (2) the nine *Minnesota Vocational Interest In-*

147

ventory (MVII) homogeneous keys, (3) the sixteen scales of the *Sixteen Personality Factors Questionnaire*, (4) the 3 scales of the 30 scale version of the *Minnesota Importance Questionnaire* (MIQ), (5) the *Minnesota Scholastic Aptitude Test* (MSAT) score and (6) 11 personal variables including work history and prior education.

A correlation program (UMST500) was used to correlate the VDI with the 74 other variables. See Table I for a list of these variables and their correlations with the VDI. Those variables which correlated significantly with the VDI at the .01 level are indicated with an asterisk.

Results

The results will be discussed in regard to one instrument at a time. Only those scales of a given instrument that were significantly correlated with the VDI at the .01 level will be discussed.

GATB

All of the seven written GATB aptitudes significantly correlated with the VDI. The highest correlations (.328, .357 and .257) were with those scales closely related to intelligence. It appears that more intelligent persons obtain higher scores on the VDI.

MVII

Six of the nine MVII homogeneous key scales were significantly correlated with the VDI. The results indicate that there are positive relationships between increases on the following scales and vocational maturity: health service, office work and sales-office. There are negative relationships between the VDI and the mechanical scale, electronics scale, and outdoors scale. Apparently the VDI considers a positive attitude as one being oriented toward professional or white collar occupations as contrasted with an attitude oriented toward skilled or blue collar occupations.

16-PF

Four of the 16 scales of the 16-PF were found to have significant positive correlations with the VDI: scale B, Scale H, Scale I and Scale Q3. The results indicate that persons who are more intelligent, venturesome, tender-minded and or controlled obtain higher scores on the VDI.

MIQ

Fourteen of the 30 scales of the 30 scale version of the MIQ were found to be s ̇gnificantly correlated with the VDI. All but the correlation with the "Company Image" scale, the moral value scale and the correlation with the "Company Practices and Policies" scale were negative. The scales which correlated negatively with the VDI were "Authority", "Compensation I", "Creativity", "Independence", "Recognition", "Responsibility", "Social

148

TABLE I

CORRELATIONS BETWEEN THE VDI AND OTHER PROJECT MINI-SCORE TEST BATTERY SCORES

Variable	Correlation	Variable	Correlation
GATB		4. Advancement	−.040
1. G-Intelligence	.328*	5. Authority	−.226*
2. V-Verbal Aptitude	.357*	6. Company Practices &	
3. N-Numerical Aptitude	.257*	Policies	.139*
4. S-Spatial Aptitude	.140*	7. Compensation I	−.090*
5. P-Form Perception	.114*	8. Co-workers	.052
6. Q-Clerical Perception	.148*	9. Creativity	−.107*
7. K-Motor Coordination	.110*	10. Independence	−.273*
		11. Moral Value	.170*
MVII		12. Recognition	−.156*
1. H-1 Mechanical	−.133*	13. Responsibility	−.162*
2. H-2 Health Service	.110*	14. Security	.047
3. H-3 Office Work	.120*	15. Social Service	.052
4. H-4 Electronics	−.095*	16. Social Status	−.251*
5. H-5 Food Service	.062	17. Supervision (Human	
6. H-6 Carpentry	−.080	Relation)	.077
7. H-7 Sales-Office	.116*	18. Supervision (Technical)	.012
8. H-8 Clean Hands	.050	19. Variety	−.088*
9. H-9 Outdoors	−.117*	20. Working Condition	.021
		21. Work Challenge	−.208*
16 PF		22. Company Image	.101*
1. A-Aloof vs. Warm, Outgoing	.076	23. Organization Control	−.170*
2. B-Dull vs. Bright	.146*	24. Feedback	−.035
3. C-Emotional vs. Mature	.022	25. Physical Facilities	−.100*
4. E-Submissive vs. Dominant	−.074	26. Work Relevance	−.030
5. F-Glum, Silent vs.		27. Company Prestige	.047
Enthusiastic	−.021	28. Company Goals	.002
6. G-Casual vs. Conscientious	−.017	29. Closure	−.036
7. H-Timid vs. Adventurous	.095*	30. Compensation II relative to	
8. I-Tough vs. Sensitive	.097*	other jobs	−.127*
9. L-Trustful vs. Suspecting	−.050		
10. M-Conventional vs. Eccentric	−.028	*MSAT*	.129*
11. N-Simple vs. Sophisticated	−.066		
12. O-Confident vs. Insecure	−.052	*PERSONAL DATA*	
13. Q1-Conservative vs.		1. Age	.064
Experimenting	.063	2. Years of Education	.079
14. Q2-Dependent vs. Self-		3. High School Graduate	.030
Sufficient	.040	4. Number of Dependents	.049
15. Q3-Uncontrolled vs. Self-		5. Married	.073
Controlled	.120*	6. Number of Trade Changes	.016
16. Q4-Stable vs. Tense	−.067	7. Prior High School	
		Vocational Training	−.013
MIQ		8. Prior Post-high	
1. Ability Utilization	.049	Vocational Training	.017
2. Achievement	.078	9. Related Work Experience	.064
3. Activity	.077	10. Unrelated Work Experience	.032
		11. Sex	−.184*

*correlation significantly different than zero at the .01 level

149

Status'', ''Variety'', ''Work Challenge'', ''Organizational Control'', ''Physical Facilities'', and ''Compensation II.'' The results imply that people who wish to work for a company with prestige and fair policies and do not aspire to a position of independence, recognition, social status and relatively large amounts of compensation receive higher scores on the VDI.

Personal Data

Sex was the only one of the 11 personal data variables which significantly correlated with the VDI. Apparently females obtained higher scores on the average than did males. This may be due to the fact that most females applied to white collar types of jobs. Age and amount of prior education did not significantly correlate with the VDI. These findings can possibly be explained by the fact that persons in the population were quite homogeneous in terms of age and prior education. Most of the persons were about 18 years of age and were high school graduates.

Ability of the VDI to Differentiate Graduates from Different Vocational-Technical Curricula

Another previously completed Project MINI-SCORE sub-study, *Differentiating Among Graduates of Vocational-Technical Curriculums* (Pucel, et al., 1970) described differences in VDI scores among persons who entered and graduated from selected groups of male and female curriculums. The results of this study indicated that significant differences existed between persons who entered and graduated from different male curricula as well as from different female curricula.

Conclusions

The attitude scale of the VDI apparently is measuring something relatively unique from any *one* of the scales of the other instruments included in the Project MINI-SCORE battery although it is significantly correlated with many of the scales. The highest correlation between any of the scales and the VDI was the correlation with the verbal aptitude scale of the GATB (.357). Four other scales had correlations with the VDI GREATER THAN PLUS OR MINUS .25: GATB-G and GATB-N and MIQ-Independence and MIQ-Social Status. A total of 33 of the 74 scales of the Project MINI-SCORE battery correlated significantly at the .01 level with the VDI. These 33 scales represent constructs which appear to be related to intelligence and aptitudes, white collar versus blue collar job interests, and or controlled behavior. Persons who have more aptitude, have white collar versus blue collar job interests and or do not aspire to increase their social and occupational levels appear to obtain higher VDI scores.

Regardless what constructs the VDI is actually measuring it does appear to be capable of distinguishing graduates from different vocational-technical curricula.

THE EFFECT OF POST-HIGH SCHOOL TRAINING
ON VOCATIONAL MATURITY

The objective of this investigation was to determine if taking part in a post-high school vocational program increases a student's vocational maturity as measured by the attitude scale of the VDI.

Population and Sample

The population for the investigation consisted of students who were originally tested by Project MINI-SCORE and applied to one of thirteen curriculums offered by the area vocational-technical schools between January and September of 1968. Three schools participated in the study: Minneapolis, St. Cloud, and Alexandria. The thirteen curriculum areas were clustered into three occupational clusters as follows: technical cluster—computer programming, electronics, data processing, offset printing; skilled cluster—carpentry, diesel mechanics, farm equipment mechanics, automotives, machine shop; and sales clerical cluster—accounting, fashion merchandising, sales & marketing, and sales management.

Each cluster was divided into two groups. One group consisted of persons who applied, were accepted for training, and were about to graduate (experimental group). The other group consisted of persons who applied and were not accepted (control group). The original control groups included 103 persons. Seventy-one per cent or 73 returned their questionnaires and are reported in the control groups of this investigation. The sample group sizes are presented in Table II.

TABLE II
SAMPLE GROUPS

CLUSTER	"EXPERIMENTAL" ACCEPTED ABOUT TO GRAD	"CONTROL" NOT ACCEPTED
TECHNICAL	48	21
SKILLED	93	37
SALES CLERICAL	44	15

Results

The experimental and control groups were compared on the basis of pre-VDI scores obtained prior to the accepted groups enrolling in vocational programs in an attempt to determine if persons were admitted on the basis of vocational maturity.

TABLE III

PRE-VDI DIFFERENCES BETWEEN THE EXPERIMENTAL ON CONTROL GROUPS

	EXPERIMENTAL	CONTROL	F-VALUE
TECHNICAL	N = 48 $\bar{x}$ = 39.041 s = 3.775	N = 21 $\bar{x}$ = 38.381 s = 3.247	.485
SKILLED	N = 93 $\bar{x}$ = 37.344 s = 4.412	N = 37 $\bar{x}$ = 35.703 s = 5.825	3.029
SALES & CLERICAL	N = 44 $\bar{x}$ = 37.818 s = 3.724	N = 15 $\bar{x}$ = 38.733 s = 4.876	.575

Table III indicates that the experimental and control groups were not different for any of the three clusters on the basis of pre-VDI scores. Therefore, vocational maturity does not appear to have been a systematic factor in admitting students.

The treatments which the experimental groups received consisted of taking part in vocational-technical training programs offered by the vocational schools. Both the experimental and control groups were re-tested with the VDI when the experimental groups were about to graduate from the vocational schools. The experimental groups were tested in the schools and the control groups were followed up with a mailed questionnaire.

A comparison was made of pre and post training VDI scores of the experimental groups. The data reported in Table IV reveal that although the post-VDI group means were higher than the pre-VDI means for each of the three groups, the difference was significant only for the technical group. Persons in the technical group had significantly higher VDI scores when they were about to leave the training programs than when they entered.

Of the 74 members of the control groups, a number had to be eliminated in order to obtain a control group composed of persons who had not received any vocational training since they had applied to the schools. Forty-eight persons or 66 per cent of the control groups indicated on their follow-up questionnaires that they had taken part in public post-high school vocational training since originally not being admitted to the vocational schools. An additional eight people did not complete their post-VDI instrument and two persons were taking part in apprenticeship programs. The remaining 15 people from the three control groups were combined into one combined group.

TABLE IV

GAIN IN VID SCORES FOR
EACH EXPERIMENTAL GROUP

	PRE	POST	F-VALUE
N = 48 TECHNICAL	$\bar{x} = 39.041$ $s = 3.775$	$\bar{x} = 41.375$ $s = 4.134$	8.344**
N = 93 SKILLED	$\bar{x} = 37.344$ $s = 4.412$	$\bar{x} = 38.237$ $s = 4.593$	1.825
N = 44 SALES & CLERICAL	$\bar{x} = 37.818$ $s = 3.724$	$\bar{x} = 38.818$ $s = 4.363$	1.338

**significant at the .01 level

In order to obtain an experimental group with a similar composition to that of the combined control group, a proportional stratified random sample was taken from the three occupational cluster experimental groups stratified according to the proportions of occupational training programs originally desired by persons in the combined control group. The results of the comparison of the combined control group and the stratified sampled experimental group are presented in Table V.

TABLE V

PRE-VDI AND POST-VDI COMPARISONS OF THE COMBINED CONTROL GROUP AND THE COMBINED EXPERIMENTAL

	N = 30 EXPERIMENTAL	N = 15 CONTROL	F-VALUE
Pre-measures	$\bar{x} = 38.87$ $s = 3.07$	$\bar{x} = 35.53$ $s = 3.80$	$F = 10.05$**
Post-measures	$\bar{x} = 38.80$ $x = 4.96$	$\bar{x} = 37.87$ $s = 5.42$	$F = .33$

**significant at the .01 level

The comparison of the two groups on the basis of pre-VDI scores indicated that the two groups were significantly different. The control group had significantly lower pre-VDI scores. A comparison of the two groups on the basis of post-VDI scores indicated that the groups were no longer significantly different when the experimental group was about to graduate. The control group scores increased on the average while the experimental group remained about the same.

Conclusions

Post high school vocational training appears to have a differential effect upon the vocational maturity of persons taking part in different types of training. Persons enrolled in the technical programs significantly increased in vocational maturity while persons enrolled in skilled and sales clerical programs did not. Also, it appears that persons with relatively low VDI scores who are not accepted for training and who enter employment do increase their VDI scores to a level similar to that of those who have taken part in training. Such a finding implies that experience in the world of work has the effect of increasing the vocational maturity of persons who originally have relatively low levels of vocational maturity as measured by the VDI.

REFERENCES

Carter, H.D., The development of vocational attitudes. *Journal of Consulting Psychology,* 1940, 185-191.

Crites, J.O., Measurement of vocational maturity in adolescence: I. Attitude test of the vocational development inventory. *Psychological Monographs,* No. 2, Vol. 79, Whole No. 595, 1965.

Crites, J.O., *The maturity of vocational attitudes in adolescence.* Iowa City, Iowa: University of Iowa, 1969a.

Crites, J.O., *Vocational psychology.* New York: McGraw-Hill, 1969b.

Ginzberg, E., and others, *Occupational Choice.* New York: Columbia University Press, 1951.

Miller, D.C. and Form, W.H., *Industrial sociology.* New York: Harper and Row, 1951.

Pucel, D.J., Nelson, H.F., and Wheeler, D.N., *Differentiating among graduates of vocational-technical curriculums.* Project MINI-SCORE, Department of Industrial Education, University of Minnesota, 1970.

Super, D.E., *The dynamics of vocational adjustment.* New York: Harper and Row, 1942.

Super, D.E., *The psychology of careers.* New York: Harper and Row, 1957.

To become merely useful may well mean in the future, if not now, to become useless. To become employable, employee, or employed will not be enough to satisfy self-fulfillment. Man must learn to make of himself the uses which can be functionally reapplied in unforeseen directions. It is not archaic to teach men merely how to work; they must be taught how to become that work.

Willers, J.C. The quality of life in the seventies and implications for vocational teacher education. In R.N. Evans and D.R. Terry (Eds.), *Changing the role of vocational teacher education.* Bloomington, Ill.: McKnight and McKnight, 1971. p. 11.

Risk Taking and Vocational or Curriculum Choice

MALCOLM J. SLAKTER and STANLEY H. CRAMER

■ Risk taking as a variable in occupational choice has been the subject of much speculation [3, 5, 8, 12] and some attempts at empirical verification [2, 7, 9, 14]. Moreover, since curriculum choice may be regarded as an intermediate step in the vocational development process, it may be inferred that individual risk-taking propensity may also be a factor in curriculum choice. The underlying rationale appears to be that an individual acts as if presented with a variety of occupational (or curricular) choices, each of which has a corresponding probability of success. Hence, if risk-taking proclivities differ among individuals, it can be conjectured that these differences should have an effect upon subsequent choice of a major field of study and/or choice of job.

Ziller [14], for example, hypothesized that individual risk-taking tendencies play a part in vocational choice. To test his conjecture, Ziller investigated the relation between vocational choice and risk-taking tenden-cies for 182 male college sophomores in an ROTC program. The risk score was derived from a true-false achievement test of military terms, and represented an estimate of the ratio of items guessed to items not known. Specifically, each S received a risk score R_Z, where

$$R_Z = \frac{2W}{2W + U},$$

W is the number of incorrect responses for the examinee, and U is the number of items omitted by the examinee.

The range of R_Z is from 0 to 1, with low values indicating low risk, and high values indicating high risk. Vocational choice was ascertained by means of a questionnaire, and 18 categories originally resulted. However, due to the small number of S's in nine groups (accounting, art, general engineering, law, medicine, ministry, armed services, physics, and physical education), and the diversity of positions possible in another group (agriculture), the final analysis dealt with only eight groups, including an "undecided" group. Using analysis of variance on the arcsine transform of the risk scores, Ziller found the relation between vocational choice and risk-taking to be significant at the 0.05

level. An examination of group means revealed that students selecting sales as a vocation had the highest mean risk, while the "undecided" students attained the lowest mean risk. Ziller [14] concluded:

> In general, the results are supporting and provocative. However, the study should be cross-validated. Moreover, a larger scale project including both men and women and a larger number of vocational areas will provide additional information upon which a theory of vocational choice based upon an individual decision-making model may be developed in greater detail (pp. 63–64).

The study described in the present paper may be considered to be an example of the larger study called for by Ziller. The problem of interest, however, was twofold: (1) What is the relation between vocational choice and risk-taking? and (2) What is the relation between curriculum choice and risk-taking?

Method

Entering freshmen in the Fall Semester of 1966 at the State University of New York at Buffalo, who were available for regular university testing during the summer of 1966, comprised the S's. Complete risk-taking and vocational choice data were obtained on 976 males and 759 females; complete risk-taking and curriculum choice data were acquired on 1,010 males and 776 females.

Vocational choice was determined by presenting each S with a list of 44 possible vocations (including "other" and "undecided" categories), and requesting that a single category be selected. In a similar fashion, curriculum choice was acquired by presenting each S with a list of 34 major fields (including "undecided"), and requesting that a single selection be made.

The risk score was obtained during a 15 minute segment of the testing period by administering the College Entrance Vocabulary Test (CEVT) to all S's. The CEVT is ostensibly a legitimate synonym-antonym type vocabulary test, but is actually composed of 20 "nonsense" items embedded in 40 legitimate items. A "nonsense" item is an item with one nonsense word paired with a legitimate word. An example of one of the nonsense items is the pair: prurient . . . praign. Since the word "praign" has no meaning, the two words do not qualify as synonyms or antonyms, and hence there is no correct or best answer. The directions for the CEVT state that there is a penalty for incorrect responses, and therefore the risk taker is one who tends to respond to the nonsense items. The "nonsense" risk score (R) assigned to each S was the proportion of nonsense items to which he responded. Since practically all of the reliable variance in R_Z is predictable from R [11], the measure of risk utilized in this study was R. As in the case of R_Z, the range of R is from 0 to 1, with low values indicating low risk, and high values indicating high risk.

Results

Table 1 presents the mean arcsine risk score for each vocational choice by sex. The number in parentheses within each cell is the sample size for that combination of sex and vocational choice. Since the cell frequencies are unequal, the sex by vocational choice factorial analysis of variance utilized an exact least squares solution [1]. The computer program for the analysis was prepared by Finn [4]. Using the 0.05 level, vocational choice (with the effects of sex eliminated), sex (with the effects of vocational choice eliminated), and the sex by vocational choice interaction (with both main effects eliminated), were each nonsignificant. However, the ratio of mean square for vocational choice to mean square within was 1.3838, while the appropriate rejection point (0.05 level) is approximately 1.3940. Stated

156

TABLE 1

Mean Arcsine Risk Score for Vocational Choice By Sex (Cell Frequency in Parentheses)

Vocational	Sex M (976)	F (759)	Total (1,735)
Accounting	0.78 (28)	0.77 (8)	0.78 (36)
Administration-Business	0.89 (27)	1.01 (4)	0.90 (31)
Administration-Education	0.00 (1)	1.57 (1)	.79 (2)
Administration-Government	(0)	0.56 (4)	0.56 (4)
Advertising	0.91 (5)	0.50 (8)	0.66 (13)
Archeologist	(0)	0.40 (2)	0.40 (2)
Architecture	0.36 (3)	(0)	0.36 (3)
Athletics-Professional	0.73 (3)	0.20 (1)	0.60 (4)
Airline Services	(0)	1.10 (5)	1.10 (5)
Commercial Aviation	0.85 (3)	(0)	0.85 (3)
Communications	0.90 (6)	(0)	0.90 (6)
Dentistry	0.82 (42)	(0)	0.82 (42)
Diplomatic Service	0.88 (9)	0.93 (14)	0.91 (23)
Dramatic Arts	0.94 (4)	0.55 (4)	0.75 (8)
Engineering	0.79 (234)	0.57 (7)	0.78 (241)
Fine Arts	0.47 (11)	0.89 (20)	0.75 (31)
Guidance	(0)	0.98 (4)	0.98 (4)
Insurance	0.52 (1)	(0)	0.52 (1)
Language Interpreter	1.57 (1)	0.84 (16)	0.88 (17)
Law	0.82 (67)	0.74 (9)	0.81 (76)
Literary Arts	0.56 (6)	0.28 (4)	0.45 (10)
Mathematics	0.59 (33)	0.55 (27)	0.57 (60)
Medical Technology	0.32 (3)	0.90 (51)	0.87 (54)
Medicine	0.66 (120)	0.66 (39)	0.66 (159)
Military Service	1.13 (14)	(0)	1.13 (14)
Nursing	0.47 (1)	0.77 (64)	0.76 (65)
Occupational Therapy	(0)	0.77 (14)	0.77 (14)
Personnel	0.00 (1)	1.57 (1)	0.79 (2)
Pharmacy	0.75 (41)	0.61 (23)	0.70 (64)
Physical Therapy	0.86 (7)	0.49 (23)	0.57 (30)
Political Science	0.76 (72)	0.62 (23)	0.73 (95)
Politics	0.38 (7)	0.36 (1)	0.38 (8)
Secretarial Science	(0)	1.15 (17)	1.15 (17)
Social Science	0.67 (11)	0.66 (37)	0.66 (48)
Social Work	1.57 (2)	0.81 (20)	0.88 (22)
Speech Therapy	(0)	0.99 (8)	0.99 (8)
Teaching-Elementary, Secondary	0.75 (42)	0.74 (154)	0.74 (196)
Teaching-College, University	0.79 (14)	1.07 (11)	0.91 (25)
Veterinary Medicine	1.12 (5)	(0)	1.12 (5)
Other	0.76 (18)	0.68 (16)	0.72 (34)
Undecided	0.76 (134)	0.65 (119)	0.71 (253)

another way, the probability of obtaining a ratio of 1.3838 or more under the null hypothesis is greater than 0.05, but is less than 0.06. Hence, while Ziller's [14] relation between vocational choice and risk-taking was not confirmed at the 0.05 level, it is perhaps worthwhile to point out the near miss. In the present study the strength of relation between vocational choice and risk-taking was estimated to be approximately 0.03.

To test the conjecture that a grouping of occupations on the basis of some tenable theory of vocational development might yield stronger and more meaningful relationships, 39 of the original 41 occupations selected were reclassified according to Holland's [6] paradigm. The two remaining categories of occupations (other, undecided) could not be reclassified. However, in a one-way analysis of variance the six resultant groupings (Realistic, Intellectual, Social, Conventional, Enterprising, and Artistic) failed to yield results significant at the 0.05 level.

The mean arcsine risk score for curriculum choice by sex is displayed in

TABLE 2

Mean Arcsine Risk Score For Curriculum Choice By Sex (Cell Frequency in Parentheses)

Curriculum Choice	Sex		
	M (1,010)	F (776)	Total (1,786)
American Studies	(0)	1.57 (2)	1.57 (2)
Anthropology & Linguistics	0.20 (2)	0.67 (3)	0.49 (5)
Art	0.69 (10)	0.71 (35)	0.70 (45)
Biology	0.74 (33)	0.65 (25)	0.70 (58)
Business Administration	0.88 (69)	0.89 (14)	0.89 (83)
Chemistry	0.61 (46)	0.80 (11)	0.65 (57)
Classics	0.05 (1)	0.46 (4)	0.38 (5)
Drama and Speech	0.87 (4)	0.81 (12)	0.83 (16)
Economics	0.29 (3)	0.54 (2)	0.39 (5)
Education	0.44 (6)	0.90 (49)	0.85 (55)
Engineering	0.82 (256)	0.53 (8)	0.81 (264)
English	0.72 (19)	0.73 (36)	0.73 (55)
Geology and Geography	0.87 (3)	0.10 (1)	0.67 (4)
History	0.92 (27)	0.71 (13)	0.85 (40)
Mathematics	0.64 (52)	0.57 (50)	0.60 (102)
Medical Technology	0.59 (9)	0.90 (55)	0.86 (64)
Modern Language & Literature	1.11 (5)	0.85 (42)	0.88 (47)
Music	0.35 (6)	0.78 (10)	0.62 (16)
Nursing	(0)	0.75 (66)	0.75 (66)
Occupational Therapy	1.57 (1)	0.67 (14)	0.73 (15)
Pharmacy	0.71 (43)	0.62 (21)	0.68 (64)
Philosophy	0.50 (2)	0.19 (3)	0.31 (5)
Physical Education & Hygiene	1.19 (10)	0.65 (9)	0.93 (19)
Physical Therapy	0.86 (7)	0.55 (26)	0.61 (33)
Physics and Astronomy	0.97 (19)	1.08 (2)	0.98 (21)
Political Science	0.49 (16)	0.74 (13)	0.60 (29)
Pre-Dental	0.81 (39)	(0)	0.81 (39)
Pre-Law	0.89 (61)	0.74 (12)	0.86 (73)
Pre-Medical	0.67 (113)	0.75 (33)	0.69 (146)
Psychology	0.71 (14)	0.67 (45)	0.68 (59)
Secretarial Science	(0)	1.19 (15)	1.19 (15)
Social Work	0.51 (2)	1.08 (9)	0.97 (11)
Sociology	0.96 (6)	0.59 (12)	0.71 (18)
Undecided	0.73 (126)	0.65 (124)	0.69 (250)

158

Table 2. Once again the cell frequencies (in parentheses) are unequal, and a least squares analysis was performed. Using the 0.05 level, curriculum choice (with the effects of sex eliminated) was significant, but sex (with the effects of curriculum choice eliminated), and the sex by curriculum choice interaction (with both main effects eliminated) were not significant. The strength of relation between curriculum choice and risk was approximately 0.03.

Discussion

It is seen that the results indicate weak relations between risk-taking and curriculum choice, and between risk-taking and vocational choice. The relation between curriculum choice and risk was significant at the 0.05 level; relation between vocational choice and risk was not significant at the 0.05 level. In each case, however, approximately 3 per cent of the variability in risk score could be accounted for by curriculum (or vocational) choice. For purposes of comparison, a reanalysis of Ziller's [14] data provided an estimate of 6 per cent for the strength of relation between risk and vocational choice.

Inspection of categories of vocational or curriculum choice in the present study, however, suggest that the differences in mean risk were not only weak, but that many were illogical. For example, with regard to vocational choice, elementary and secondary school teaching received a higher mean risk score than politics or medicine, while secretarial science emerged with a higher mean risk score than college or university teaching. With respect to curriculum choice, education received a higher mean risk score than pre-medical. Thus, while the overall relationship between risk-taking and curriculum choice (or vocational choice) is significant (or just "missed" significance) at the 0.05 level, the comparative mean risk scores of the various categories appear to be somewhat unexpected and irrational.

These data may be a result of several factors inherent in the population of the study and the instrument employed. For example, some vocational and curriculum choice categories contain an extremely small number of S's. Too, the research on change of major in college rather strongly points to the tenuous nature and instability of freshmen curriculum and vocational choice through the first two years, at least, of the college experience. Since the S's in the present study were college freshmen who had not yet even commenced their first college semester, the choices made were undoubtedly less realistic than the college sophomores used by Ziller [14]. Finally and perhaps most important, the CEVT, like the instrument used by Ziller [14], is a measure of risk-taking on *examinations,* and hence may not be the risk measure most appropriate for use with vocational or curriculum choice.

In conclusion, while there is some evidence to indicate that risk-taking is related to vocational or curriculum choice, it would appear that the Ziller approach and similar modifications such as that utilized in the present study, may be inappropriate to capitalize on this relation. Indeed, when one keeps in mind that the present study investigated the relation between risk-taking on an objective examination and stated curriculum (or vocational) choice at the pre-freshman level, it is perhaps somewhat surprising to find that the strength of relation even approached 3 per cent. It is, therefore, certainly reasonable to conjecture that other measures of risk, more appropriate to vocational or curriculum choice, can be constructed [13]. In addition, because of the instability over time (especially in the college years) of curriculum and vocational choice, it may prove more efficacious for researchers to develop empirically-keyed measures of risk-taking which are validated on existing occupational groups, much in the manner

159

of the Strong Vocational Interest Blank. In short, while there exists some evidence for a relation between risk-taking and curriculum choice or vocational choice, it remains for future research to find a better method to capitalize on this relation.

REFERENCES

1. Bock, R. D., "Programming Univariate and Multivariate Analysis of Variance," *Technometrics*, 1963, 5, 95–117.

2. Burnstein, E., "Fear of Failure, Achievement Motivation, and Aspiring to Prestigeful Occupations," *Journal of Abnormal and Social Psychology*, 1963, 67, 189–193.

3. Clarke, R. Gelatt, H. B., and Levine L., "A Decision-Making Paradigm for Local Guidance Research," *Personnel and Guidance Journal*, 1965, 40–51.

4. Finn, J. D., *Multivariance—univariate and multivariate analysis of variance and covariance: A Fortran IV program*, Unpublished manuscript, State University of New York at Buffalo, 1967.

5. Hilton, T. L., "Career Decision-Making," *Journal of Counseling Psychology*, 1962, 9, 291–298.

6. Holland, J. L., *The Psychology of Vocational Choice: A Theory of Personality Types and Model Environments*, Waltham, Massachusetts: Blaisdell, 1966.

7. Mahone, C. H., "Fear of Failure and Unrealistic Vocational Aspiration," *Journal of Abnormal and Social Psychology*, 1960, 60, 253–261.

8. Meadow, L., "Toward a Theory of Vocational Choice," *Journal of Counseling Psychology*, 1955, 2, 108–112.

9. Morris, J. L., "Propensity for Risk Taking as a Determinant of Vocational Choice," *Journal of Personality and Social Psychology*, 1966, 3, 328–355.

10. Slakter, M. J., "Risk Taking on Objective Examinations," *American Educational Research Journal*, 1967, 4, 31–43.

11. Slakter, M. J. and Koehler, R., "A New Measure of Risk Taking on Objective Examinations," *California Journal of Educational Research*, 1968, 19, 132–137.

12. Super, D. E., "A Theory of Vocational Development," *American Psychologist*, 1953, 8, 185–190.

13. Williams, L. K., *The Measurement of Risk Taking Propensity in an Industrial Setting*. Doctoral Dissertation, University of Michigan, Ann Arbor, Michigan: University Microfilms, 1961. No. 61–1810.

14. Ziller, R. C., "Vocational Choice and Utility for Risk," *Journal of Counseling Psychology*, 1957, 4, 61–64.

THEORIES OF VOCATIONAL BEHAVIOR

by

Larry J. Bailey

The present theories of vocational development trace their roots to the beginning of the present century with the birth of the vocational guidance movement. Frank Parsons, director of the first vocational guidance center in the United States, provided the framework for the first theory of occupational choice. Parsons (1909) advocated a scientific approach to vocational counseling which he outlined in a three-phase approach: (1) study and understanding of self, (2) study of the requirements of occupations, and (3) "true reasoning" about the relationships among the facts obtained.

The development of this approach was characterized by a concern with measurable attributes as predictors of educational and vocational success. As a result, the psychology of individual differences, which underlies the method of determining occupational ability, became the basis of vocational psychology. Super (1954) and Pepinsky and Pepinsky (1954) have called this practice the actuarial method. They defined the underlying theory as the trait theory of vocational guidance. Katz (1963) provides a concise definition of this theory:

> To oversimplify, this theory holds that first, the individual is in effect 'keyed' to one or a few 'correct' occupational positions; second, if left to his own devices, he would probably gravitate toward the right choice, but with some wasted motion and time and some possibility of missing the proper target altogether; third, the 'key' should therefore be learned—and can be learned—quite early in adolescence; fourth, all educational decisions should be determined by the requirements and characteristics imputed to this 'appropriate' vocation; fifth, the occupational goal should remain constant over a period of time and subsidiary decisions should accordingly be consistent. In short, the final goal can be known early and can—and should—determine all preliminary decisions (for example, choice of high school curriculum and other educational alternatives) leading up to it. (p. 6)

One of the first applications of the psychology of individual differences was the emphasis on intelligence testing. Mental tests were first used to discover students' general level of intelligence for guidance purposes. Proctor (1920) ascertained that intelligence level could be used as a means of selecting school subjects and was a "significant" predictor of success in a particular subject. He concluded that "the best way in which to arrive at an estimate of a given pupil's probable success in a specific high school subject (was) to discover the general level of his intelligence." (p. 381)

Use of the Army Alpha Intelligence Test with soldiers during World War I gave the intelligence testing movement the greatest stimulus it has ever had There can be no doubt that the experience of the Army demonstrated the value of the various tests which were used. Some people were so impressed by the success of the Army tests that they believed a method had been found of classifying all human beings for all sorts of purposes. (Super 1957c)

The need for successful placement of men in the armed services resulted in studies designed to link intelligence levels with occupational classifications. One such study, on the basis of psychological examinations, classified the alpha grades of "literate white men" into fifty-five occupations. Each occupation was then ranked according to median intelligence scores. This ranking illustrated that there seemed to be "four or five" primary levels. The researchers concluded that "from the practical point of view. . . the table of occupational standards could be used in the Army with resulting increased efficiency in the placement of men." (Yerkes 1921, p. 837)

The classification of occupations by intelligence levels resulted in attempts by vocational counselors to establish occupational-intelligence standards to assist in the process of vocational counseling and in the selection of personnel. Fryer (1922) established five occupational levels (Professional, Technical, Skilled, Semi-skilled, and Unskilled) with intelligence as the basis for grouping. He then developed a table listing the occupational-intelligence standards for ninety-six occupational designations. The occupations were indexed according to the average intelligence scores of a "few hundred cases." The intelligence mean for the occupation was presented as the "score average", and the "score range" indicated the range of intelligence within which one could expect success in that occupation. Examples, with score averages indicated, are as follows: Engineer 161, Clergyman 152, Teacher 122, and Fireman 27, Sheet metal worker 22, Fisherman 20. On the basis of his classification, Fryer concluded:

A classification of occupations with intelligence as the basis for the grouping is essential information for a vocational office. . .The occupational territory of an individual is bounded by his intellectual capacity; he is blocked off into an occupational field with intelligence as the standard for classification. . .The scores are so presented as to indicate that in all probability an individual must have an intelligence rating within the score range for achievement in the occupation, with the further probability that he should be above the score average to be sure of sufficient intellectual capacity for the occupation. (p. 275)

During the 1920's a team of researchers at the University of Minnesota were in the process of constructing broad outlines for a scientific vocational testing and counseling program. (Paterson 1949) When the disastrous depression began in 1929, this group undertook to apply their newly discovered techniques to the study of hundreds of cases of unemployed workers. This work was carried on by the Committee on Individual Diagnosis and Training of the Minnesota Employment Stabilization Research Institute, and one of the first large-scale attempts to utilize a variety of psychological tests and measurements.

Throughout their five-year study numerous independent studies were undertaken and completed. The program of individual diagnosis and training involved the principles and techniques of various related fields including industrial social work, vocational psychology, industrial medicine, industrial education, and personnel administration and management. This approach to problems of unemployment may be best described as that of "human engineering." Out of this research came increased knowledge of the vocational significance of standard intelligence tests, clerical aptitude tests, mechanical ability tests, tests of manipulative dexterities, vocational interest blanks, and personalities. Occupational ability profiles were developed so that the individual psychograph could be interpreted in a limited way in terms of occupational requirements. The idea was itself a forerunner of the notion of job families as developed by the Occupational Research Program of the United States Employment Service. The Institute not only made an important contribution in itself, but also set a pattern for studies of occupations that served as the foundation for nationwide occupational research, both civilian and military. (Paterson 1949, Paterson and Darley 1936).

In the late 1930's increasing attention was given to the measurement of basic psychological functions in aptitude tests and aptitude test batteries. (Stuit 1949) The United States Employment Service (USES), in 1933, launched a five-year study to develop a test battery through a process of job and worker analysis. The resultant USES General Aptitude Test Battery (GATB) was a combination of tests which measured a number of important aptitudes. The basic assumption underlying the GATB was that a large variety of tests could be boiled down to several factors, and that a large variety of occupations could be clustered into groups according to similarities in the abilities required. (Dvorak 1956)

The battery was standardized by first identifying jobs to serve as the basis for the selection of an experimental sample. Persons who were performing that same kind of job and who were regarded as proficient (by foreman or supervisors) on that job were included in the sample. This group was then administered the GATB consisting of fifteen subtests chosen as a result of factor analysis studies. Occupational Aptitude Patterns were established after analysis of test data and job analysis schedules showed that certain occupations required a similiar minimum amount of the same combination of aptitudes. The GATB could then be administered to a counselee to determine his Individual Aptitude Profile. The Individual Aptitude Profile was then compared with the twenty Occupational Aptitude Patterns to determine the fields of work that were most suitable for the person's abilities. (Dvorak 1947)

The major purpose of the Occupational Research Program of the USES was to furnish public employment offices and other co-operating agencies with operating tools to facilitate the proper counseling, classification and placement of workers. Thus, this technique was a testimonial to the widespread acceptance of vocational counseling as a process of "matching" abilities and interests with occupational requirements and trends. (Crites 1965, Stead and Shartle 1940, Super 1954)

During the years preceding World War I the primary motive of test constructors appeared to be that of building tests which would measure specifiic psychological variables, regardless of the tests' predictive value. In the years between the two world wars, the primary concern was constructing tests to predict success in particular areas of study or vocational activity. This approach, in other words, was empirical and not based on any formalized theory of aptitude or mental organization. (Guilford 1948, Stuit 1949)

With the outbreak of World War II, the importance of problems of selection and classification accentuated a further development of the trait approach. Consistent with previous studies, the results of Army General Classification Test scores virtually duplicated the occupational hierarchies constructed from World War I Army Alpha scores. (Stewart 1947) There was a realization, however, of the posibility that the GCT was a "measure of ability to manipulate words, numbers and space relations, . . . and those occupations with the lowest averages on the test (were) the occupations least concerned with words, numbers or space relations." (Harrell and Harrell 1945, p. 239)

The second type of emphasis in occupational counseling was given to experimental and theoretical studies of the nature of abilities. (Stuit 1949) Work-sample tests were designed to present a task that resembled the features of a job or some elementary components of the job. An example of a work-sample test was the Army Air Force Classification battery that was designed to present a task analogous to that of a pilot operating an airplane in flight. (Guilford 1948) The Aviation Psychology Program of the AAF utilized an array of aptitude tests for predicting success in a pilot selection program. Using multiple-regression techniques derived differentially from weighted combinations of test scores, assignments were made to pilot, navigator, or bombardier training. (Katz 1963)

The evolvement of the trait centered approach to vocational counseling culminated in the years following World War II. The early results of factor analysis studies indicated that there was considerable duplication in what was measured by different psychological tests. The number of functional units (factors) which accounted for variation in test scores was actually much smaller than the total number of tests. As the intercorrelational information regarding test and criteria grew, the basis for increasing use of factor analysis theory and practice was strengthened. (Pepinsky and Pepinsky 1954, Stuit 1949) Guilford (1948) presents an excellent discussion of the factor-analysis technique:

> The first assumption of the factorial approach is that tests and criteria alike can be statistically analyzed into a limited number of basic traits that additively make up the total variance of each test or criterion. The term 'variance' may be regarded roughly and simply, as merely a more exact expression for the idea of 'individual difference.' It should be emphasized that the analysis is statistical rather than observational in the ordinary sense. One reason why more of the factors have not been detected without the use of statistical procedures is that they are not obvious to surface inspection. For the most part, owing to the extreme complexity of the person observed and of his activities, they have eluded even the sophisticated observer. They are, however, usually recognizable and acceptable to most observers when they are pointed out after having been discovered by statistical analysis. The hiatus between a list of ordinary job-analysis traits and a list of statistically derived factors is most striking. They conclude at some points, but are generally divergent. (p. 82)

Based on results of factor analysis studies, the emphasis approaching mid-century was primarily on the measurement of "pure factors" for the differential prediction and selection for civilian occupations. In regard to theory:

. . . the predominant conception of vocational choice was essentially a cross-sectional, nondevelopmental one . . . it emphasized the historical, instantaneous, nondynamic elements in vocational decision making. Resolution of the problem of choosing an occupation, whether before or after entry into the world of work, was seen as a point-in-time event when the individual, more or less consciously and rationally, appraised his personal assets and liabilities, surveyed the employment opportunities open to him, and decided upon the one which offered him greatest chances for job satisfaction and success. (Crites 1965, p. 1)

While guidance practices during this era were aimed at differential prediction through the application of trait-and-factor theory, there was growing concern that deficiencies existed in both theory and practice. Thorndike and Hagen (1959) conducted a study in 1955 of 10,000 men who had been given a battery of aptitude tests in 1943. Their investigation was based on tests administered to applicants for Aviation Cadet status in the Army Air Force in World War II. The analysis of aptitude test scores for these men was compared with information collected concerning their educational and vocational history.

The results showed that occupational groups differed with respect to personal background variables as well as aptitude test scores. The patterns were, in most cases, sensible and in accord with what might be expected. The authors rationalized that these differences should be "thought of as chance variables and ones that probably would not hold up in another sample." (p. 50)

With respect to the prediction of success within an occupation, however, their conclusions were quite different.

As far as we were able to determine from our data, there is no convincing evidence that aptitude tests or biographical information of the type that was available to us can predict degree of success within an occupation insofar as this is represented in the criterion measures that we were able to obtain. This would suggest that we should view the long-range prediction of occupational success by aptitude tests with a good deal of skepticism and take a very restrained view as to how much can be accomplished in this direction. (p. 50)

In general, our conclusions must be that although the differentiation between occupations with respect to score on a group of tests is real, still this differentiation is less sharp than the test enthusiast would suggest, in this case when the occupations are all at approximately the same level and when the tests are limited to a battery of tests of abilities. We can hardly assert that the evidence presented in our results gives strong support for using tests to guide individuals into one or another of a set of occupations all at approximately the same level in the occupational hierarchy. (p. 323)

In the final statement of their book, the writers summarized their notions concerning the value of test batteries for predictive differentiation.

Individuals get into occupations for a great variety of reasons, many of which may be completely unrelated to their abilities or appropriateness for the occupation. Insofar as this is the case, we can hardly expect our tests to predict this event. (p. 323)

As concern grew about the appropriateness of trait-and-factor theory, methodology based on this approach continued to dictate vocational guidance practice. Barry and Wolfe (1962) refer to this method as "the greatest myth in vocational guidance. . . . The repetition of the same theoretical position creates the myth that a single, universally accepted theory exists and the corollary myth that vocational guidance practices have a sound theoretical base." (p. 3)

During the early 1950's, alternative theories of vocational behavior began to emerge. These theories attempted to establish generalizations and patterns that give knowledge about occupations and the people in them. They were referred to as "pattern" theories and were extremely important because they furnished the basis for the eventual destruction of antiquated methodological theory and practice. (Barry and Wolfe 1962)

The best-known theories are those dealing with "life stages." Super (1954, 1960) credits two Austrians, Buehler and Lazarsfield, with laying the groundwork for the modern theories. Lazarsfield supplied research methods and forces for later pattern investigations and raised important issues about choices. Buehler's study had a more direct influence on later American theories. She traced the processes of development throughout the entire life span. Her theory of life stages (growth, exploration, establishment, maintenance, and decline) was to serve as a framework for the organization of data concerning vocational choice and adjustment. A person's vocational development as well as other aspects of his life was assumed to fit into this same developmental pattern.

Two different theories of vocational life stages were formulated in 1951. The first was by a research team composed of Ginzberg, Ginsburg, Axelrad, and Herma; the second by two industrial sociologists, Miller and Form. The theory of Ginzberg et al. (1951) clearly reflects the influence of Buehler's study of life stages. This research team reviewed earlier theories of occupational choice and then interviewed sixty-four students at Horace Mann-Lincoln School and Columbia University, both in New York City. Their purpose was to establish generalizations about the types of occupational choices young people make before and after college. They found that the process of occupational decision-making could be analyzed in terms of three periods. These periods could be differentiated by the way an individual "translates" his impulses and needs into an occupational choice.

The first stage they refer to as the "fantasy" period. During this time (childhood thru age eleven) an individual thinks about an occupation in terms of his wish to be an adult. His translations are arbitrary, and he believes he can be whatever he wants to be. Next comes the "tentative" period (age eleven to seventeen) when a person recognizes the problem of deciding on a future occupation. His choices are determined by interests, by capacities, and then by values. The "realistic" period begins at about age seventeen and is composed of stages of exploration, crystallization, and specification. During this period, the translation is so heavily weighted by reality considerations that a synthesis is difficult. Following is their general theory:

First, occupational choice is a process which takes place over a minimum of six or seven years, and more typically, over ten years or more.

secondly, since each decision during adolescence is related to one's experience up to that point, and in turn has an influence on the future, the process of decision-making is basically irreversible. Finally, since occupational choice involves the balancing of a series of subjective elements with the opportunities and limitations of reality, the crystallization of occupational choice inevitably has the quality of a compromise. (p. 198)

The significance of Ginzberg's study was the emphasis on a concept of occupational choices, not just one, and the undermining of the idea that a vocational decision is a single reasoned process. "The study also pointed out the great variety and number of factors that influence the young person's job choices, the shifting nature of these choices, and the interelationships of an individual's vocational decisions and his personality development." (Barry and Wolfe 1962, p. 11)

Miller and Form (1951), in their book *Industrial Sociology*, describe life stages from the point of view of work characteristics. They define five work periods as preparatory, initial, trial, stable, and retirement. These designations are quite similiar to Buehler's life stages except that progression from one period to another is not necessary. Their interest is in describing kinds of work periods which are characteristic of various occupational patterns. After an investigation of career patterns, Miller and Form concluded that:

. . . personal motivation and hard work explain the career pattern and that occupational success can be attained regardless of social background. This kind of thinking might be called the *individual* causation theory of career patterns. In contrast, the network of interrelated social factors that have been demonstrated to be associated with occupational levels might become the basis of a *social* causation theory of career patterns. . . . Relationships can be demonstrated between occupational level of a worker and (1) the father's occupation, (2) the historical circumstances, (3) the father's income and education, (4) financial aid and influential contacts, (5) social and economic conditions. An accurate weighing of the facts will demonstrate that the social background of the worker is a base of opportunities and limitations. As opportunities are enlarged the possibilities of occupational mobility are increased. Personal motivation and native ability are necessary to an enlarging career pattern. However, there is good evidence that the social backgrounds of workers are the crucial determiners in the number who are able to come into various occupational levels.

Forces making for the location at various occupational levels have been identified and described. *Social background, native ability, historical circumstance, and acquired personality traits* are the influences determining a given career pattern. These forces may be considered as intertwined and pulling upon each worker with different intensities at various times in his career. (pp. 583-585)

The most extensive and oldest sustained program of research on vocational behavior is a result of the efforts of Donald Super. Although he attempted to combine earlier (Super 1942), the then available facts concerning the psychology, sociology, and economics of vocational development, it was not until the middle fifties that he began development of a theory.

167

Super (1953) prepared an article which attempted to synthesize current knowledge and to begin formulation of a comprehensive theory of vocational development. He critized Ginzberg's theory of occupational choice because it failed "to take into account the continuity of the development of preferences and of the differences in the stages, choices, entry, and adjustment; it (should) explain the process through which interest, capacities, values, and opportunities are compromised." (p. 187) He then sketched the main "elements" of a theory of vocational development as they appeared in the literature. There seemed to be a dozen elements to such a theory: (1) individual differences (2) occupational multi-potentiality of the individual (3) occupational ability patterns (4) identification with parents and the role of models (5) continuity of the adjustment process (6) life stages (7) career patterns (8) development can be guided (9) development is the result of interaction (10) dynamics of career patterns (11) job satisfaction (12) work as a way of life.

Following this enumeration of the diverse elements of a theory, he organized these elements into a summary statement of a comprehensive theory. His theory was stated in a series of ten "propositions."

1. People differ in their abilities, interests, and personalities.
2. They are qualified, by virtue of these characteristics, each for a number of occupations.
3. Each of these occupations require a characteristic pattern of abilities, interests, and personality traits . . .
4. Vocational preferences and competencies, . . . and hence their self concepts, change with time and experience, making choice and adjustment a continuous process.
5. This process may be summed up in a series of life stages . . .
6. The nature of the career pattern (that is, the occupational level attained and the sequence, frequency, and duration of trial and stable jobs) is determined by the individual's parental socioeconomic level, mental ability, and personality characteristics, and by the opportunities to which he is exposed.
7. Development through the life stages can be guided . . .
8. The process of vocational development is essentially that of developing and implementing a self concept . . .
9. The process of compromise between individual and social factors, between self concept and reality, is one of role playing . . .
10. Work satisfactions and life satisfactions depend upon the extent to which the individual finds adequate outlets for his abilities, interests, personality traits, and values . . . (pp. 189-190)

In order to clarify and test his theoretical model, Super began, in 1951, a long-term research project entitled the Career Pattern Study. A developmental approach was adopted due to the impact of developmental psychology in the form of Buehler's life stages, and the variations suggested by Ginzberg et al. and Miller and Form. The research was a project of the Horace Mann-Lincoln Institute of School Experimentation, Teachers College, Columbia University, and utilized a sample of 142 eight-grade and 143 ninth-grade boys. (Super 1954, 1955, 1957c)

Although basic field work for the Study was conducted in 1951-52, it was not until 1957 that the first of a series of monographs appeared. Based on previous research findings and experience, Super (1957c) attempted to identify relevant areas of study. He therefore proposed a series of "working principles" to explore the nature of vocational development theory. The first three "postulates" are as follows:

Proposition 1. Vocational development is an ongoing, continuous, and generally irreversible process.

Proposition 2. Vocational development is an orderly, patterned process and thus predictable.

Proposition 3. Vocational development is a dynamic process of compromise or synthesis. (pp. 89-90)

The next three propositions aimed to determine the nature of the occupational choice-making process; the effect of role-taking upon the development of the self-concept; and the effects of these factors.

Proposition 4. Self-concepts begin to form prior to adolescense, become clearer in adolescense, and are translated into occupational terms in adolescense.

Proposition 5. Reality factors (the reality of personal characteristics and and the reality of society) play an increasingly important part in occupational choice with increasing age, from early adolescence to adulthood.

Proposition 6. Identification with a parent or parent substitute is related to the development of adequate roles, their consistent and harmonious interrelationship, and their interpretation in terms of vocational plans and eventualities. (pp. 91-92)

The factors that affect the patterning of careers and the relationships among certain psychological, sociological, and economic factors were dealt with next.

Proposition 7. The direction and rate of the vertical movement of an individual from one occupational level to another is related to his intelligence, parental socioeconomic level, status needs, values, interests, skill in interpersonal relationships, and the supply and demand in the economy.

Proposition 8. The occupational field which the individual enters is related to his interests and values, the identifications he makes with parental or substitute role models, the community resources he uses, the level and quality of his educational background, and the occupational structure, trends, and attitudes of his community. (pp. 93-94)

The last three propositions were concerned with the way satisfactory careers for an individual can be predicted. The ninth element presented the concept of occupational multipotentiality of the individual.

Proposition 9. Although each occupation requires a characteristic pattern of abilities, interests, and personality traits, the tolerances are wide enough to allow both some variety of individuals in each occupation and some diversity of occupations for each individual. (p. 94)

Multipotentiality implies two different relationships: (1) the relationship of the individual's abilities to success or satisfaction with an occupation, and (2) the relationship between individual characteristics and occupational ability patterns is one of belonging. These facts suggested the last two propositions.

169

Proposition 10. Work satisfactions depend upon the extent to which the individual can find adequate outlets in his job for his abilities, interests, values, and personality traits.

Proposition 11. The degree of satisfaction the individual attains from his work is related to the degree to which he has been able to implement his self-concept in his work. (pp. 95-96)

In 1956 the National Science Foundation invited Dr. Super to submit a proposal dealing with the "identification of scientific capabilities and motivation in scientific career selection." To develop a research methodology, Super (1957a) invited a distinguished panel (noted for their independent contributions to this area) to read papers representing the major types of theoretical approaches to occupational research. The presentations, and the discussion that followed, resulted in an "integrated approach to vocational development." Also, as a result of suggestions by the panel, another proposition concerning the nature of career development was adopted.

Proposition 12. Work and occupation provide a focus for personality organization for most men and many women, although for some persons this focus is peripheral, incidental, or even non-existant, and other foci such as social activities and the home are central. (p. 120)

In setting up a model for the Career Pattern Study, Super (1957c) synthesized previous generalizations of life stages into the following:

1. Growth Stage (Birth-14), Self-concept develops through identification with key figures in family and in school; needs and fantasy dominate early in this stage; interest and capacity become more important in this stage with increasing social participation and reality-testing. Substages of the growth stage are; Fantasy (4-10), Interest (11-12), and capacity (13-14).

2. Exploration Stage (Age 15-24), Self-examination, role tryout, and occupational exploration take place in school, leisure activities, and part-time work. Substages of the exploration stage are: Tentative (15-17), Transition (18-21), and Trial (22-24).

3. Establishment Stage (Age 25-44), Having found an appropriate field, effort is put forth to make a permanent place in it. There may be some trial early in this stage, with consequent shifting, but establishment may begin without trial, especially in the professions. Substages of the establishment stage are: Trial (25-30) and Stabilization (31-44).

4. Maintenance Stage (Age 45-64), Having made a place in the world of work, the concern is now to hold it. Little new ground is broken, but there is continuation along established lines.

5. Decline Stage (Age 65 on), As physical and mental powers decline, work activity changes and in due course ceases. New roles must be developed; first that of selective participant and then that of observer rather than participants. Substages of this stage are: Deceleration (65-70) and Retirement (71 on). (pp. 40-41)

According to Super this outline gives a description of the nature of vocational behavior which seems characteristic of each life stage and it indicates the approximate age limit of the stages. The importance of this synthesis is that it furnishes a research base for two major concepts: (1) that vocational development is "an ongoing, continuous, generally irreversible process" and (2) that it is "an orderly, patterned process." (Super 1957c, p. 42)

The concept of vocational development as used by Super (1957b, 1957c) led to a completely new set of behavioral definitions. The term "vocational choice," which was borrowed from differential psychology, conveyed a misleading notion of neatness and precision of time of singleness and uniqueness in the life of the individual. "Choice is, in fact a process rather than an event." (p. 184b) For these reasons, a new term was adopted.

Vocational development is conceived of as one aspect of individual development. Like social development, emotional development, and intellectual development, it has both distinctive characteristics which make focusing on it worth while and common characteristics which reveal it as one way in which the general development of the individual manifests itself. Work, like social life and intellectual activity, is one specific medium through which the total personality can manifest itself. Like other aspects of development, vocational development may be conceived of as beginning early in life, and as proceeding along a curve until late in life. . . Just as general development can be broken down into major life stages placed sequentially on a continuum, each stage having characteristics which are peculiar to it and which justify singling it out, so the continuum of vocational development can be broken down into vocational life stages, each defined by its peculiar characteristics. (p. 185b)

The concept of vocational development leads logically to that of vocational maturity. . . *Vocational maturity* is used to denote the degree of development, the place reached on the continuum of vocational development from exploration to decline. Vocational maturity may be thought of as vocational age, conceptually similar to mental age in adolescence, . . . (pp. 185-186b)

The next revision of Super's vocational development theory occured in the early 1960's. In a monograph consisting of five essays, Super (1963) presented his model for explaining vocational behavior. He viewed an individual's occupational preference as an attempt to implement a self-concept. He maintained that a person selects a vocation whose requirements provide a role consistent with his self-image. The processes by which self-concept affects vocational development are identified as the processes of formation, translation, and implementation. The *formation* stage includes exploration of the world and of the self, self-differentiation, identification, role playing, and reality testing. *Translation* occurs in various ways: (1) Through identification with an adult, (2) Experience in a role in which one is cast may lead to the discovery of a vocational translation, and (3) Awareness that one has attributes which are important in a certain field may lead to an investigation of that occupation. The *implementation* of the self-concept is the end result of the process. The person begins his professional training, completes his education, and ultimately goes on into the world of work. According to Super, the process of forming a concept of self begins in infancy. "This is essentially an exploratory process which goes on throughout the entire course of life . . ." (p. 11)

171

The writings of Super provide a clear outline of the process and investigation of vocational development. The work of Tiedeman (1960, 1961) has attempted to furnish an explicit statement of the process of decision in vocational development. "The structure of decision must be specified before investigations of the theory of vocational development can enter new phases. . . The set of decisions and the context of relevance for the anticipation and implementation of each constitutes the essence of vocational development." (1960, p. 50)

Tiedeman asserts that the vocational development process is oriented by each of several decisions with regard to school, work, and life. With respect to each decision, the problem may be divided into two periods: (1) The period of anticipation which may be analyzed into subaspects of exploration, crystallization, and choice. (2) A period of implementation and adjustment which may be further specified as stages of induction, transition, and maintenance. Each decision potentially consists of these stages. In addition, each decision may be considered within the context of several decisions. It is the organization and order of "sets" of action, therefore, that specify vocational development. The career evolves in a time pattern in intimate association with the evolution of other aspects of life. "Vocational development then is self-development viewed in relation with choice, entry, and progress in educational and vocational pursuits." (Tiedeman 1961, p. 18)

Like Super, Tiedeman maintains that the goal of his research efforts is to predict and understand the individual's career pattern. In the pursuit of this goal, Tiedeman has explored many theoretical models (as opposed to one for Super) and developed new statistical techniques. (Tiedeman 1960) He, more than anyone else, has emphasized the work history as the criterion for the study of vocational behavior. Accordingly, the elements of work history are: (1) the kinds of positions chosen; (2) their sequence; and (3) the duration of stay in each. (Holland 1964)

According to Barry and Wolfe (1962), motivational theories represent another attempt to explain vocational behavior. "Motivational theory came into being as investigators began to concern themselves with the intriquing question, Why do men work?" (pp. 16-17) The most significant attempt to relate motivational speculations to vocational behavior is found in the work of Anne Roe.

Roe (1956, 1957) schematized a theory of vocational choice that is explained in terms of child-parent relationships. Her hypotheses are based on the assumption that parental attitudes and home atmosphere in early childhood are crucial forces in determining adult choices. More explicitly, "warmth or coldness" of parental attitude is thought to shape one's orientation toward persons or nonpersons. This orientation toward persons ramifies into patterns of special abilities and interests which are given expression in the pattern of the adult's life; in his personal relationships; in his emotional reactions, in his activities; and in his vocational choice. "More than any other aspect of life, the occupation usually reflects most clearly the coalescence of the genetic and experiential variables . . ." (1957, p. 217)

A similiar orientation is presented by Bordin et al. (1963) which attempts to set up a series of dimensions to account for all of the gratifications which work can offer. They illustrate that any occupation can be described in terms of the "relative strength of component dimensions and their relation to a series of modifying characteristics." The structure of dimensions of work has to be carried out via a repeated weaving back and forth between job analysis, personality traits, and the assumptions regarding childhood experiences. Their theory attempts to link the adoption of an occupational role to personality organization by: (1) Presenting a scheme which identifies the gratifications that varieties of work can offer, and (2) Tracing these gratifications to the infantile psysiological functions necessary to their achievement. The importance of early experiences that lead to investments in particular modes of obtaining gratification is particularly emphasized.

To explain his theory, Holland (1959) has classified all of the major kinds of American work environments. Concurrent with this, a given person has a set of adjustive orientations designated as motoric, intellectual, supportive, conforming, persuasive, and esthetic. Each orientation represents a life style characterized by preferred methods of dealing with daily problems. The person making a vocational choice in a sense "searches" for situations which satisfy his hierarchy of adjustive orientations. Within a given class of occupations, the level of choice is a function of intelligence and self-evaluation. "Essentially, the theory assumes that at the time of vocational choice the person is the product of the interaction of his particular heredity with a variety of cultural and personal forces including peers, parents, and significant adults, his social class, American culture, and physical environment." (p. 35)

The present paper has been concerned with the attempt to find some rational explanation for the process of choosing an occupation. Following the classification of Barry and Wolfe (1962), this author has summarized the main elements of three types of theories. Methodological theories are the simplest and most familiar and are characterized by the use of trait-and-factor methods. The second group, pattern theories, contains the modern attempt to establish generalizations about occupations and the people in them. The third group deals primarily with the reasons people work and what satisfaction means. Some are pioneeer attempts at theory building, while some borrow elements from other theories and incorporate them into new approaches. The value of all of these theories lies in their potential usuage for developing models to study the vocational behavior process.

Recent emphases on career development programs stimulated Borow (1960) to assess the various theories. Although each theory represents a slightly different approach, he summarized the distinguishing characteristics of all theories of vocational behavior into the following:

1. Emphasis is upon the generation of hypothetical constructs and the consequent use of explanatory principles and causal connections rather than exclusively upon the invention and use of intervening variables in the testing of response-response laws.

2. Current formulations in psychodynamics are invoked to account for vocational development and choice in terms of the subject's need structure.

3. Ego psychology (self theory) is employed both to specify an important source of knowledge about the subject's behavior and to hypothesize about the relations between his perceptions and his social choices . . .

4. Movement through major prevocational choices and subsequent vocational choices is postulated as a lawful, hence, hypothetically predictable process. The term *career pattern* has been invented to convey the notion of this orderly progression from position to position . . .

5. Vocational development theory emanates from general developmental theory and its derivable laws hold a formal relationship to those of general developmental theory . . .

6. Life-long vocation-related behaviors occur within an ordered sequence of life stages and are to be interpreted with references to the *vocational developmental tasks* which each successive life stage poses in the culture.

7. Childhood experiences contribute importantly to the differentiation of capacities and motives and, consequently, to the history of the individual's career development.

8. Longitudinal research design is generally preferable to cross-sectional research design since the evolution of adequate career development theory requires the continuous mapping of the linkage between antecedent conditions and consequent behavior. (pp. 63-64)

In the same article, Borow reviewed several empirical studies designed to test their respective theories. His conclusions reflect the complexity of the nature of vocational behavior. "That none of these (studies) generally affirms the claims of the particular theory under investigation speaks convincingly of the tenuous character of current theoretical formulations." (p. 63)

References

Barry, R. and Wolfe, B. EPITAPH FOR VOCATIONAL GUIDANCE. New York: Bureau of Publications, Teachers College, Columbia University, 1962.

Bordin, E. et al. "An Articulated Framework for Vocational Development." JOURNAL OF COUNSELING PSYCHOLOGY, 1963, 10, 107-117.

Borow, H. "Research Programs in Career Development." JOURNAL OF COUNSELING PSYCHOLOGY, 1960, 7, 62-69.

Crites, J. "Measurement of Vocational Maturity in Adolescense: 1. Attitude Test of the Vocational Development Inventory." PSYCHOLOGICAL MONOGRAPHS, 1965, 79 No. 1, 36p.

Dvorak, B. "The New USES General Aptitude Test Battery." OCCUPATIONS, 1947, 26, 42-44.

Dvorak, B. "The General Aptitude Test Battery." PERSONNEL AND GUIDANCE JOURNAL, 1956, 35, 145-152.

Fryer, D. "Occupational Intelligence Standards." SCHOOL AND SOCIETY, 1922, 16, 273-277.

Ginzberg, E. et al. OCCUPATIONAL CHOICE: AN APPROACH TO A GENERAL THEORY. New York: Columbia University Press, 1951.

Guilford, J. "Factor Analysis in a Test Development Program." PSYCHOLOGICAL REVIEW, 1948, 55, 79-94.

Harrell, T. and Harrell, M. "AGCT Scores for Civilian Occupations." EDUCATIONAL AND PSYCHOLOGICAL MEASUREMENT, 1945, 5, 229-239.

Holland, J. "A Theory of Vocational Choice." JOURNAL OF COUNSELING PSYCHOLOGY, 1959, 6, 35-44.

Holland, J. "Major Programs of Research on Vocational Behavior." In Henry Borow (Ed.), MAN IN A WORLD OF WORK. Boston, Mass.: Houghton Mifflin, 1964, 259-284.

Katz, M. DECISION AND VALUE. New York: College Entrance Examination Board, 1963.

Miller, D. and Form, W. INDUSTRIAL SOCIOLOGY. New York: Harper, 1951.

Parsons, F. CHOOSING A VOCATION. Boston: Houghton Mifflin Co., 1909.

Paterson, D. "Developments in Vocational Counseling Technique." In E. Williamson (Ed.), TRENDS IN STUDENT PERSONNEL WORK. Minneapolis: University of Minnesota Press, 1949, 80-96.

Paterson, D. and Darley, J. MEN, WOMEN, AND JOBS. Minneapolis: University of Minnesota Press, 1936.

Pepinsky, H. and Pepinsky, P. COUNSELING: THEORY AND PRACTICE. New York: Ronald Press, 1954.

Proctor, W. "Psychological Tests and Guidance of High School Pupils." JOURNAL OF EDUCATIONAL RESEARCH MONOGRAPHS, 1920, 1 No. 5.

Roe, A. THE PSYCHOLOGY OF OCCUPATIONS. New York: John Wiley & Sons, Inc., 1956.

Roe, A. "Early Determinants of Vocational Choice." JOURNAL OF COUNSELING PSYCHOLOGY, 1957, 4, 212-217.

Super, D. DYNAMICS OF VOCATIONAL ADJUSTMENT. New York: Harper, 1942.

Super, D. "A Theory of Vocational Development." AMERICAN PSYCHOLOGIST, 1953, 8, 185-190.

Super, D. "Career Patterns as a Basis for Vocational Counseling." JOURNAL OF COUNSELING PSYCHOLOGY, 1954, 1, 12-20.

Super, D. "Dimensions and Measurements of Vocational Maturity." TEACHERS COLLEGE RECORD, 1955, 57, 151-163.

Super, D. and Bachrach, P. SCIENTIFIC CAREERS AND VOCATIONAL DEVELOPMENT THEORY. New York: Bureau of Publications, Teachers College, Columbia University, 1957. (a).

Super, D. THE PSYCHOLOGY OF CAREERS. New York: Harper & Brothers, 1957. (b).

Super, D. et al. VOCATIONAL DEVELOPMENT: A FRAMEWORK FOR RESEARCH. New York: Bureau of Publications, Teachers College, Columbia University, 1957 (c).

Super, D. and Overstreet, P. THE VOCATIONAL MATURITY OF NINTH-GRADE BOYS. New York: Bureau of Publications, Teachers College. Columbia University, 1960.

Super, D. et al. CAREER DEVELOPMENT: SEIF-CONCEPT THEORY. Princeton, N. J.: College Entrance Examination Board, 1963.

Stead, W. and Shartle, C. OCCUPATIONAL COUNSELING TECHNIQUES. New York; American Book Co., 1940.

Stewart, N. "AGCT Scores of Army Personnel Grouped by Occupations." OCCUPATIONS, 1947, 26, 5-41.

Stuit, D. "Significant Trends in Aptitude Testing." In E. Williamson (Ed.), TRENDS IN STUDENT PERSONNEL WORK. Minneapolis: University of Minnesota Press, 1949, 62-79.

Thorndike, R. and Hagen, E. 10,000 CAREERS. New York: John Wiley & Sons, Inc., 1959.

Tiedeman, D. and O'Hara, R. "The Harvard Studies in Career Development: In Retrospect and in Prospect." HARVARD STUDIES IN CAREER DEVELOPMENT, No. 15A, August 1960.

Tiedeman, D. "Decision and Vocational Development: A Paradigm and Its Implications." PERSONNEL AND GUIDANCE JOURNAL, 1961, 40, 15-21.

Yerkes, R. (Ed.) "Psychological Examing in the U. S. Army." MEMOIRS OF THE NATIONAL ACADEMY OF SCIENCE, Washington: Government Printing Office, 1921, 15, 819-837.

Vocational Choice

DEVELOPMENT OF THE SELF-CONCEPT: A THEORETICAL FRAMEWORK AND SUGGESTIONS FOR CLASSROOM ACTION RESEARCH

by Frank C. Pratzner

It is becoming increasingly clear that one of the responsibilities of the educational researcher is to facilitate the process of educational change. In an attempt to meet this responsibility, the researcher presumably clarifies and investigates problems which have been identified as being of broad interest and of immediate or longer-range concern to the educational community. A second way by which the researcher can attempt to induce change and persuade adoption of the results of research into the school program is through dissemination of systematic, in-depth reviews of research on particular problems, or by in-depth reviews of literature relevant to particular topics (e.g., journal articles, textbooks, other publications).

This article, presenting a theoretical framework for self-concept development with related hypotheses and suggested procedures for investigating them, is intended to employ a third, interest arousing technique. It attempts to utilize less systematically reviewed data, or perhaps incomplete data, to arouse an interest in a particular topic and/or to entice educators, who are involved on a day-to-day basis in the school program, to become actively engaged in classroom action research. This latter technique may be helpful in the diffusion process and may, at the same time, suggest possible and immediate, first-hand approaches to persistent teacher questions (e.g., How to improve instructional methods? . . . What can be done to influence not only skill development or subject matter mastery, but to help development of the "whole" learner, for "life"?).

There is a vast literature available dealing with the self-concept in a variety of contexts which will not be reviewed here. Suffice it to say, that Blocher (1959) and Garrad (1968) are two of many authors who present exemplary reviews, and both authors include extensive bibliographies. Levenstein (1965) and Michael (1965), in separate discussions of technological and societal change, have more than adequately pointed out many problems resultant from this rapid change and have cited some of the educational implications of change (e.g., less meaningful and inherently less satisfying jobs, the need to specifically educate for empathy and rapport among people, the need for changing jobs several times in a life-time and the concomitant problems of adjusting the self-concept). It also seems increasingly more apparent that a learner's self-concept will be shaped in part by school experiences, regardless of whether the shaping is done consciously or unconsciously on the part of educators, and its development and maturation is typically interpreted to be one of the individual's goals of a formal education. The relationship among society, the school, and the individual self-concept might thus be depicted as follows.

FIGURE 1

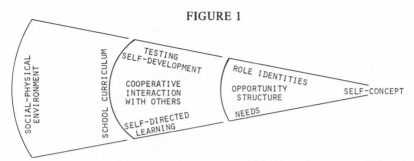

The figure is intended to summarize and show that, (a) the school curriculum has been singled out from among the many aspects of the social-physical environment, and (b) three functions of the curriculum have been identified which, it is felt, influence several characteristics of the individual, and thus self-concept. The self-concept, in this sense, is seen to be more the product of the social development of the individual than an innate attribute of personality. This view of the self-concept is analogous to the concept of "leadership" discussed by Hollander (1967) and Bavelas (1960) who point out that:

> . . . if any point stands forth in the modern day view of leadership it is that leaders are made by circumstances even though some come to those circumstances better equipped than others . . . the situational approach conceives of leadership in terms of function performed, rather than in terms of persisting traits of the leader (Hollander & Hunt, 1967, p. 486).

Both William James (1890) and G.H. Mead (1934) have contributed significantly to an understanding of self-concept and it is their thinking which has contributed substantially to the present behavioristic view. Mead considered the awareness of self as ". . . growing out of the observations which an individual makes of the reactions which others make to his personality" (Blocher, p. 9). In discussing Mead's theory of self, Blocher points out further that:

> The attitudes which others communicate to him, and the evaluations which they make, gradually become assimilated into the persons own perception of himself. The self is thus considered to be a purely social product arising out of communication between individuals. From this point of view the self could only arise in a social setting, and without social communication there could be no awareness of self (Blocher, 1959, p. 9).

This position would seem to be somewhat substantiated by the extensive studies of the development of the self-concept of the child, particularly by the work of Piaget and Horowitz.

In analyzing the self, Goffman (1959) asserts that the means for producing and maintaining selves do not reside inside the possessor. He claims that the self is a thing of "colloborative manufacture," and goes on to say that:

> There will be a team of persons whose activities on stage in conjunction with available props will constitute the scene from which the performed character's self will emerge, and another team, the audience, whose interpretive activity will be necessary for this emergence. The self is a product of all of these arrangements, and in all of its parts bears the marks of this genesis (in Hollander & Hunt, 1967, p. 327).

179

Dewey (1961) has repeatedly stressed that society exists through, and indeed in, communication. That is, common ideals, standards, and views originate in and are transmitted through participation in common channels of communication. He frequently and forcefully makes the point that group perspectives are internalized through social participation.

Each of these positions regarding the self-concept places emphasis upon the importance of the social "group." The particular group under consideration here is that of the school population, and more specifically, the classroom group. It is this group which will be referred to as the "reference group" and "interaction group." The former case denotes that it is one of the most important and influential groups for most children until the age of approximately eighteen years and it frequently serves as the point of reference in making comparisons or contrasts, especially in forming judgements about one's self. (It provides what B.F. Skinner and others have called a "reinforcing community."). The latter connotation emphasizes " . . . the reciprocal influence of individuals upon one another's actions when in one another's immediate physical presence" (Goffman, 1959, in Hollander & Hunt, 1967, p. 323).

An additional point about the reference group grows out of the extensive work of the Research Center for Group Dynamics which dates back to 1945.
. . . it is remarkable to what extent a strong, cohesive group can control aspects of a member's behavior traditionally thought to be expressive of enduring personality traits. Recognition of this fact rephrases the problem of how to change such behavior. It directs us to a study of the sources of the influence of the group on its members (Cartwright, 1951, in Hollander & Hunt, 1967, p. 523).

One of the several ways in which the industrial arts program attempts to foster the development of an increasingly more mature and accurate self-concept is through activities exploratory of the student's relation to work and leisure. The activities engaged in typically require use of the tools and processes of industrial occupations as facilitating teaching techniques. It has already been noted that the nature of work is rapidly changing and that as these changes continue to have an effect on the individual, his problems of developing an adjustable and mature self-concept become confounded. The industrial arts program in the high school might therefore profitably direct a part of its effort toward designing activities aimed primarily at self-concept development.

One of the principles which emerge regarding the self-concept and the impact of the group on its development might be phrased as follows: *The maturity of an individual's self-concept tends to vary directly with active participation in group interaction and communication relevant to one's self.* There are innumerable problems growing out of this principle (e.g., problems relevant to group dimensions and characteristics, problems related to individual differences within groups, etc.). Perhaps more important from a curriculum and teaching methodology point of view are the problems of defining and describing classroom group activities which are most likely to facilitate the development of a more mature self-concept. A specific researchable problem for classroom action research and several subsequent hypotheses are summarized in FIGURE 2. Each of the hypotheses is somewhat related to the others, in the sense that each specifies a measure of self-other agreement about one's self as the indicator of self-concept, and in that it would be possible to design one procedure which would attempt to investigate several of the hypotheses. The use of a measure of self-other agreement about one's self would seem to be an appropriate indicator of the self-concept because it most directly reflects what has already been discussed regarding the notion of self-concept more as a social group phenomenon than a personality trait. Newcomb (1956), in discussing the prediction of interpersonal attraction, refers to "attraction" as attitudes toward persons as a class of objects. The results of his research indicate that:

... attraction varies with perceived cognitive agreement about the self ... All persons, at all times, are liked according as they are judged to agree with one's self about one's self (in Hollander & Hunt, 1967, p. 300).

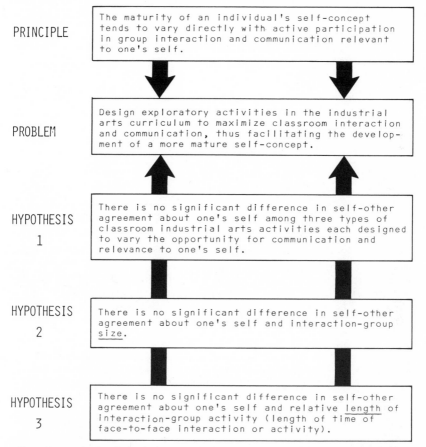

PRINCIPLE

The maturity of an individual's self-concept tends to vary directly with active participation in group interaction and communication relevant to one's self.

PROBLEM

Design exploratory activities in the industrial arts curriculum to maximize classroom interaction and communication, thus facilitating the development of a more mature self-concept.

HYPOTHESIS 1

There is no significant difference in self-other agreement about one's self among three types of classroom industrial arts activities each designed to vary the opportunity for communication and relevance to one's self.

HYPOTHESIS 2

There is no significant difference in self-other agreement about one's self and interaction-group size.

HYPOTHESIS 3

There is no significant difference in self-other agreement about one's self and relative length of interaction-group activity (length of time of face-to-face interaction or activity).

Based upon the forgoing, several possible measurement instruments of self-other agreement have been identified by the writer which could be used by the teacher alone, used concurrently as posttests, and/or used as pretests for assigning individuals to groups or verifying equality of randomly determined groups.

Harrison Gough Adjective Check List (1955)—cognitive similarity regarding self and other persons; subject describes himself, his ideal self and himself as he thinks others would describe him.

The Berger Scales (1952)—Likert type rating method on two scales on self-acceptance and acceptance of others.

Leary Interpersonal Check List (1957)—an inventory of 128 descriptive words and phrases; level of conscious description reflects how subject chooses to present himself and his views of the world; level of values-ego ideal or what he would like to be.

Kuder Preference Record, Form A - Personal (1953)—set of forced-choice items measuring preference among sociable, intellectual, etc. activities.

Edwards Personal Preference Schedule (1959)—paired comparisons yield scores on 15 needs as they relate to interest &/or occupational preference.

The first of the three hypotheses noted in FIGURE 2 will be discussed further to serve as an illustration. A procedure which would attempt to systematically explore this hypothesis should have the following considerations.

	Independent Variables		Dependent Variable
Groups	Relevance to self	Opportunity for communication	Self-other agreement
1	high	high	(high, medium or low self-
2	low	high	other agreement scores)
3	irrelevant	low	

Group 1—A treatment with high relevance to self and high opportunity for communication would consist of exploratory communication within the group centering on the role expectations, requirements, and interrelationships among *individuals* in various occupations. The emphasis here would be on what Samler (1961) has referred to as "The Psychological Man" and the group's interest would be directed toward:
> ... the worker's role, his ability to work at a task that is congruent with his identity, the exercise of his values and attitudes, consideration of status, ways of meeting anxiety, patterns of interaction with others, out-of-work style of life, and totally, the way in which his personality needs will be met (Samler, 1961, p. 459).

In addition, continuous encouragement by the teacher of active participation of all members of the group would help to maximize communication.

Group 2—A treatment with low relevance to self and high opportunity for communication would be designed to provide for exploratory communication within the group centering on the nature, economic requirements and societal needs for *occupations*. Here again Samler (1961) provides additional guides, which might be useful in determining appropriate interests, when he characterizes "The Economic Man" as being concerned with:
> ... economic considerations, wages, competitive conditions of training and education, duties performed in payment for wages received, lines of advancement, certification and union membership conditions, and so

182

on (Samler, 1961, p. 459).

Group 3—A treatment with both irrelevance of group activity to the self and low opportunity for communication could be considered a control group against which differences in the dependent variable can be guaged. The activity of this group could be the typical industrial arts shop activities: learners working on separate and individual shop projects with little need for, or encouragement of, group interaction and communication.

The three group activities have thus been determined so that they control for two selected independent variables. Differences in the two independent variables should be reflected in measures of self-other agreement. If the principle under investigation is an accurate statement, we would expect that Group 1 would score highest, relative to the other two groups, in terms of self-other agreement and in terms of having developed a more mature self-concept. If, in fact, this was the finding, it would have significant implications for the industrial arts program, some of which have previously been noted.

SUMMARY

It has been suggested that there are several alternative techniques for stimulating the diffusion and adoption of the findings of research and research-related experiences. The article has employed one technique in an attempt to draw out of prior research a framework for thinking about self-concept development and has suggested a method for operationalizing this theoretical framework. The method has been illustrated so that it can be readily applied by the teacher in an action research program. If utilized in a spirit of research and systematic inquiry, the suggested method should provide for a conscious effort on the part of the teacher to shape self-concept development in accord with experimental results.

SELECTED REFERENCES

Blocher, D.H. *A Study of the Relationship Between Self Descriptions and Stereotypes of Occupations With High and Low Claimed Interests.* Unpublished Doctoral Dissertation. Minneapolis: University of Minnesota, 1959, 94p.

Cartwright, D. "Achieving Change in People: Some Applications of Group Dynamics Theory," in Hollander, E.P. and Hunt, R.G. *Current Perspectives in Social Psychology.* New York: Oxford University Press, 1967, p. 520-29.

Dewey, J. *Democracy and Education.* New York: The Macmillan Company, 1961, 378p.

Garrard, J. *Development of the Self Concept of the Child.* Unpublished Course Paper. Minneapolis: University of Minnesota, 1968, 28p.

Goffman, E. "The Presentation of Self in Everyday Life," in Hollander, E.P. and Hunt, R.G. *Current Perspectives in Social Psychology.* New York: Oxford University Press, 1967, pp. 318-28.

Hollander, E.P. and Hunt, R.G. *Current Perspectives in Social Psychology.* New York: Oxford University Press, 1967, 685p.

James, W. *Psychology.* New York: Henry Holt, 1890.

Levenstein, A. "Work and Its Meaning in an Age of Affluence." Mimeographed Paper Delivered at a Vocational Guidance Association Conference at Airlie House, Warranton, Virginia, December 12-15, 1965, 7p.

McCall, G.J. and Simmons, J.L. *Identities and Interactions*. New York: The Free Press, 1966, 278p.

Mead, G.H. *Mind, Self and Society*. Chicago: University of Chicago Press, 1934.

Newcomb, T.M. "The Prediction of Interpersonal Attraction," in Hollander, E.P. and Hunt, R.G. *Current Perspectives in Social Psychology*. New York: Oxford University Press, 1967, pp. 292-304.

Michael, D.M. "The Plausible Future: Some Trends, Some Questions, and Some Answers," Mimeographed Copy of a Paper Delivered at a Vocational Guidance Association Conference at Airlie House, Warranton, Virginia, December 12-15, 1965, 12p.

Samler, J. "Psycho-Social Aspects of Work: A Critique of Occupational Information," *Personnel & Guidance Journal*, 34:458-65, February, 1961.

OBTAINING TEST INFORMATION
RELEVANT TO VOCATIONAL PROGRAM CHOICE[1]

by

Dale J. Prediger

Most vocational educators justifiably believe that a student's aptitudes and interests are among the characteristics relevant to his choice of a vocational program. However, counselors have very little information on this point that is directly relevant to vocational guidance. Almost all of the standardized tests used in vocational guidance were normed and validated with a different purpose in mind.

Some evidence of the relationship between ability measures and success in vocational programs has finally begun to accumulate. Reviews by Prediger, Waple, and Nusbaum (1968) and Stock and Pratzner (1969) have shown that: (a) success in vocational education programs is predictable to an extent that has practical significance; (b) the level of predictability depends upon the vocational area and the predictors that are used; and (c) the nature of effective predictors and the level of effectiveness vary widely from one vocational training setting to another. These reviews point to the need for determining the effectiveness of tests in the locale in which they are used. During the past five years The Penta-County Vocational High School has been engaged in such a study.

The primary focus of Penta-County's efforts has been to develop concrete test information that can be used by Penta-County District Counselors in helping students explore and select appropriate vocational education programs. By taking a close, statistical look at what happened to a large number of students who were tested prior to entry, Penta-County determined just what the tests can tell counselors about potential Penta-County students. In addition, test interpretation aids were developed to help counselors and students translate test scores into information directly related to choice of vocational program. This report presents examples of the interpretive aids along with a summary of counselor and student reactions to their use with more than 900 students in 12 high schools. Details have been discussed by Prediger (1971).

OVERVIEW OF SETTING AND ANALYSES

The Penta-County Vocational High School is an area vocational school serving 14 feeder high schools surrounding Toledo, Ohio. Penta-County offers

[1] The project described in this article was partially supported by a contract with the Office of Education, U.S. Department of Health, Education, and Welfare.

24 vocational programs, most of which are two-year programs open to high school juniors. Since early in 1966, scores on ten aptitude and ten interest measures were accumulated for each of approximately 1600 prospective Penta-County students. Included were eight scores from the General Aptitude Test Battery, the Mechanical Reasoning score from the Differential Aptitude Test Battery, grade-point-average earned in the freshman and sophomore years of high school, and the ten interest scores from the Kuder Preference Record-Vocational.

For each student who entered Penta-County, vocational program success (as measured by instructor grades) and satisfaction (as measured by a satisfaction inventory) were noted and a record was kept of whether or not the student persisted to the point of graduation. Data from post-program follow-up studies will also be analyzed when a sufficient amount has accumulated. Student progress records were then compared by means of statistical analyses, with the test scores obtained prior to entering Penta-County. For purposes of the analyses, the 24 vocational programs were organized into 12 areas: 4 enrolling primarily boys, 4 enrolling primarily girls, and 4 enrolling a substantial number of boys and girls.

The statistical analyses showed definite and useful relationships between the counseling measures and student progress at Penta-County. Two types of interpretation aids—similarity scores and experience tables—were developed to make practical use of these relationships.

SIMILARITY SCORES—AN EXPLORATORY TOOL

Similarity scores were used to show the similarity of a prospective Penta-County student's aptitudes and interests to the aptitudes and interests of successful and satisfied students in the various vocational program areas. For boys, similarity scores were developed for the eight areas appropriate to males. The eight programs appropriate to females were covered in the similarity score reports for girls. The most recent version of the score report form is presented in Figure 1. The similarity scores for Fred Cartesian, a fictitious, prospective Penta-County student, are shown on the ''computer-printed label'' near the center of the form. The vocational program areas are listed to the left of this label.

The report form describes the meaning and use of the similarity score in language the student can understand. In summary, the higher a student's score for a vocational area, the more similar he is to successful and satisfied students in that area. Similarity scores can range from zero to one hundred. Fred's highest score (87) is in area E, Vocational Horticulture. His next highest area is Carpentry (area A), and his third highest area is the Commercial Art, Printing, and Drafting area (area G). As instructed on the report form, Fred has ranked these areas from one to three and has placed a check mark beside area names on the list to the left of the label.

FIGURE 1

SIMILARITY SCORE REPORT FORM

EXPLORING PENTA-COUNTY VOCATIONAL PROGRAMS

If you are thinking about going to Penta-County, you probably face a difficult decision—the choice of which vocational program you wish to enter. This report won't tell you what to do. But it will provide some information that can help you explore what Penta-County has to offer. The vocational programs at Penta have been grouped into the 12 areas listed to the left of the box below. Your counselor will give you a label that fits over the box. This label contains scores giving a rough estimate of your *similarity* to students in the different programs. These "similarity scores" are based on aptitude and interest tests you have taken in the last year.

THE KEY POINT IS THIS: The higher your score for an area, the more *similar* you are to students in that vocational area. The highest score you can get is 100. The lowest score is zero. A zero score for area E would mean that your test scores do not look like the scores made by students in vocational horticulture. It's still O.K. to consider horticulture, however. Test results, after all, don't give the whole picture. You must consider them *along with all the other things* you know about yourself and Penta-County programs.

THE BEST WAY TO USE THIS REPORT is to find the vocational programs in which you score the highest. These are programs you might want to explore—find out more about. Perhaps you would not have thought of them otherwise. You certainly don't want to overlook a good possibility. There's too much at stake.

VOCATIONAL AREAS

Mostly boys enroll

√A. Carpentry
B. Auto & Ag. Mechanics, Machine Trades
C. Radio & TV, Electronics
D. Auto Body, Welding

Both boys & girls enroll

√E. Vocational Horticulture
F. Distributive Education
√G. Commercial Art, Printing, Drafting
H. Data Processing, Account Clerk

Mostly girls enroll

I. Child Care Aide or Ass't, Community & Home Service, Dietary Aide
J. Cosmetology, Dental Assistant
K. Co-op Office Education, Office Machines
L. High Skill Steno

SAMPLE LABEL

032154	FRED E CARTESIAN	10/14/69

Student Similarity Scores for P-C Voc. Programs

AREA=	A	B	C	D	E	F	G	H	I	J	K	L
SCORES=	41	14	03	26	87	25	28	01				
RANK=	2				1		3					
AREA=	A	B	C	D	E	F	G	H	I	J	K	L

PROFILE FACTOR SCORES: 56, 36

SO HOW DO YOU USE THE SCORES ON YOUR LABEL?

First, paste your label on the box shown above. Next, find and rank your top 3 or 4 scores. Give the highest score a rank of 1, etc., and write the ranks on the line below your scores. Finally, put a check mark beside the *names* of the 3 or 4 areas ranking the highest. These are the areas that your test results suggest you might want to find out more about. Some students receive low scores in all of the areas. This simply means that the test results aren't of much help in suggesting areas to explore. Whether your scores are "high" or "low," your counselor can help you figure out why they came out the way they did.

In order to judge *how successful* you might be in a program, you must also consider if you have the course work, aptitudes, and personal desire that is needed. This report does *not* tell you that. However, with the help of your counselor and your parents, you *can* use it along with other information as you explore the programs available at Penta-County.

TABLE 1

EXAMPLE OF EXPERIENCE TABLES FOR ESTIMATING STUDENT PERFORMANCE IN VOCATIONAL PROGRAMS

Prior grade average	Vocational grades at Penta-County			
	0.0-2.0	2.1-3.0	3.1-4.0	Number of students
Distributive Education Area				
2.0-4.0	36%	57%	7%	28
1.5-1.9	67	33	0	24
0.0-1.4	70	30	0	27
Data Processing and Account Clerk Area				
2.7-4.0	20	31	49	35
2.1-2.6	18	61	21	38
0.0-2.0	50	48	3	40

Note.—The distribution of vocational course grades for former Penta-County students is shown for each of three categories of prior grades. About one-third of the students fall in each of the three prior grade categories. On both grading scales, 2.0 = C.

The point emphasized in the report form is that a student's highest similarity scores indicate vocational programs which he might want to explore—find out more about—before making a definite choice. The function of similarity scores, then, is to widen the range of programs considered by the student and, at the same time, stay within the context of programs that appear to be appropriate to the student's aptitudes and interests. Program exploration at Penta-County was accomplished by a variety of procedures, e.g., leaflets, slides, a "Tour-Penta Day," and discussions with students already enrolled in various programs.

As noted on the bottom of the report form, similarity scores do not give estimates of how successful a student will be in a given vocational area. Being similar to successful and satisfied students in an area indicates reasonable chances for successful completion of the program. Actual level of performance, however, is not specified. EXPERIENCE TABLES WERE DEVELOPED to provide more precise information on level of performance.

PERFORMANCE ESTIMATES VIA EXPERIENCE TABLES

Table 1 provides examples of the experience tables used to obtain performance estimates. The experience tables shown for the Distributive Education area and the Data Processing and Account Clerk area were

188

developed by observing the vocational course grades earned by students having various grade averages prior to entering Penta-County. In each of the 12 areas, prior grade average was found to have a higher relationship with vocational area grade average than any of the aptitude measures. Thus, in Distributive Education, we see that 70 per cent of the students with a prior grade average between 0.0 and 1.4 obtained vocational course grades at Penta-County of 2.0 or less. No one in that prior grade category received a 3.1 or higher at Penta-County. Similar comparisons can be made for other categories of prior grades.

Experience tables were used by feeder school counselors to provide students with estimates of how they might perform in the various vocational areas. Once the grade average a student earned in his feeder school was calculated, the appropriate experience table categories could be consulted in order to see what happened to previous Penta-County students with similar grades. Because the experience tables provide a picture of the actual relationship between prior grades and vocational area grades, the degree of certainty (and uncertainty) in performance estimates obtained from the tables could be readily seen both by the counselors and the prospective Penta-County students.

Counselors were encouraged to use the performance estimates in conjunction with the similarity scores. A two-stage strategy was suggested with similarity scores being used to stimulate and facilitate vocational program exploration and success estimates being one of the many things to be considered during the process of exploration.

COUNSELOR AND STUDENT REACTION TO FIELD TESTS

Field trials of the interpretative aids involved approximately 900 students attending 12 of the 14 feeder high schools during the 1969-70 school year. Surveys of counselor and student reaction have been summarized by Prediger (1970). In general, counselors felt that the interpretative aids were much more useful than the usual score reports received for the tests. Student reaction to the similarity scores was particularly encouraging. Of the 154 students surveyed, 132 saw the similarity scores serving an exploratory or confirmatory role.

IMPLICATIONS

The procedures employed by Penta-County to provide feeder school counselors with useful test information have been described in detail elsewhere (Prediger, 1971). Through use of computer programs already in existence, it is possible for any educational unit having access to a computer to employ similar procedures. As a result, counselors and students would know much more about the relevance of aptitudes and interests to choice of vocational program.

189

REFERENCES

Prediger, D.J. Converting test data to counseling information: System trial—with feedback. *Journal of Educational Measurement,* 1971, 8, 161-169.

Prediger, D.J. Validation of counseling-selection data for vocational school students. Toledo: University of Toledo, 1970. (Grant No. OEG-3-6-551169-0379, Bureau of Research, USOE).

Prediger, D.J., Waple, C.C., &Nusbaum, G.R. Predictors of success in high school level vocational education programs: A review, 1954-67. *Personnel and Guidance Journal,* 1968, 47, 137-145.

Stock, W.E., &Pratzner, F.C. Review of research on student selection and the prediction of success in occupational education. Minneapolis: Minnesota Research Coordination Unit in Occupational Education, University of Minnesota, 1969.

THE ROLE OF THE SELF-CONCEPT IN DETERMINING AN ADOLESCENT'S OCCUPATIONAL CHOICE

by

Norman W. Sievert

Students in many of today's school systems are usually required during the second semester of ninth grade to choose a specific direction from among the academic, vocational, general or other curriculums. For those students who choose the vocational program, it means stating in order of preference three and sometimes four occupational choice areas in which they would like to study and later work. Prospective vocational students then discuss with the guidance counselor their interests, aptitudes, and the like in relation to their stated choices. Occupational areas in which they finally enroll usually are retained throughout the tenth, eleventh, and twelfth grade years.

The question that one could then ask is whether these students when making a choice to study a particular occupational area are in fact translating their concept of self into occupational terms. One may also ask what effect their self-occupational congruencies have on certain dependent variables such as shop achievement and sociability.

Although a few studies have been conducted on self-occupational perceptions, it has not been investigated to any great extent. The literature reviewed (Super, 1957; Englander, 1960; O'Hara, 1962; Combs 1962) seemed to suggest that future research emphasis should be in the direction of high school students, especially those enrolled in vocational-technical programs. Research in this area could also help vocational counselors and coordinators who are confronted with the arduous task of properly guiding students headed toward the vocational-technical program areas.

The present study investigated various relationships between the perceived self and the perceived occupational concept as inferred through self sorts by adolescents who have made an initial exploratory choice of a specific vocation in a vocational program. Specifically, the four questions answered in this study are the following:

1. What is the range of congruencies between the self-concept and occupational identity for a group of occupational students selected at random from each of three grade levels, ten through twelve?

2. What is the difference between the observed congruencies of youngsters in tenth, eleventh, and twelfth grades?

3. Within each of grades ten through twelve, do students' shop achievements increase as the congruence between their perceived self-concepts and their perceived occupational concepts increases?

191

4. As the congruence between students' perceived self-concepts and perceived occupational concepts increases, do students' social interactions with the group increase?

POPULATION

The population consisted of 516 subjects enrolled in nine occupational areas (auto mechanics, auto body, machine trades, basic electricity, basic electronics, mechanical drafting, sheet metal, welding, and printing) in the Altoona Area Vocational-Technical School, Altoona, Pennsylvania. This group included 190 tenth graders, 173 eleventh graders, and 153 twelfth graders. A random sample of 100 students with five replacements was drawn from each of the grade levels, or a combined total of 315 students was selected for the study. The stratified random sampling procedure (Cochran, 1957) was used to select the sample.

DESIGN

A Q-sort instrument consisting of 80 self-referent items was administered twice to each of the subjects involved in the study. It was first administered to the subject to determine his inferred self-concept, and second to determine his inferred occupational concept. Pearson product-moment correlations were then computed for the subjects' two sorts (self-concept and occupational concept) within each grade (10 through 12). A subject was classified as ''congruent'' if the correlation between his two sorts was above the median correlation for all subjects at his grade level.

Shop numerical grades for tenth graders and *Ohio Trade and Industrial Education Achievement Test Battery* (OTAT) score totals for eleventh and twelfth grade provided the basis for assessing students' shop achievement. Tenth grade shop grades and OTAT total scores were then transformed into a standard score distribution with a mean of 50 and a standard deviation of 10. An independent pooled t-test for equal N's was applied to the mean differences in shop achievement between congruent and non-congruent subjects for each of the grades. To justify the use of the independent t-test, the F-max was applied for testing homogeneity of variance.

A three-statement sociometric instrument generated for the study was administered to each of the subjects along with his peers in his own occupational area to determine his sociability within that group. Data thus obtained were translated into a sociometric matrix. A quantitative index of social attractiveness was obtained from the matrix. Quantitative indices for each occupational class were then also converted to standard scores with a mean of 50 and a standard deviation of 10. Independent pooled t-tests for equal N's were also applied to the mean differences in the sociability indices between congruent and non-congruent subjects for each of the three grades.

RESULTS

Correlation coefficients between the self-concept and occupational concept sorts for each of the 300 subjects ranged from −.30 to .99. Ranges of the correlation coefficient intervals for each of the grade levels were as follows: tenth grade − .20 to .89; eleventh grade −.30 to .99; and twelfth grade − .01 to .99.

Tests for the differences between each pair of mean correlation coefficients (converted to Fisher Z's) for grades ten through twelve were conducted. The z transformation test formed the basis for the statistical analysis between the correlcation coefficient means. Low and non-significant ($p > .05$) z values of .42, .59, and .17 respectively were found for each of the three comparisons (ten-eleven, ten-twelve, and eleven-twelve).

An independent pooled t-test for equal N's was employed to determine possible differences in sociability and shop achievement between congruent and non-congruent groups. The resultant t-ratios for the two criterion variables showed that shop achievement ($t = 4.44$, 2.73, and 3.42) and sociability ($t = 3.42$, 3.05, and 2.23) differed between the two groups ($p < .05$) for each of the grades ten through 12.

DISCUSSION

The first question asked what the range of the self-concept and occupational identity congruencies would be for a group of occupational students selected at random from each of three grade levels, ten through twelve. Results of the correlation coefficients presented in Table 1 show that a wide range of congruencies existed for each of the grades, ten through twelve. The range of the correlation coefficients was greatest for the eleventh grade subjects and least for the twelfth grade subjects. Since a previous pilot study indicated a test-retest stability of approximately .77 for the Q-sort instrument, the researcher assumed that the range of correlation coefficients though affected by some instability, was a good representation of the true range of correlations.

The substantial number of low correlation coefficients and negative ones indicates that some of the subjects had made an unrealistic occupational choice according to the self-concept proposition. Since 70 percent of the correlation coefficients, however, were different from zero ($r = .22$, $p < .05$), it would appear that the majority of the students were capable of expressing their self-concepts in occupational terms. The ability of the subjects to sort the self-referent items twice—first, in terms of their perceived self and second, their occupational concept—also indicates that adolescents seem to have some personal standards for the selection of an occupation in their early teens.

In terms of the self-concept proposition, the results indicated that many of the students were not perceiving themselves as being similar to their perceptions of the worker's role in their chosen occupational field. In fact, 30

TABLE 1

DISTRIBUTION OF CORRELATION COEFFICIENTS BETWEEN SELF-CONCEPTS AND OCCUPATIONAL CONCEPTS AT EACH OF THE GRADE LEVELS, TEN THROUGH TWELVE

Correlation Coefficient Intervals	Distribution (in %'s) by Grades		
	Tenth	Eleventh	Twelfth
—.30 - —.39	0	1	0
—.20 - —.29	3	0	0
—.10 - —.19	0	-	2
—.01 - —.09	4	3	2
.00 - .09	7	4	9
.10 - .19	14	9	8
.20 - .29	8	13	12
.30 - .39	16	14	13
.40 - .49	14	17	14
.50 - .59	16	16	12
.60 - .69	14	10	17
.70 - .79	3	4	10
.80 - .89	1	3	2
.90 - .99	0	3	1
Total	100	100	100
Mean	.385	.435	.455
Median	.394	.415	.449

percent of the subjects perceived no relationship between their perceived selves and their perceptions of a worker in their chosen occupation. Although the subjects were in the early stages of vocational development, one must conclude according to the self-concept proposition that subjects who demonstrated low positive or negative correlation coefficients were not making a realistic occupational choice.

This conclusion is supported further by self-concept theorists (Wylie, 1957; Wrenn, 1958) who state that an individual develops a more refined and clearly defined self-concept as he grows older. Super (1957) himself states that the process of career development is one of developing images of the world and then comparing these images to one's self-image in trying to make career decisions. Appropriateness of the occupational choice is then determined by the similarity between the individual's self-concept and the vocational concept of the chosen career. Therefore the data indicate that many of the subjects in the tenth, eleventh, and twelfth grades are now functioning in an occupational role that is not consistent with their perceived self-concept.

A vocational student encountering difficulties in attempting to translate his concept of self into occupational terms based on a particular choice may subsequently transfer to another vocational program. This type of change is

194

considered part of his normal development. When well-planned and based on previous experiences, this type of exploration—whether it be in the first vocational program area chosen or successive ones—helps the individual to formulate a realistic concept of the kind of person he is. It also aids in his identifying that type of occupation which will allow him to express his concept of self, and thus assume his desired occupational identity in the world of work.

The results also suggest that industrial coordinators, teachers, and the like when assisting students in stating an occupational preference or making an occupational choice should place more emphasis on the student's perception of the kind of person he is and type of vocational environment (vocational class) that would allow him to properly develop and translate his concept of self into occupational terms. Greater emphasis on the student's self perceptions should prevent the placement of students in vocational environments that are negative to them. High school students having limited experiences with the world of work may still develop negative attitudes toward a vocational area that was previously considered to be congruent with their self-concept. As stated earlier, a student with these self-occupational discrepancies (a common occurrence) should transfer to another vocational environment that is more consistent with his self-concept.

The role of the vocational program in terms of fostering self-occupational perceptions of students in the secondary school should be seen as an opportunity for the student to develop properly his self-concept as it relates to the world of work, to translate his self-concept into occupational terms, and to identify with the occupational area. Primary emphasis of the instructional program should be on the developing nature of the student and how his development relates to the occupational area. As the student builds his cognitive structure and resolves any incongruities that may have affected his identifying with the occupational area, a greater emphasis would gradually be placed on the development of skills and subject knowledge.

It is the responsibility of the teacher education institutions to develop courses that will enable teachers to identify students who are encountering difficulties in identifying with the occupational area. These courses must also allow teachers to teach the proper work role of a person in the occupation as part of the course content. The vocational teacher must also be familiar with the vocational behavior of students in the various stages of development.

Results for question two showed no significant difference in the mean correlation coefficient between the pairs of grades. This suggests that tenth grade students are just as apt to view themselves as similar or different from their perceived occupational roles as are senior students. According to the self-concept proposition, one would have thought that subjects with large discrepancies between the self-concept and occupational identity would have either changed their perceptions of self or perceptions of a worker in the occupational field, or would have transferred to another occupational program by their senior year. Since the data are cross-sectional and not longitudinal, no further inferences can be drawn at this time.

Results for question three indicated that the more congruent subjects generally attained a higher level of shop achievement than those who were less congruent. This was true for all three grades, ten through twelve.

The positive relationship found between the self-occupational congruencies and shop achievement indicated that shop instructors should observe and counsel students who are below average in achievement for their shop area. Through discussions with such students the instructor could ascertain whether it was a problem of a lack of ability or the inability of the student to identify with the occupational area. If the problem was identified as one of translating the self-concept into occupational terms for that particular occupational area alternative programs may be recommended to the student. An additional implication for the shop or laboratory instructor involves his attitudes toward low achievers. It appears to be equally plausible that low achievement is due to a student's inability to identify with the occupational field, than it is due to his inability to do the work required.

The finding that shop achievement is related to the degree of congruency between the self-concept and the occupational concept of the subject indicates that shop instructors must place additional emphasis on the appropriate work role of an individual in that occupational field. The vocational instructor must include as part of his course objectives the development of proper attitudes, values, and other traits of a person working in the occupational field. Until an individual identifies with the occupational area, he most likely will not understand the need for the learning of theory and skills that the shop instructor is attempting to teach, and therefore will attain a lower level of shop achievement.

Results obtained in answering question four provide some indication that a subject's social interaction while in the occupational class may be dependent upon the degree of congruency between his perceived self-concept and his perceived concept of his occupational field. Interpreted within this frame, it may be that a partial reason for a student's acting out against his environment in the school shop or laboratory is due to the placement and retention of the student in a setting that is not congruent with his perceived self-concept. Shop instructors should therefore adopt appropriate procedures for periodically evaluating student sociability in their classes to identify which students are liked or disliked by others, and which students participate in group activities, or not. It may be that such evidence may be utilized by the instructor to uncover possible student difficulties.

REFERENCES

Cochran, W.G. and Cox, G.M. *Experimental designs.* New York: John Wiley and Sons, 1957.

Combs, A. A perceptual view of the adequate personality. *Perceiving, behavior, becoming: A new focus for education.* Washington D.C.: Association for Supervision and Curriculum Development, National Education Association, 1962.

Englander, M.E. A psychological analysis of a vocational choice: Teaching. *Journal of Counseling Psychology,* 7 (1960) 257-264.

O'Hara, R.P. Vocational self-concepts and high school achievement. *Vocational Guidance Quarterly,* 16 (1966), 106-112.

Super, D.E., Crites, J.O., Hummel, R.C., Moser, H.P., Overstreet, PlL. And Warnath, C.F. *Vocational development: A framework for research.* New York: Bureau of Publications, Teachers College, Columbia University, 1957.

Wrenn, C.G. The self-concept in counseling. *Journal of Counseling Psychology,* 5 (1958), 104-109.

Wylie, R.C. *The self-concept.* Lincoln: University of Nebraska Press, 1961.

APPRAISING
THE APPRAISAL INSTRUMENTS

John O. Crites

THE APPRAISAL instruments which vocational counselors may use to assist students in their career decision-making encompass a variety of more or less objective techniques, ranging from interviews and oral trade questions to records of classroom and on-the-job achievement. But usually what is meant are standardized psychological tests.

More specifically, these tests would include measures of general intelligence, special aptitudes, vocational interests, and various aspects of personality functioning and structure.

In the discussion which follows, the development of some of the more common tests which have been constructed over the years will be presented first, in order to gain an historical perspective upon their value and usefulness. Then, some of the practical and theoretical shortcomings in traditional tests, in light of contemporary theories of vocational choice as a developmental process,

will be identified and enumerated.

Finally, some new appraisal instruments which are being constructed as part of the Vocational Development Project at the University of Iowa and are designed to measure the maturation of decision-making attitudes and competencies during late childhood, adolescence, and early adulthood, will be described.

Through such a consideration of both old and new assessment devices, implications may be drawn for their more effective application in vocational education by counselors and teachers alike.

Historical Review. When Frank Parsons, the acknowledged father of vocational guidance, wrote his handbook in 1909 on "Choosing a Vocation," there were no standardized tests, as we think of them today, to assist in the appraisal of an individual's career prospects.

It was not until the First World War that some real progress was made in what are known now as "group intelligence" tests. The *Army Alpha* and *Beta* tests, measures of verbal and nonverbal intelligence, respectively, were constructed by Yerkes and his co-workers and were administered to thousands of draftees. From the data gathered, the first analyses of differences between occupations in intelligence were made by Fryer and Sparling.

Soon afterwards, in 1927, Strong published the first edition of his *Vocational Interest Blank,* and the vocational testing movement was well on its way. Still, there were very few adequate measures of special aptitudes, although Parsons as well as others had long recognized their importance in vocational adjustment.

It was not until the establishment of the Minnesota Employment Stabilization Research Institute (MESRI) in 1931 that the first significant work was initiated on the assessment of special aptitudes. Under the direction of the Committee on Individual Diagnosis and Training, which included such pioneer vocational psychologists as Paterson, Darley, and Dvorak, such measures of special aptitudes as the *Minnesota Mechanical Assembly Test, Minnesota Rate of Manipulation Test,· Minnesota Spatial Relations Test, and Minnesota Clerical Test* were constructed and extensively studied.

It should be noted also that it was in the early 1930's that two personality tests, the *Bell Adjustment Inventory* and the *Bernreuter Personality Inventory*, which were to become well-known in the years to· follow, were first published.

Thus the First World War, the Aspirin Age of the 1920's, and the Great Depression marked the beginning of the development of general intelligence, special aptitude, vocational interest, and personality tests.

Factor Analysis Ushered In. The next stage in the vocational testing movement largely involved the activities of the Aviation Psychology Program of the Army Air Forces during the Second World War, although individual researchers such as Dvorak, were also making significant contributions.

The primary task with which such vocational psychologists as Flanagan, Super, and Thorndike were confronted was the selection of personnel for Air Cadet training and their classification as pilots, navigators, and bombardiers. Many tests of intelligence, special aptitudes, interests, and personality were devised and tried out, and eventually a battery of measures which had considerable predictive validity for success in training was developed.

Our interest is not so much in what these tests were, since the content of most of them is not appropriate for civilian counseling purposes. But we are interested in the implications of their construction for subsequent developments in testing.

The major impact of the Aviation Psychology Program was to emphasize the application of factor analysis as a method for not only identifying the relatively unique dimensions of ability, interest, and personality but also for isolating the basic components in criteria of performance. It was found, for example, that many special aptitudes, such as spatial perception and visualization, which vocational psychologists had previously assumed to be unitary abilities, could actually be broken down further into more basic factors.

Thus, we now distinguish among two-dimensional spatial relations perception, three-dimensional spatial visualization, horizontal and vertical spatial orientation; spatial aiming and positioning, and other spatial aptitude factors. Similarly, criteria of training and job success were factor analyzed into their component parts and "criteria" for criteria were established.

In short, it can be said that the Second World War ushered in the era of factor analysis in the construction and validation of tests.

Trends Traced. Today, our inheritance of tests from the past half century reflects many of these historical trends. First, most of the assessment devices, which we use in counseling are of the pencil-and-paper, group type, as were the Army intelligence tests of the First World War.

Second, we have tests which have been developed in accordance with both the so-called "empirical" approach, as exemplified by the *Strong Vocational Interest Blank*, and the "rational" approach, as illustrated by *the Kuder Preference Record—Vocational*.

Finally, we now have a host of aptitude, interest, and personality tests which have been developed through factor analytic procedures. Among these are several multi-factor aptitude batteries, such as the *General Aptitude Test Battery* of the U.S. Employment Service; a number of interest inventories, such as the *Guilford-Zimmerman Interest Inventory;* and, a few personality tests, such as the *Sixteen Personality Factor Questionnaire*.

In addition, current trends in test development have produced such instruments as the *Edwards Personal Preference Schedule*, which was designed to control the effects of social desirability upon item endorsement, and the *Minnesota Vocational Interest Inventory*, which, for the first time, provides measures of the preferences of nonprofessional workers.

Unlike Parsons, who had no tests with which to assess the vocational capabilities of his clients, present-day counselors are faced with the problem of which tests to use out of the multitude available. In Buros' compilation of *Tests in Print* (1961), he indexes over 2,100 which have been published, and undoubtedly more have appeared since his survey.

Shortcomings. When we ask which of these hundreds of tests should be used in counseling, we are usually posing the question: Which of these tests will best predict the future vocational adjustment of a client? By vocational adjustment we generally mean the client's success and satisfaction on the job after he has entered the world of work.

The sad but true conclusion which we must draw is that most of our assessment instruments have little or no predictive validity in forecasting these two major criteria of vocational adjustment.

Intelligence tests *do* differentiate between occupations at different levels of education, responsibility, and skill, as the data from both world wars indicate, but there is also a great deal of overlap between them, so that the brightest lumberjack is about as intelligent as an average accountant.

At best, there is only a low to moderate positive correlation between intelligence and success, and no correlation between intelligence and satisfaction. Vocational interest inventories have even lower correlations with success and satisfaction, although the latter criterion of vocational adjustment, in particular, should be predicted by them.

The highest correlations which Strong obtained, however, between his Blank and ratings of satisfaction were in the .20 to .30 range. He concluded that interest inventories predict occupational stability, i.e., staying in an occupation for a long period of time, but not occupational satisfaction.

Finally, the evidence on personality tests is even more negative. There are only scattered instances of either objective or projective personality measures being related to success and satisfaction.

Aside from the problem of how well tests can predict vocational adjustment, there is aonther shortcoming of our traditional assessment instruments which may be even more serious. These measures of ability, interest, and personality were developed within a conceptual framework which has come to be known as the "matching men and jobs" or "trait-and-factor" approach, which consists of three assumptions or principles: first, that by virtue of his unique psychological characteristics each worker is best fitted for a particular type of work; second, that groups of workers in different occupations have different psychological characteristics; and, third, vocational adjustment varies directly with the extent of agreement between worker characteristics and work demands.

Outmoded Concept. This way of conceptualizing vocational adjustment is basically sound as far as it goes, although the empirical evidence for differential patterns of occupational aptitudes, interests, and especially personality characteristics is often equivocal or lacking. What the "matching men and jobs" or "trait-and-factor" concept of vocational adjustment overlooks is the developmental nature of choosing, entering, and progressing in an occupation. Within the past decade and a half, vocational psychologists have become increasingly aware that vocational choice and adjustment are not just point-in-time events; they are processes which begin early and continue until late in life.

More and more we *talk* about the vocational maturity of our clients, whether they are fifth graders, high school seniors, or middle-aged workers. But, we cannot *measure* vocational maturity as yet, because our traditional assessment instruments are inappropriate. They are from another era—that of "matching men and jobs," not that of contemporary vocational development theory.

Wrong Use. It must not be concluded, however, that the tests which have been developed for so many years have no utility for counseling. They do, but it is of a different kind than we have usually assumed. A client generally comes for counseling not only to solve a problem, such as the choice of a vocation, but also to find out what kind of person he is—to understand himself better.

In fact, it can be argued that self-understanding, rather than specific decision making, may be the more important outcome of counseling, whether it is vocational or personal. For, if a client can know himself better—acquire a realistic picture of his assets and liabilities—he should be better prepared not only to solve his immediate problems, but also those he may encounter in the future, after he leaves counseling.

Our traditional tests can provide a client with the information he needs, if they are used for *description* rather than *prediction*. By description is meant the client's standing in the various norm groups for the tests he has taken. Thus, he may be above average in general intelligence; average in most special aptitudes, except for superior clerical speed and accuracy; interested primarily in Things rather than People; and, introverted in interpersonal relationships.

Once a description of a client has been made, it may then be possible to identify through analysis and inference the problems which he is experiencing or may experience as he develops vocationally. But our existing tests cannot give us an estimate of either a client's *degree* of vocational development—the vocational life stage he has reached; or his *rate* of vocational development— the extent to which he has matured vocationally relative to his peers. For this purpose new assessment instruments are needed.

New Instrument. To fill this need, at least in part, the *Vocational Development Inventory* (VDI) has been constructed at the University of Iowa as part of the Vocational Development Project sponsored by the U. S. Office of Education. The VDI consists of two parts, the Competence Test and the Attitude Scale, which are designed respectively to assess the aptitude and attitude dimensions of vocational development.

The Competence Test has five subtests, each comprised of 30 multiple-choice items with five foils. Part 1

is the "Problems" test and supposedly measures the ability to resolve conflicts between the factors in vocational choice. Part II is the "Planning" test, in which the task is to order the steps leading to a vocational goal in a logical or chronological sequence.

Part III is a test of occupational information covering knowledge of job duties and tasks, trends in the occupational distribution of workers, and employment opportunities for the future. Part IV is the "Self-Knowledge" test, scored against objective test information for accuracy of estimated aptitude, interest, personality, and social traits and characteristics. And, Part V is the "Goal Selection" test, the items of which require the examinee to choose the "best" (most realistic) occupation for the hypothetical individual who is described in terms of his aptitudes, interests, and personality characteristics.

The functions or processes which are supposedly involved in taking the Competence Test, then, are largely what might be designated as comprehension and problem-solving abilities, as they pertain to the process of vocational choice.

Combines Best Features. In contrast, the Attitude Scale is composed only of self-descriptive statements about an individual's vocational attitudes and behaviors. It was designed to elicit the dispositional response tendencies in vocational maturity which are nonintellective in nature, but which may mediate both choice behaviors and choice aptitudes.

The items for this scale were developed from a combination of the best features of the rational and empirical methods of test construction.

Ten to 20 items were written for each of the following dimensions of vocational maturity; involvement in the choice process, orientation to work, independence in decision-making, bases for choice (i.e., interests, capacities, and values), and conceptions of the choice process.

From this initial item pool, a scale was then constructed, each item of which was empirically related to age and grade between the upper elementary school years and the senior year of high school. Illustrative of the items which were finally included in the Attitude Scale are the following:

1. Once you make an occupational choice, you can't make another one.

2. Work is drudgery.

3. You get into an occupation mostly by chance.

4. I plan to follow the occupation my parents suggest.

5. I seldom think about the occupation I want to enter.

An examinee responds to 50 items like these by indicating whether he agrees or disagrees with them, and his vocational maturity score is the total number of responses he makes which are like those of 12th graders, the criterion group used in standardizing the scale.

Trial Period. Considerable research must be done before the VDI is ready for use in counseling, but a start has been made. Experimental forms of the Competence Test will be administered in the near future to 5th through 12th graders to determine which items differentiate among these educational levels. Also, the Attitude Scale will be administered for the eighth consecutive year next spring, and sufficient data will then be available to begin longitudinal analyses of its validity.

A large number of studies (over 100) of its reliability and relationships to other variables have already been completed, and the results have been encouraging.

A preliminary manual on the Attitude Scale to be published in early 1969 will report normative and research data from several independent projects, including investigations of specialty-oriented students in business, technical, and trade schools; evaluations of the effects of Neighborhood Youth Corps programs; prediction of college achievement; outcomes of secondary school guidance activities; and, correlations with intelligence, interests, personality characteristics, family background, school experiences, and vocational success and satisfaction.

Summary. To briefly summarize, the main point of this discussion of appraisal instruments for the vocational counselor has been that our traditional measures of aptitudes, interests, and personality are not sufficient, either practically or conceptually, to do the job that needs to be done in counseling. These tests may best be used for descriptive rather than predictive purposes, and they need to be supplemented with reliable and valid measures of vocational maturity.

MAIN QUESTION IS:
DID THE PROGRAM MAKE A DIFFERENCE?

A Systematic Approach to Statewide Evaluation of
Career Guidance, Counseling and Placement

FRANK E. WELLMAN & NORMAN C. GYSBERS

P ROCEDURES employed to evaluate career guidance, counseling
and placement have generally
resulted in positive indications, but
the results have been inconclusive in
answering the question: Did career
guidance, counseling and placement
programs make a difference?

Federal and state funding of those
programs have placed added respon-
siblity on the profession to demonstrate that the results of expending
the allocated funds are in line with
the purposes for which they were
appropriated. This is particularly true
at state and local levels.

This article will propose and discuss some aspects of a systematic
approach to monitoring the effectiveness of career guidance, counseling, and placement programs on a
statewide basis.

State-level evaluation should follow
a systematic pattern of (1) determining needs, (2) reporting resources,
and (3) assessing outcomes. The evaluative questions pertinent to these
three areas should provide the basis
for determining (1) the information
needed, and (2) the most feasible
sources and procedures for collecting
it.

State vocational advisory committees and program administrators
should formulate evaluative questions
regarding the most pressing career
guidance, counseling, and placement
concerns in their state and local programs. Most questions need to be
reduced to specifics that can be answered from available information on
state and local programs and from
students. Such information will be descriptive in nature, but will permit the

evaluators to relate bodies of descriptive data and thus to draw inferences pertinent to the basic questions asked, as well as the broader question of: What needs to be done?

Determining Needs. The social, economic, and educational needs upon which career guidance, counseling, and placement are predicated have been enumerated in the legislative history of the most recent vocational education and manpower acts. The existence of these needs in every state and local school system is assumed; however, each state should examine the nature and severity of needs which are indigenous.

Among examples of questions that may be suggestive for state-level examination of needs, along with possible sources of information, are these:

Question: Do youth stay in school to complete their educational preparation for work or further education?

Information Source: Statewide data on enrollments and completions of programs by grade level and type of program.

Question: Are there segments of the youth population that show high concentrations of unemployment or underemployment among students after they leave school?

Information Source: Statewide (or sample) follow-up data on students one, three, and five years after leaving school (differentiated by minority groups, urban-rural, dropouts, vocational programs, etc.).

Question: Do students, counselors, and teachers have an appropriate awareness and understanding of educational and occupational opportunities and the relationships between education and employment?

Information Source: Sample survey of relevant knowledge possessed by students and by those in a position to assist students in career development and decision-making.

State-level attempts to answer such questions will enable state advisory committees and program administrators to define career guidance, counseling, and placement needs more clearly and to implement program provisions designed to meet those needs. The information collected will provide baseline data for the assessment of the effectiveness of programs (vocational guidance, vocational education, and program innovations) in terms of change subsequent to implementation.

An adequate description of needs provides the point of reference for looking at programs and program-related resources that are available to serve students and those that are still needed.

Reporting Resources. Information describing certain aspects of career guidance, counseling, and placement resources is usually included in the annual reports of local school systems, and is available for evaluative purposes. All too often, however, such information is too general and lacks the comprehensiveness necessary to make evaluative judgments.

The description of career guidance, counseling, and placement resources should be comprehensive and extensive enough to answer the general question: "What changes need to be made?." Information for this type of program decision-making must be more than a quantitative enumeration; it must also include qualitative estimates.

State and local program deficiencies can be identified by evaluating the quantity and quality of available resources against criteria derived from professional standards and guidelines such as those provided in state plans, state accreditation standards, and legislative regulations.

One structure for determining the information needed to survey resources might include data on (1) program provisions, (2) program operation, and (3) program use and participant reaction. These three categories can serve to formulate correlated questions that should be answered in the process of describing resources.

Program Provisions. This category lends itself to the collection of objective information somewhat better than the other two categories. The information collected should provide a comprehensive account of the specific vocational guidance resources available (both in and out of school), including such items as personnel, materials, equipment, physical facilities, and budget.

This information serves three evaluative purposes: (1) to describe the status of provisions for career guidance, counseling, and placement in the state; (2) to identify variations in resources among schools in the state; and (3) to provide a basis for evaluating the effectiveness of different types of program provisions in achieving specified outcomes.

Examples of specific questions that should be answered from information collected in this category include:

Question: What are the numbers and qualifications of professional personnel specifically assigned responsibilities for career guidance, counseling, and placement activities at the various grade levels?

Information Source: Local school system—information collected from local schools, special surveys, or site visitations.

Question: What occupational information materials are available at the respective grade levels?

Information Source: Local school system—information reported for regular programs or for special projects, special surveys, or site visitations.

Question: What community resources are made available for career guidance, counseling, and placement activities?

Information Source: Surveys of community agencies, reports of special projects, or site visitations.

Program Operation. The concern here is how the program operates, who participates, and how various aspects and levels of the program are coordinated. Information in this category will indicate the major emphases and continuity of the program.

Examples of questions and sources of information are as follows:

Question: What are the assigned functions of the school counselors? What is the nature of counselor-student contacts?

Information Source: Local administrators, counselors, and students—special surveys, interviews, and specific daily-log studies of counselor activities.

Question: What activities are carried out to orient the student to the world of work? Group, individual, levels, resources used, etc.?

Information Source: Local school system—detailed program reports, special surveys, and site visitations.

Question: How are teachers, parents, community agencies, and business and industry involved in the career development activities of the school?

Information Source: Local community—school program reports; surveys of community agencies and leaders; interviews with students, counselors, teachers, parents, and others in the school and community.

Program Use and Participant Reaction. This category collects information on how students and others involved in the program use the resources offered and how they respond to the program as a whole. The information should give evidence of how well the program is accepted and provide estimates of its effectiveness from those it is intended to serve.

While variations among local programs make generalizations of such information difficult, the data can be helpful in identifying the types of programs and activities that are most highly valued by those who participate in them.

Examples of questions and sources of information follow:

Question: To what extent is the counseling service used by students seeking assistance in making vocational decisions?

Information Source: Counselors' records and surveys of students.

Question: How do students, counselors, teachers, and parents perceive the purposes and functions of the career guidance, counseling, and placement program in their school?

Information Source: Survey of samples of students, counselors, teachers, and parents.

Question: How do students evaluate the effectiveness of career guidance, counseling, and placement in helping them to make career decisions and manage placement procedures?

Information Source: Survey of samples of students who have received services from the program.

The resources information should meet the criteria of providing a comprehensive description of organized efforts to facilitate career guidance, counseling, and placement through the school. It should describe the process or the means used to achieve stated needs, goals, and objectives. It is a crucial part of the evaluation model in that it describes what was done, but it is insufficient to answer the most penetrating evaluation question: Did it make a difference in the career development of students? This question can be answered only by assessing outcomes and by being able to attribute the outcome to what was done in the program or process.

Thus two major types of evaluation emerge (1) process evaluation, or comparing what is provided with some set of professional standards; and (2) outcome evaluation, or determining whether the process contributed to the observed outcomes.

Assessing Outcomes. Evaluation based on outcomes is the only approach that can provide answers to the question: Did career guidance, counseling, and placement make a difference in the career development of those the program served?

Evidence from evaluation studies indicates that the extent to which desired outcomes are achieved varies among students and situations. Students with different characteristics respond differently to career guidance, counseling, and placement activities. The situation in which students function and in which these activities are carried out seems also to be associated with variations in outcomes.

A definitive assessment of outcomes must therefore attempt to answer the question: What kind of guidance activities produce specified outcomes with a particular type of student in a given situation?

Many of the differentiations in programs and situations can be determined from information collected to describe program provisions and program operations; and the school often has the information needed to differentiate students by such characteristics as ability, interests, socioeconomic status, handicaps, and ethnic groups.

The specification of outcomes to be assessed (outcome criteria) is one of the most difficult and important steps in evaluation procedures. The needs that career guidance, counseling, and placement programs are designed to meet serve as the point of departure for the stating of goals, objectives, and outcomes.

Goals usually are stated in global terms with one or more objectives stated in specific terms so that the objectives serve as an operational definition of the goal. Each objective should have one or more specified outcomes so that its achievement can be determined from an assessment of the outcome or outcomes.

Outcomes must therefore be stated in terms (usually behavioral) that will permit the measurement (or observation and reporting) of specific student knowledge, skills, performance, or attitudes.

The individual nature of good outcome data and the collection methods used limit the number of students and programs about which such information can be gathered. Samples of students in particular types of programs and in delineated situations can however provide sufficient data for state-level evaluation and subsequent program decisions.

Career development theory and research can provide the basis for the specification of behavioral objectives and outcomes at various age and grade levels. (Other social, educational, and psychological bases may also be used as a point of departure.) The following examples illustrate the stating of objectives and outcomes at different levels of career development.

MIDDLE CHILDHOOD (Grades K-3)
Objective: To be aware of jobs and differentiating characteristics of jobs.
Outcome: Ability to tell something about the jobs of parents and about ten different occupations in the immediate community.

LATE CHILDHOOD (Grades 4-6)
Objective: To understand the concept of job families.
Outcome: Ability to list at least one classification system for job families.

EARLY ADOLESCENCE (Grades 7-9)
Objective: To differentiate educational opportunities and related vocational preparation available in the community.
Outcome: Ability to give a general description of the major curricular programs and to indicate at least one occupational area related to each program.

ADOLESCENCE (Grades 10-12)
Objective: To learn the fundamental knowledge and skills of applying for a job.
Outcome: Ability to demonstrate (1) appropriate grooming to apply for a specified job; (2) satisfactory completion of a job application form; and (3) appropriate job interview behavior in a simulated situation.

There are a variety of designs for outcome evaluation. Most, however, draw conclusions or inferences from analyses of (1) comparisons among groups, (2) changes within groups, or (3) comparison of outcomes with a predetermined standard. The design used should fit the kinds of evaluation answers sought and the student and situational variables to be analyzed.

Baseline Comparison Group. This evaluation procedure uses measures of the outcomes for a comparable group of students prior to the initiation of the activities being evaluated. For example, the 1969-70 ninth grade students in X high school might serve as a comparison group for the 1970-71 ninth grade students in the same school. If career guidance, counseling and placement activities were introduced in 1970-71 for the purpose of reducing dropouts, the dropout incidence of the 1969-70 group would provide a bench mark from which to estimate the effectiveness of the processes being evaluated.

This design is open to serious question if (1) other program changes such as curricular modification were introduced for the 1970-71 group, or (2) the two groups differed in personal characteristics which might induce dropout tendencies, such as level of mental ability.

It has the advantage, however, of permitting the introduction of new program activities for all students in a specified service group without requiring the denial of services to a concurrent control group.

Within Group Design. This procedure focuses on behavioral changes or behavioral manifestations over time, or at a given point in time, from which inferences can be made about the effect of the guidance process. The two types of analyses most applicable are (1) changes in behavior as a function of career guidance, counseling, and placement activities introduced between pre- and post-tests of the criterion behaviors; and (2) comparisons of post-process student behaviors with a predetermined behavioral goal or "hit rate."

The second of these analyses permits the evaluator to establish the kind, level, or frequency of behavior expected and then compare the outcome with the expectancy. For example, the expected behavioral goal for a group of third-grade pupils might be that 75 percent will be able to name ten occupations that serve people. This expectation serves as a "hit rate" standard for the evaluation of

actual behavioral outcomes.

This design has the advantage of providing new input for the modification of goals and objectives as the result of experience gained. In a sense it provides reality testing of guidance objectives.

On the other hand, it has limitations with respect to the kinds of conclusions that can be defended from the evidence produced. For example, in the absence of other controls, it is not possible to conclude that the guidance activities caused the observed outcomes. Maturation, other classroom activities, community experiences, or a host of other factors may have influenced the outcomes. With this type of design, we can't know.

Experimental Design. Properly planned and executed, this design can provide the best evidence of a cause-and-effect relationship between guidance processes and observed outcomes. The experimental design ordinarily permits the evaluator to compare the behavioral outcomes of a group subjected to guidance activities with one or more control groups that have the same basic characteristics and who have had the same opportunities for other learning experiences.

Matching or random assignment to groups is essential to this design. The added work required will be rewarded by the confidence that can be placed in the results.

Any of the three suggested designs, or combinations of them, can be used for outcome evaluation. They will all permit the investigation of student and situational sub-sets and the interactions of these categories of variables. Where possible, however, the experimental design is recommended. The issue of temporarily denying

209

services to a control group is greatly diminished when weighed against the possible future benefits to many students and to the profession. ∎

Occupational Information

Should we teach career information?

David C. Bjorkquist and H.C. Kazanas

On the assumption that individuals will not select careers about which they are uninformed or toward which they have an avoidance attitude, a presentation to describe careers in industrial education teaching was developed with the intent of attracting potential teachers to this field. This was not an attempt at "hard sell" but was designed to be informative and factual.

The present study was concerned with the effectiveness of information about careers in industrial education teaching in increasing knowledge and changing attitudes about those careers. These measures were compromises in assessing the influences of the occupational information on career choices, but they were estimates of the students' receptivity to the information. To the extent that the originally-stated assumption of this article is true, these measures provided an assessment of the effectiveness of the occupational information.

Entrants into an occupational field could be increased efficiently if characteristics of those likely to be receptive to the occupational information were known. Philippus and Fliegler (1962) suggested, ". . . it would appear that an informative study concerned with personality, values and interest patterns would be revealing, attempting to determine the types of individuals entering the teaching field". [p. 247]

The findings of Carruthers (1968), in which university students within different curricula and with different occupational objectives were shown to have different value hierarchies, further encouraged the exploration of the relationship of students' values to their receptivity of occupational information.

Therefore, the purpose of the study was to measure the effectiveness of a 15-minute tape-narrated slide presentation, about careers in industrial education teaching on students with differing values, as measured by the *Scale of Interpersonal Values* (1963).

Method. The 15-minute tape-narrated slide presentation about industrial education teaching was prepared by graduate students enrolled in a seminar in industrial education at the University of Missouri-Columbia. A set of objectives and an outline of the topics to be covered were developed and evaluated by the group prior to writing of the script. Photographic slides were made to accompany the script.

Senior high schools to participate in the study were selected from an 18-county area in central Missouri. This area included St. Louis and Kansas City and the more rural area between. All schools were rated AAA by the Missouri State Department of Education. A random sample of 12 schools was selected after which the remaining schools were placed in random sequence as alternates.

It was assumed that to become an industrial education teacher, the student must first attend college. For this reason the industrial education teaching information was presented to college preparatory students. Through contacts with school administrators, arrangements were made to present the slide-tape program to two classes in each school. The classes were identified by the administrator according to the requirements of the study, and the experimental or control treatments were randomly assigned to the intact classes.

The experimental treatment was conducted by graduate students in industrial education. Following an introduction to the class, the slide-tape presentation was made. Immediately after, each student completed a 33-item five-point Likert-type attitude scale. The scale was designed to measure attitude toward industrial education teaching as a career and was developed by the graduate seminar group. Each item on the scale was scored on a five-to-one basis, with five representing a most positive attitude. Items included in the scale were selected on the basis of a pilot study.

A 30-item true-false test of knowledge about industrial education teaching and the program of teacher preparation followed the attitude scale. The true-false test was also developed by the students in the graduate seminar and consisted of items selected by means of pilot study. Each correct item in the test was scored one, with incorrect items scored zero.

After the attitude and knowledge measures, Gordon's *Survey of Interpersonal Values* (SIV) was completed by the students. The SIV contains six scales: 1) Support; 2) Conformity; 3) Recognition; 4) Independence; 5) Benevolence and 6) Leadership. Each of these scales was used to separate the respondents into high and low scoring groups for the purpose of analyzing scores on the attitude and knowledge measures.

Attitude scores were compared in six two-way analyses of variance. The effect of the treatment on attitude scores and the relationship between high and low value scores for each of the six SIV scales were tested. A similar procedure was used for the knowledge scores in testing the effects of the treatments and the relationship of value scores to knowlege scores.

Findings and conclusions. There was significant difference in attitude scores dependent on the treatment. Students in the experimental group had a mean attitude score of 123.4, while those in the control group had a mean score of 117.2. A total attitude score of 165 was possible.

Attitude scores also varied significantly between students with high and low values as measured by three of the six SIV scales. In the cases of .the Support and Independence scales, low-scoring students had significantly higher attitude scores than their high-value-scoring counterparts. Students with high Conformity scores had significantly higher attitude scores than did those with low Conformity scores.

Scores representing knowledge about careers in industrial education teaching were significantly affected by the experimental treatment. Students who were exposed to the slide-tape presentation (Experimental Group) had a mean score of 28.5, while those in the control group had a mean score of 25.6. It was possible to score a total of 30 on the knowledge test.

In no case was there a significant relationship between knowledge test scores and scores on one of the six SIV scales.

Although the tape-narrated slide presentation about careers in industrial education teaching was only 15 minutes, it did have an effect on the attitude and knowledge of high school students about those careers, according to the criterion measures. In actual point separation, the difference in attitude scores between experimental and control groups was 6.2. The knowledge point total for the experimental group was 2.9 higher than for the control group.

Analysis of individual items on the attitude scale indicated the items most likely to distinguish between experimental and control groups were:

1. The salary for industrial education teachers is too low for my standard of living. (negative item)

2. Student teaching has little value for the prospective industrial education teacher. (negative item)

3. Industrial education teachers should require less formal education than other teachers. (negative item)

4. Numerous vacations make industrial education teaching an attractive career. (positive item)

5. I feel that techniques in industrial education courses do not parallel the techniques of industry. (negative item)

6. Working conditions for industrial education teachers are generally very undesirable. (negative item)

Students in the experimental group had more negative attitudes toward the negative items and more positive attitudes toward the positive items than did students in the control group.

The six most discriminating attitude items represented four general facets of the field of industrial education teaching. One item (1) was concerned with teachers' salaries, two items (2 and 3) were about the preparation of the industrial education teacher, two items (4 and 6) dealt with the conditions of employment, and one item (5) had to do with the curriculum. The tape-narrated slide presentation influenced a variety of attitudes about industrial education teaching.

The knowledge items most likely to distinguish between experimental and control groups were:

1. The shortage of industrial education teachers is due to poor pay. (false)

2. A look at teachers' salaries over the last 10 years indicates that little change has actually occurred. (false)

3. The Industrial Education Department of the University of Missouri-Columbia lacks modern laboratories. (false)

4. Salaries for industrial education teachers are lower than for teachers of other subjects. (false)

In each case, students in the experimental group more frequently answered these items correctly than did students in the control group.

In contrast with the variety of the most discriminating attitude items, three of the four most discriminating knowledge items (1,2 and 4) had to do with salaries. The other knowledge item which was most likely to distinguish between experimental and control groups was about the teacher education facilities.

The relationships between attitude scores and measured values suggest that students who value support and independence less and conformity more have more favorable attitudes toward industrial education teaching. It may be that students with this value pattern tend to have more favorable attitudes as measured on other attitude scales as well. However, Clark (1968) did not find significant relationships between SIV value scores and Minnesota Teacher Attitude Inventory scores for college freshmen and seniors in teacher education.

According to Gordon's (1960) definitions, students whose attitudes are changed by a presentation about careers in industrial education teaching are more likely to have certain values. These students place less value on "being treated with understanding, receiving encouragement from other people, being treated with kindness and consideration", and "having the right to do whatever one wants to do, being free to make one's own decisions, being able to do things in one's own way." "Doing what is socially correct, following regulations closely, doing what is accepted and proper, being a conformist", (Gordon, 1969, p. 3) is more valued by those with more favorable attitudes toward industrial education teaching.

Implications. The conclusions of this study suggest that information about industrial education careers can be broadly influenced by a tape-narrated slide presentation. At the same time, there is a misunderstanding about the salaries of industrial education teachers. It would be of interest to learn the degree to which attitudes are influenced by the understanding of salaries.

The 15-minute tape-narrated slide presentation had an immediate effect on attitudes and knowledge. Further research should be conducted to test the durability of those attitudes and knowledge and their relationship to career choices.

Students with certain values developed more favorable attitudes toward industrial education teaching than did others. This suggests that efforts to recruit prospective teachers could be more efficient if directed toward those individuals. It also suggests that teacher educators should examine the values of their incoming students and judge whether these are compatible with the philosophy of their programs and the characteristics desired in teachers entering the field. It may be incumbent on industrial teacher educators to make deliberate efforts to influence the values of those they prepare to teach.

References

Philippus, M. S̆., and L. Fliegler. "Study of personality, value and interest patterns of student teachers in the areas of elementary, secondary and special education." *Science Education,* 1962, 46 (3), 247-252.

Carruthers, T. E. "Work values and chosen careers: Note on a trial of an American work value inventory with British subjects." *Occupational Psychology,* 1968, 42 (2-3), 111-117.

Clark, W. B. *An empirical study of attitudes toward teaching selected values, and demographic information of freshmen and seniors.* (Doctoral dissertation, Auburn University) Ann Arbor, Mich.: University Microfilms, 1968, No. 68-5900.

Gordon, L. V. *Manual for survey of interpersonal values.* Chicago: Science Research Associates, Inc., 1960.

A Five-Year Study of Students' Educational Aspirations

WARREN D. GRIBBONS AND PAUL R. LOHNES

■ Data analyzed in this paper were collected in a longitudinal study of career development of a group of boys and girls covering the period from early eighth grade to late twelfth grade. The purpose of this analysis was to examine the relationship between educational aspirations and personal-social variables. Educational aspirations are among the most vital aspects of early career development because curriculum choices prefigure a youngster's vocational future to a considerable degree.

The data reported here are only a small part of the data collected and reported covering the eighth to twelfth grades. Other aspects of the longitudinal study data have been reported in Gribbons [2] and Gribbons and Lohnes [3, 4, 5, 6, 7].

This paper examines the relationship between educational aspirations and the following variables:

1. Type of curriculum
2. Intelligence
3. Socio-economic level
4. Mother's and father's attained education

Methodology

Three personal interviews in the eighth, tenth, and twelfth grades were conducted with each of the 110[*] students (56 boys and 54 girls) from five communities in the metropolitan Boston area. Eighth-grade Otis I.Q. scores were obtained for all subjects.

Findings

Curriculum

In the eighth grade more students (58 per cent) expressed a desire to go to college than were likely to enter and remain in college. The percentage

This research was supported through the Cooperative Research Program of the Office of Education, U. S. Department of Health, Education and Welfare.

[*] One student dropped out of school and, although he is still in the sample, is not included in this analysis because most questions in the interview were not appropriate in his case.

218

of boys outnumbered the percentage of girls (75 per cent to 41 per cent). There was a definite downward trend for the total group over the high school years, indicating that perhaps social forces and reality were beginning to take effect. By the twelfth grade, for example, eleven boys and seven girls changed their aspirations to a level below a four year college.

In the eighth grade, 37 of the 38 boys planning to enroll in the college preparatory curriculum aspired to college while only one boy in the other curricula aspired to college. At the same time, 19 of 32 girls in the college preparatory curriculum planned to attend.

A steady decrease in college attendance aspirations for the college preparatory group was noted and by the twelfth grade the total number desiring to go to college was 40 of 46 (26 boys and 14 girls). Students in the business curriculum for the most part were not aspiring to college; only two of 25 in the eighth grade and two of 34 in the twelfth grade had college aspirations.

Although the N is extremely small, the IA group showed a sharp increase in college aspiration over the high school years—from none of seven in the eighth grade to four of sixteen in the twelfth grade.

Intelligence and educational aspirations

When the relationship between I.Q. and level of aspiration was studied over the five year period, it was noted that both sexes in the 121 I.Q. plus group were very consistent (thirteen of eighteen in the eighth grade and fourteen of eighteen in the twelfth grade) in aspiring to college, with no difference between number from each sex in the twelfth grade. The 111–120 I.Q. group decreased in number aspiring to college (sixteen of twenty-two in the eighth, to nine of twenty-two in the twelfth grade) over the high school years. Again there was practically no difference to be found

between the sexes. In the 106–110 I.-Q. group however, the *total* decrease (from eighth to twelfth grade) was four boys and one girl. The 101–105 group showed little fluctuation throughout, but the boys once again accounted for most of the decrease. In the 100 and below I.Q. group, it was interesting to note that the number aspiring to college decreased from a total of twelve to a total of seven, but in this case it was the girls who lowered their level of aspiration. It should be noted that even as late as spring of the twelfth grade, six of twelve boys in the 100 and below I.Q. group still desired college educations.

Data obtained from the guidance counselors in their respective schools indicated that fourteen in the 121 plus I.Q. group (evenly divided between sexes) who aspired to college at the twelfth grade applied and were admitted to four year colleges. In the 111–120 I.Q. group, seven of nine (four girls and three boys) were accepted. Of the remaining two who were not accepted (both girls), one is in high school, and one has been accepted at a junior college. Thus, of the total group of twenty-three with I.Q.'s of 111 plus, all but two were accepted and not one boy who aspired to this level failed to make it!

In what might be called, from a prediction standpoint, a "borderline" I.Q. group, (106–110), it is noteworthy that three boys were accepted by colleges and five students were not (two boys and three girls). Of these five who were not accepted by any college, one is going to a school of dental hygiene and one will attend a prep school.

The 101–105 group has one boy (I.Q. 102) accepted to college and seven boys and girls who have not been accepted. In the 100 I.Q. and below group, one boy and one girl were accepted and five boys were not. Of these five students, one is going to prep school, and two have been accepted at two year technical institutes.

It was also interesting that the average I.Q. for college aspirations was 111; those who aspired to three years of training, 107.6; two year institutes, 107.7; one year, 105; and those having no plans for further education, 104.

Socio-economic level and aspirations

Socio-economic status, rated by Hamburger's revision of Warner's scale, indicates that all major occupational groups were included among the parents of students in the sample, and there was a tendency for the occupations to fall at the middle of the scale.

Seventy-nine per cent (nineteen of twenty-four) of the boys and girls in classes one and two (indicating high socio-economic level) planned to go to college with only a slight decrease in the number (nineteen to eighteen) over the five year period. Levels 3 and 4 which are closer to what Warner called middle class, with nine students lowering their aspirations, showed a decrease from sixty-six per cent to forty-six per cent planning college. It is interesting that in the eighth grade, of the nine students in level 3 aspiring to college, six were girls (same ratio holds in the twelfth grade, two boys to four girls) while in the eighth grade, level 4 had sixteen boys of twenty looking forward to college with five of eleven girls in this level aspiring to college. Level 5 was fairly consistent throughout the study. The smallest percentage of any group aspiring to college came from level 6, with only six of nineteen thinking about college in the eighth grade and decreasing to three of nineteen in the tenth and twelfth grades. One of the two students (a girl) in level 7 aspired to college in the tenth grade, but lowered her aspirations when interviewed in the twelfth grade.

Father's and Mother's educational level

Only one eighth grade boy and five eighth grade girls aspired to educational levels below that of their fathers. The number in the "below" categories increased by one in the tenth grade and by four in the twelfth grade. The general tendency for educational aspirations equal to or higher than parents is also quite prominent when mothers' educational level is examined (N equals 4, 3, and 8 aspiring to lower levels at eighth, tenth, and twelfth grades).

The category "same level" has about the same N for father's and mother's educational level throughout the high school years. In large part this is accounted for by the fact that most of the fathers and mothers in the "same level" category have at least a college education. The sons and daughters are aspiring to the same level, so that this category leaves little room for a higher level of aspiration for many students. For example, in the eighth and tenth grades, nine of eleven fathers of boys in the "same level" categories had a college education and this number decreased to eight in the twelfth grade. The same trend holds for the boys whose mothers had a college education (eight of ten in the eighth and tenth grade, and seven in the twelfth grade).

Discussion

It is quite clear that if a student wants to go to college he must either be forced to think about the possibility by his parents or some other agent of society (e.g., counselors), decide by himself, or haphazardly drift into it by choosing the "correct curriculum." With seventy of 110 (63 per cent) planning to enter the college curriculum and with sixty-four of 110 (58 per cent) indicating a preference for college (in the eighth grade), it appears that societal forces are operating on these students early in their career development.

The verbalized expression of a desire for a college education is, as expected, stronger with boys than with girls. That some of these youngsters were behaving in fantasy fashion in the eighth grade was indicated by the decrease in the number of college aspirers over the five year period. One can assume that, at least in some cases, forces in the student's environment have resulted in a more realistic self-appraisal, or appraisal of the difficulties facing him if he continued to think of going to college.

It is encouraging to note that most of the college preparatory students were planning to go to college, and that few students in other curricula were planning a college education. It matters little, from a career development point of view, whether these plans were fulfilled. The important thing is, as Tiedeman [10] suggests, that these youngsters, in choosing the college preparatory course, were keeping the door open and thus, were operating with some flexibility.

A certain amount of realism of aspiration is also noted when intelligence and level of aspiration were examined. In the eighth grade almost all of the students with an I.Q. of 111 plus were thinking of going to college. Again, concerning the process of career development, of importance is that boys and girls with college potential were considering college as a possibility. It is also apparent, however, that some youngsters are not acting in what an outside observer would consider a realistic manner. For example, as late as the spring of the twelfth grade, fifteen students with I.Q.'s of 105 and below were still aspiring to college. It is true that three of these students were accepted. That still leaves twelve students, however, who are going to have to change their level of aspirations. This is especially apparent in the 100 I.Q. group and below where there are still six boys expressing a desire to enter college. That these results are indicative of a national problem may be seen in the recent conclusion of the Project TALENT staff, arrived at from a study of 440,000 youth in a national sample, that "We may tentative-

ly conclude that students at the lowest aptitude levels expect more education and think that their parents want them to have more education than is realistically possible or even beneficial to them " [1].

The analysis of socio-economic level shows, as might be expected, that those in the higher levels are aspiring to college while those in the lower socio-economic group do not, in general, think in these terms. Most of the students aspired to the same level or a level above their parents, indicating some evidence for upward socio-economic mobility through education.

This group, for the most part, was behaving in a realistic way with regard to educational aspirations, or showed a trend in that direction as they progressed through high school. This trend may indicate some empirical evidence to support Super's statement that occupational choices always reflect compromises between preferences and expectations [8]. There were, however, students whose pre-vocational behavior (choice of curriculum) indicated that they faced frustrations as they moved through the stages of vocational development.

It seems that parents, schools, and other forces in society are doing a good job in encouraging bright students to take advantage of the opportunities available to them. It does seem, however, that perhaps too little time and attention is directed toward the less academically able student. We should re-examine our programs to guarantee that these youngsters are given opportunity to develop to the greatest degree whatever potentials they have, within a framework of realistic self-appraisal.

REFERENCES

1. Flanagan, J. C., et al., *The American High School Student*, Pittsburgh: University of Pittsburgh, 1964.

2. Gribbons, W. D., "Changes in Readiness for Vocational Planning from the 8th Grade to the 10th Grade," *Personnel and Guidance Journal*, 1964, *42*, 908–913.

3. Gribbons, W. D., and Lohnes, P. R., "Relationships Among Measures of Readiness for Vocational Planning," *Journal of Counseling Psychology*, 1964, *11*, 13–19.

4. Gribbons, W. D., and Lohnes, P. R., "Validation of Vocational Planning Interview Scales," *Journal of Counseling Psychology*, 1964, *11*, 20–26.

5. Gribbons, W. D., and Lohnes, P. R., "Predicting Five Years of Development in Adolescents from Readiness for Vocational Planning Scales," *Journal of Educational Psychology*, 1965, *56*, 244–253.

6. Gribbons, W. D., and Lohnes, P. R., "Occupational Preferences and Measured Intelligence," *The Vocational Guidance Quarterly*, 1966, *14*, 211–214.

7. Gribbons, W. D., and Lohnes, P. R., "Shifts in Adolescents: Vocational Values," *Personnel and Guidance Journal*, 1965, *44*, 248–252.

8. Super, D. E., and Overstreet, P. L., *The Vocational Maturity of Ninth Grade Boys*, New York: Bureau of Publications, Teachers College, 1960.

9. Tiedeman, D. V., and Bryan, J. G., "Prediction of College Field Concentration," *Harvard Educational Review*, 1954, *24*, 122–139.

OCCUPATIONAL VERSATILITY: KEY TO CAREER

JOHN LAVENDER

J EFF RAYMOND, an eighth grade student, enters the industrial arts shop at Chinook Junior High School in the Highline District. Jeff takes red notebook #12 from the bookcase. The notebooks are color-coded by period, with the color "red" signifying first period, and "12" being Jeff's student number. Today is the second day of the fall term, and of Jeff's first full year in shop after a nine-week session as a seventh grader.

In his notebook are the record sheets which Jeff will maintain during the term. Jeff knows he is responsible for selecting the area in which he wishes to work and for electing or designing the project he wishes to make. Jeff also knows he is to manage all his activities in the shop. These management responsibilities include his attendance record, his material purchases record, his planning records, his power equipment usage record, and his performance record.

The shop is a large single room with a team of three teachers available to the students. Eleven activity areas are available for

223

Jeff to explore: woods, plastics, general industries, graphics, electricity/electronics, drafting, power, foundry, welding, cold metals, and career guidance. Notebook in hand, he wanders about looking at the brightly colored tool panels and the many project ideas displayed throughout the shop.

A 16-gauge sheet metal candlestick holder catches his eye. "My mother would like one of those, but I think she would like it a little taller," Jeff tells a girl looking at the same project. "I think I'll redesign it and make her one."

On his plan sheet, Jeff draws a sketch of the holder 12 inches high instead of the 10-inch height indicated on the shop plan. He then determines the procedural steps which he will follow, and he also calculates the total price of his project from the metals price list. Jeff asks Mr. Fowler to check his planning and then selects the material he is going to use.

After cutting and rolling the three pieces of metal to the desired shape, Jeff checks his plan. The next step is to cut an oval-shaped hole in each piece, which will require the use of an oxyacetylene torch. After using self-instructional materials for learning how to use the shears and forming rolls, Jeff knows he also must prepare himself to use the torch. He goes to the book on torch operation and reads the safety rules and operating procedures. He looks at the loop films on how to light the torch and on how to cut metal with it. From the chart posted by the torch, he determines the pressures required. A ninth grader using the torch gives him some helpful advice. When Jeff believes he is ready, he fills in his power equipment record, indicating where he received his instructions, and asks Mr. Boe to check him out on the torch.

After his demonstration has been approved, Jeff then uses the torch to cut the three oval holes. When he is ready to weld his project, he goes through a similar self-instructional process.

Upon completion of his project, Jeff fills in the blanks on his performance record indicating the processes he used and the machines he operated. Jeff also completes a satisfaction index form on which he expresses how he felt about the work he did. Jeff knows that he is not working for a grade, but for the experience and the pride of accomplishment. The students in the program work independently or team together, without peer competition. The experience itself is the reward, and satisfaction comes from a job well done.

Choice of a Career

Looking back on his experience, Jeff thinks that he rather liked operating the oxyacetylene torch. It was hot and smoky, but he felt like an artist flowing the metal together with the flame. The burning was interesting too, but it surely took a steady hand. "What type of education is needed to be a welder," Jeff wonders, "and what kind of life does a welder live?"

Jeff looks at the two large boards in the career guidance area of the shop and he finds that the career of welding is colored green. The color-coding instructions tell him that "green" means post-high school training in the form of apprenticeship or technical school is necessary for this career. The directory also indicates there is a film he can watch on the welding profession, and a taped interview with a welder to which he can listen. After the film and tape are played, Jeff checks the apprenticeship requirements and the available technical programs in the Seattle area. This information, plus the experience of operating a torch, gives Jeff much of the background that he needs to analyze the welding profession.

225

This type of brief episode in Jeff's exploration of the industrial arts area at Chinook Junior High is repeated many, many times in the shop program. Jeff is learning how to function in the shop environment; he is learning to be responsible for all of his activities and to solve his problems himself. As the director of his own learning, there are many decisions he must make and be accountable for.

Many times, after completing his candlestick holder, Jeff selects the area in which he desires to work, chooses a problem he wishes to solve, develops a plan and a procedure for the solution, teaches himself the processes he needs, manufactures the project, and evaluates the results. Jeff has found his identity in the industrial arts environment and has developed the abilities to be self-sufficient, productive, and adaptable. He has developed his own mode of operation and has become "Occupationally Versatile." He is ready for advanced or specialized training.

This is true career guidance at the exploratory level. The problems and questions are very real to the student as he initiates them. The solutions come about through student involvement in relevant situations. The degree of thinking often extends to, and sometimes beyond, the analysis level defined in Bloom's taxonomy. The key to such learning is the establishment of an environment where the student will be naturally motivated to learn—and responsible for his learning.

At the awareness and preparatory level, the following considerations must also receive attention. The learning method—where the student is responsible—should be consistent, but the content (what the student is involved in) should be different and varied. The awareness level of career development should be integrated into the regular program and not be treated as a special program of study; it should be a natural aspect of all activities.

Goal must replace role at the preparatory level as the major emphasis. Skills, in terms of both quality and quantity, become significant. Each student should be able to identify what his own goals are and should also be able to evaluate how well he is doing in reaching these goals. This self-evaluation is the final aspect of career analysis which the student needs—"How well can I do what I want to do?" A student who has had worthwhile awareness, exploratory, and preparatory career experiences will likely know what he can do—and will do it well. □

AUTHOR INDEX

KEY-WORD TITLE INDEX